From her years of experience feeding her family as a mother of four and now a grandmother of nine, Barbara Costello has perfected her roster of comforting and delicious family-approved meals. Now all the mealtime ingenuity that has been passed down to her, or that she's earned through trial and error, is here in this book, for you! *Every Day with Babs* will be your go-to dinner resource, with Babs as your surrogate mom or grandma helping to get delicious meals organized, prepped, and on the table in no time, every night of the week.

In these pages, Babs has done all the thinking for you because with so much on your plate already, you shouldn't have to stress about dinnertime! The chapters are organized by day, each with a particular theme or cooking method that keeps in mind the rhythm of the week. We all know making dinner on a Monday feels very different than on a Sunday, so there are recipes to suit everyone's mood, schedule, and cooking style.

No matter how you're feeling by dinner, there is a recipe in here that will fit the bill. Your family will soon be part of the clean plate club, and *you* will be considered a virtual magician in the kitchen, too! Don't panic, it's easier than you think. Babs has you covered!

EVERY DAY WITH BABS

♥

EVERY DAY
with BABS

101 Family-Friendly Dinners for Every Day of the Week

BARBARA COSTELLO

Photographs by Dane Tashima

Clarkson Potter/Publishers
New York

To my wonderful husband, Bill, and our incredible children, Bill, Shawn, Erin, and Elizabeth: A family history was written around our old pine dinner table. You are my treasures and the reason my life is so richly blessed. I love you.

And a special note to my youngest daughter, Elizabeth, my co-captain during this unexpected journey. Your vision and guidance are what keep me young and energized for the next adventure.

Contents

Recipes by Chapter   8

Introduction: What's for Dinner   11

How to Use This Book   14

The Art of Everyday Cooking   17

Bums in Seats, Everybody Eats!   20

GET YOUR "SHEET" (PAN) TOGETHER MONDAY   23

EAT TWICE TWOSDAY   51

ONE AND ONLY WEDNESDAY   79

THRIFTY THURSDAY   109

FRI-YAY!   137

LOW AND SLOW SATURDAY   173

SUNDAY SUPPERS   201

SWEET TOOTH   233

What's in Babs' Refridge & Freezer?   257

Babs' Toolbox   258

Dressings for Days   260

Acknowledgments   263

Index   265

RECIPES BY CHAPTER

MONDAY

25 | Roasted Sausage, Peppers & Gnocchi

26 | Lemon-Basil Chicken & Couscous

29 | Pork Tenderloin with Peach Glaze

30 | Maple-Lime Salmon Bowls with Coconut Rice

33 | Family Fajita Night

34 | Olive Bar Chicken

37 | Samuel's Chicken Shawarma with Roasted Cauliflower

38 | Baked Shrimp with Feta & Tomatoes

41 | Snappy Kielbasa with Sauerkraut & Potatoes

42 | Zesty Chili-Lime Shrimp & Corn Salad

45 | Put-Your-Kids-to-Work Crispy Bean & Cheese Tacos

46 | Curried Fish Bites with Chickpeas & Carrots

49 | Sheet-Pan Dumpling Stir-Fry

TUESDAY

53 | Grammie's Chicken Cutlets

54 | The Ultimate Red Chimichurri Sauce with Skirt Steak

56 | Two Birds, One Oven

58 | Lick-Your-Plate-Clean Green Goddess Salmon

61 | Bourbon-Glazed Pork Chops

62 | Mom's Meatloaf

65 | Finally, I Nailed Falafel with Tzatziki Slaw

68 | Breakfast-for-Dinner Sandwiches

71 | Vincenza's "Scarole" Soup with Sausage & White Beans

73 | Minnie's Meatballs

75 | Refridge-Friendly Sheet-Pan Farro & Kale Salad

76 | Sesame Chicken Noodle Salad

WEDNESDAY

80 | Fully Loaded Cheeseburger Soup

83 | Minivan Pepperoni Pizza Chicken with Garlic Bread

84 | Skillet Orange-Sesame Beef

87 | Chicken with Orzo, Corn & Goat Cheese

88 | Salsa Verde Fish Tostadas

91 | Easiest Chicken Pot Pie

92 | Hoisin Turkey Lettuce Cups

95 | Kids' Favorite Broccoli Pasta

96 | Warm Hug Bacon Pasta

99 | Don't Knock It 'Til You Try It Stuffed Cabbage Soup

100 | Picky-Eater Pasta with Sausage & Peas

103 | Honey Mustard Salmon with Brussels Sprouts

104 | Cheater's Cheesy Pasta Bake

107 | Spinach-Artichoke Rice & Bean Bake

THURSDAY

110 | Dad's Away Sausage, Egg & Cheese Skillet

113 | Shake-It-Up Garlic Knot Drumsticks

114 | Beth's Sloppy Joe Casserole

117 | Better Than Boxed Mac & Cheese

118 | Cook's Secret Weeknight Beef Stew

121 | Takeout Lovers' Sticky Chicken Fried Rice

122 | Pasta "Fazool"

125 | Chicken & Rice Casserole for the Soul

126 | Food Truck Tamale Pie

129 | Lemony Chicken Soup

130 | Clean-Your-Refridge Frittata

133 | Aunt Mimi's Mujaddara

134 | The Classic Tuna Noodle Casserole

FRIDAY

138 | Spicy Tuna Sushi Bake

141 | Reuben Pastry Pockets

142 | Sheet-Pan Shrimp Boil

145 | Chicago Dogs with Fries

149 | Grandma's Grandma Pie

150 | Pimento Cheese Patty Melts

153 | The Ultimate Grilled Cheese Tomato Soup

154 | "We Have Food at Home" Giant Crunchy Taco Wrap

157 | "Revenge" Big Italian Sub Salad

158 | Jalapeño Popper Taquitos

161 | Oven-Fried Chicken & Waffles

163 | Not a Philly Cheesesteak–Stuffed Bread

168 | Chipotle Chicken Nachos

169 | The Best Fish & Chips

SATURDAY

174 | Not-to-Be-Missed Moroccan Chickpea Apricot Stew

177 | Matt's Favorite Finger Lickin' Good Sweet & Sour Ribs

178 | Slow Cooker Chicken Enchilada Casserole

181 | French Onion Soup Pot Roast

182 | Mrs. Murphy's Italian Cousins Chicago Beef Sandwiches

185 | Lamb Lovers' Ragu

186 | Chicken Tikka Masala

190 | Fun with Fondue Baked Potato Bar

193 | Stout Brisket Chili

194 | Love by the Spoonful Chicken Noodle Soup

197 | Dr Pepper Pulled Pork

198 | Bread Bowl Broccoli-Cheddar Soup

SUNDAY

202 | Easy Roast Chicken

205 | Roast Beef with Roasted Garlic Red Wine Sauce

207 | Homemade Ricotta Gnocchi with Sage Butter and Mushrooms

211 | My Super Cheesy Lasagna

213 | Cousin Jim's Chicken Cacciatore

217 | Lobster Roll Cobb Salad

218 | My Grandma's Greek Chicken & Potatoes

221 | Chicken Cordon Bleu Pasta

222 | Pesto Rack of Lamb with Tomato-Mozzarella Salad

225 | Kiss of Summer Shrimp & Grits

226 | Mama's Stuffed Peppers

229 | Pork Tenderloin Marbella

230 | Aunt Louise's Eggplant Parmesan

DESSERTS

234 | Famous Chocolate Chip Cookies

237 | Babs' Favorite Key Lime Icebox Cake

238 | Turtle Date Bark

240 | The Most Delicious Pound Cake

243 | Caramel Apple Crisp

245 | Strawberry Shortcake Sheet Cake

248 | Chocolate Mayonnaise Snack Cake

251 | Cookie for Breakfast Oatmeal Raisin Bars

252 | Confetti Skillet Cookie

255 | Scotcheroos

What's for Dinner?

My mother was a working mom long before it was generally accepted. I remember that, when we were living in my grandfather's apartment building in Chicago in the 1950s, my mother would walk to Sears for her part-time job, so she could make extra money to buy my sister and me Christmas presents. Later, she went to beauty school and, after graduating, started working full-time as a hairdresser.

No matter how busy she was, she always had dinner on the table for us. She was a virtual magician, feeding her family really delicious dinners in the evening, even when she was out working most of the day. Looking back on those years, I sometimes wonder how she was able to do all that. My mother is part of a generation long gone, but I still have cherished memories of those meals together.

I also worked as I was raising my four children. Being a preschool teacher and director was more than a full-time job. "What's for dinner?" was a question I had to have an answer for . . . every . . . night . . . of . . . the . . . week. At the time, I didn't think of dinner duty as a chore; it was just part of my routine.

I had a weekly rotation of chicken dishes, naturally, but I also had pasta, pot roasts, and casseroles—like my spaghetti and meatballs, my Lipton onion soup mix and cream of mushroom pot roast, the tuna-noodle casserole, or my mother's chicken and rice casserole. I cooked very tasty, very easy meals with no frills. When we sat down for dinner, we went to our designated seats. They weren't assigned, but we just always sat in the same place. Mom and Dad were at the head and foot of the table, Bill and Shawn were on one side, and Erin and Elizabeth were on the opposite side. We were blessed to be able to gather around the table at the end of the day and share stories from school, work, church—basically whatever was going on in our lives at the time. Sometimes we had to really juggle to make family dinner happen, and when my kids got into serious sports, it wasn't always achievable. That's just how the seasons of life ebb and flow. We still tried our best to gather one day a week, usually Sunday. Now that my children are adults and out of the house, those times we were able to share dinner as a family are some of my fondest memories.

For so many of you, life is even more complicated now than it was for me back then. I see it with my grown children and grandchildren. Schedules are hectic; parents are working in and out of the home to keep the family afloat; kids are busy from morning until evening. It's *a lot*!

I know that overwhelming feeling. Just remember that feeding your family is an art of the soul. It's an extension of your love. The benefits of gathering your loved ones around the table and sharing a meal are endless.

And the good news is, you don't have to do it alone. *Every Day with Babs* is here!

After the success of my first cookbook, *Celebrate with Babs*, which focused on family traditions and meals around holiday celebrations, many of my online family had a similar reaction: "Thanks, Babs! Now what do we do for *every day*? Help!"

With this book, think of me as your surrogate mom or grandma, helping you get delicious weeknight dinners organized, prepped, and on the table in no time, every night of the week. After many decades, I've learned all the shortcuts and tips. So, I'm sharing those here, as well as giving some tried-and-true classic recipes and some new favorites I've created along the way. All the mealtime ingenuity that has been passed down to me, or I've earned through trial and error, is now here in this book, for you! Your family will soon be part of the clean plate club, and *you* will be considered a virtual magician in the kitchen, too! Don't panic, it's easier than you think. I've got you covered!

—XO, Babs

How to Use This Book

In the pages of *Every Day with Babs*, I've tried to do all the thinking for you. With so much on your plate already, you shouldn't have to stress about dinner! I've organized the book by days of the week. Each day has a particular theme or cooking method that keeps in mind the rhythm of the week—because we all know a Monday feels very different from a Sunday.

The Monday through Thursday chapters get you through the bulk of your work and school days. All the recipes for these days are quick to put together from start to finish, and they are also easy on clean-up. The goal is to get *delicious* food on the table, fast, so you have a little time to breathe.

The Friday through Sunday chapters have a different tempo from the rest of your week. It's time to wind down and have some fun, and it's a great time to gather with family and friends. The recipes in these chapters reflect every weekend mood.

No matter how you're feeling by dinnertime, there is a recipe in here that will fit the bill. You can just flip this book open and go!

GET YOUR "SHEET" (PAN) TOGETHER MONDAY: What better way to start the week than with an easy meal and an even easier clean-up? Enter the humble sheet pan, where you can prep and cook everything in one place. It's a must-have kitchen item that will get you through the longest of days. Did you know you could make a salad with a sheet pan? You can! Try the Zesty Chili-Lime Shrimp & Corn Salad (page 42). In the mood for something more traditional? Roasted Sausage, Peppers & Gnocchi (page 25) is to die for!

EAT TWICE TWOSDAY: The recipes in this chapter make double the portions but without double the effort. The proteins are simple, and

you will be able to store them in the refridge or freezer for future meals. The idea is to make more now to enjoy later—batch-cooking at its best! Just think of it: you'll have a refridge and freezer full of dinner options whenever you're in a pinch. Grammie's Chicken Cutlets (page 53) are as versatile as they are delicious; you'll be stocked up for weeks. Of course, I had to add the ultimate "grab-and-go" recipe, Breakfast-for-Dinner Sandwiches (page 68).

ONE AND ONLY WEDNESDAY: As you might be able to guess from the chapter title, these recipes require only one pot or skillet to get the job done! It's another great way to streamline dinner. The recipes are packed full of flavor, since all the ingredients mingle in the same pan. Who doesn't love a one-pot meal? I've included my Picky-Eater Pasta with Sausage & Peas (page 100), as well as some delicious soups like my Fully Loaded Cheeseburger Soup (page 80), and definitely don't skip the Minivan Pepperoni Pizza Chicken with Garlic Bread (page 83).

THRIFTY THURSDAY: Pantry staples are life savers. They cut down on prep, save time, and are a little easier on the wallet. That's what Thrifty Thursday is all about! The recipes in this chapter rely on pantry staples, and they showcase how to get the most out of what you probably already have on hand, just as the weekly grocery haul starts to dwindle. Here you'll find delicious options, and you won't feel like you're skimping or sacrificing a thing! Cook's Secret Weeknight Beef Stew (page 118), The Classic Tuna Noodle Casserole (page 134), or Takeout Lovers' Sticky Chicken Fried Rice (page 121) are just a few examples of how you'll turn humble pantry ingredients into dinnertime legends.

FRI-YAY!: Hip, hip, hooray—it's Fri-Yay! Kick back and celebrate the end of a busy week. These recipes are perfect for family movie or game nights. Some of them are finger foods—no utensils required! They're crowd-pleasing and easy to serve. Many are yummier versions of restaurant dishes you might get on a night out with friends, like "We Have Food at Home" Giant Crunchy Taco Wrap (page 154), Spicy Tuna Sushi Bake (page 138), and Oven-Fried Chicken & Waffles (page 161), to name just a few. They are full of fun and a little more laid back. So, let your hair down and enjoy the end of the week—you've earned it!

LOW AND SLOW SATURDAY: Let's be honest, Saturday is different for everyone. Sometimes it's running errands, crossing things off your to-do list; maybe it's taking the kids to sporting events or birthday parties. Other times, Saturdays can be a bit more mellow. Whatever the rhythm of *your* Saturday, hands-off meals work best here, and the magic of a slow cooker or Dutch oven can make that happen. I've included an incredible French Onion Soup Pot Roast (page 181), Matt's Favorite Finger Lickin' Good Sweet & Sour Ribs (page 177), and a Fun with Fondue Baked Potato Bar (page 190). So, go out and do what needs to be done, or get cozy and take a nap. Either way, dinner will be ready whenever you are.

SUNDAY SUPPER: When I was growing up, Sunday supper meant a gathering of my extended family at Grandma's house. When raising my own family, if no other day could accomplish it, Sunday was also the day to gather around the table. Some of the recipes here are *slightly* more elaborate and special but still completely practical. You have to try My Super Cheesy Lasagna (page 211)—it's a classic.

For something a little lighter, there's my Lobster Roll Cobb Salad (page 217) or the Kiss of Summer Shrimp & Grits (page 225), inspired by my time in the South. This chapter is where I share my traditions with you and from where I hope you'll be able to create your own!

SWEET TOOTH: It would be a crime to have a cookbook without desserts, so I've compiled a list of my favorite nostalgic recipes to satisfy those sweet cravings. The recipe for my Famous Chocolate Chip Cookies (page 234) is here in this chapter, and you *need* to make them! Strawberry Shortcake (page 245) on a sheet pan? Yes, that's in here, too. The goal here is to make things easy—and, of course, super delicious!

There are some extras in this book, too! I've included a section about my favorite kitchen tools, called Babs' Toolbox (page 258)—nothing fancy, just practical. And what do I keep stocked in my refridge? I'll show you in What's in Babs' Refridge & Freezer (page 257). I even assembled some sample weeknight menus for you (see page 18). I know it's not always easy to gather your family and friends around a table for dinner, especially where there's young children, so I've incorporated some tips and tricks (see Bums in Seats, Everybody Eats!, page 20) to help you reach that goal.

Throughout the book, you'll see "Babs Says" notes that give extra tips, tricks, and suggestions to help walk you through the recipe process or to spark new ideas. Think of this as the cooking version of a self-help book!

Most important, I want to make weekly dinners something you'll actually look forward to by keeping them simple, fun, and, of course, super delicious. You can follow the book *or* you can mix and match. Cook a Thursday recipe on a Tuesday—get crazy!

The Art of Everyday Cooking

Once you master the art of everyday cooking, you'll never dread the chore of getting dinner on the table again. It's really as simple as 1-2-3:

STEP 1.
Plan your menu for the week

Menu planning is easy. Just write down what you want to make for dinner each night of the week ahead. By planning your menu, you'll save time, which is precious, and money on things like fast-food runs or pizza pickups. You'll also save your sanity! Don't forget, check your schedule because there may be nights when you won't be eating at home. Here are some sample weekly menus I've put together to get you started (see page 18).

STEP 2.
Go grocery shopping

Look at your menu for the week and figure out what ingredients you already have on hand and what you need. Then, here's the trick: Make a list using the Babs method! Organize your list by the layout of *your* grocery store. Fold a piece of paper into sixths and write the name of the departments at the top of each section: Produce, Bakery/Deli, Meat/Seafood, Dairy, Dried & Canned Goods, and Frozen. Next, write each grocery item you need in its appropriate section. You won't miss a thing and you'll save a ton of time.

STEP 3.
Prep your meals

The recipes in this book are very easy, so in many cases, you won't need to do this, *but* on nights when you find yourself pressed for time, you'll be glad you prepped a few ingredients ahead and stored them in the refridge. Just look at the recipes on your weekly menu and ask yourself: Are there veggies I could cut in advance and store? Dressings or marinades I could make ahead? Then, when you have a little extra time, tackle those small tasks to make dinnertime less stressful when it's actually time to cook.

Sample Weekly Menus

	SAMPLE MENU 1	SAMPLE MENU 2	SAMPLE MENU 3
MONDAY	Roasted Sausage, Peppers & Gnocchi (page 25)	Olive Bar Chicken (page 34)	Lemon-Basil Chicken & Couscous (page 26)
TUESDAY	Two Birds, One Oven (page 56)	Minnie's Meatballs (page 73)	Refridge-Friendly Sheet-Pan Farro & Kale Salad (page 75)
WEDNESDAY	Salsa Verde Fish Tostadas (page 88)	Skillet Orange-Sesame Beef (page 84)	Picky-Eater Pasta with Sausage & Peas (page 100)
THURSDAY	Lemony Chicken Soup (page 129)	Dad's Away Sausage, Egg & Cheese Skillet (page 110)	Shake-It-Up Garlic Knot Drumsticks (page 113)
FRIDAY	"We Have Food at Home" Giant Crunchy Taco Wrap (page 154)	Spicy Tuna Sushi Bake (page 138)	Not a Philly Cheesesteak-Stuffed Bread (page 163)
SATURDAY	Fun with Fondue Baked Potato Bar (page 190)	Mrs. Murphy's Italian Cousins Chicago Beef Sandwiches (page 182)	Slow Cooker Chicken Enchilada Casserole (page 178)
SUNDAY	My Super Cheesy Lasagna (page 211)	Mama's Stuffed Peppers (page 226)	Pork Tenderloin Marbella (page 229)

SAMPLE MENU 4	SAMPLE MENU 5	SAMPLE MENU 6	SAMPLE MENU 7
Zesty Chili-Lime Shrimp & Corn Salad (page 42)	Sheet-Pan Dumpling Stir-Fry (page 49)	Maple-Lime Salmon Bowls with Coconut Rice (page 30)	Pork Tenderloin with Peach Glaze (page 29)
Grammie's Chicken Cutlets (page 53)	Finally, I Nailed Falafel with Tzatziki Slaw (page 65)	Sesame Chicken Noodle Salad (page 76)	Vincenza's "Scarole" Soup with Sausage & White Beans (page 71)
Minivan Pepperoni Pizza Chicken with Garlic Bread (page 83)	Cheater's Cheesy Pasta Bake (page 104)	Warm Hug Bacon Pasta (page 96)	Honey Mustard Salmon with Brussels Sprouts (page 103)
Cook's Secret Weeknight Beef Stew (page 118)	Aunt Mimi's Mujaddara (page 133)	Food Truck Tamale Pie (page 126)	Takeout Lovers' Sticky Chicken Fried Rice (page 121)
Chipotle Chicken Nachos (page 168)	The Ultimate Grilled Cheese Tomato Soup (page 153)	Reuben Pastry Pockets (page 141)	Sheet-Pan Shrimp Boil (page 142)
Dr Pepper Pulled Pork (page 197)	Not-to-Be-Missed Moroccan Chickpea Apricot Stew (page 174)	Chicken Tikka Masala (page 186)	French Onion Soup Pot Roast (page 181)
Lobster Roll Cobb Salad (page 217)	Homemade Ricotta Gnocchi with Sage Butter and Mushrooms (page 207)	Kiss of Summer Shrimp & Grits (page 225)	Easy Roast Chicken (page 202)

Bums in Seats, Everybody Eats!

Beyond offering easy and delicious recipes for whatever your week throws at you, I've tried to use this book to really stress the importance of family dinners. It turns out that sitting around the dinner table with the people you love the most in the world has amazing benefits, and those benefits are scientifically proven! Massachusetts General Hospital's "Family Dinner Project" found that, after twenty years of research, family dinners are not only associated with "higher rates of resilience and higher self-esteem" but also a myriad of other benefits too long to list. Amazing! It's incredible when you think about the power family dinner holds in impacting our lives for the better, not to mention the memories we make along the way.

It may take some time to establish a regular rhythm of eating together, but you'll be rewarded with the benefits of your efforts, and that is the case even if your family can sit down together only one night a week. Don't feel guilty if life sometimes gets in the way! So, put down those phones and iPads, and turn off those TVs. Dinner will soon be the time your family looks forward to the most and what they will remember for years to come!

So, we have a plan of attack for getting those delicious meals on the table, but how do we get everyone in their chairs and truly engaged? Trust me, I've had to parent through every life stage and every attention span—everything from getting little bums in chairs to managing devastating teenage eye rolls. Think of this section as a collection of helpful ideas, based on my own experience, to get everyone around the table, share a meal, and connect. Feel free to add your own into the mix!

TWO TRUTHS AND A FIB

Some people call this game "Two Truths and a Lie," but I never liked using the word *lie* in my house, so we put a spin on "True or False?" To play, just go around the table and take turns sharing two things that really happened to you that day and one that didn't happen. It's everyone else's job to guess which stories are true and which is *not*. This engages everyone's creativity, and you may actually learn something about someone else's day that you might not have otherwise. This will even work with middle school kids, the toughest of crowds!

TALK JAR

Do you have an old pasta sauce jar? Or maybe a mason jar? Have your family decorate it however you like. You've now just created a new family tradition. Everyone gets a few strips of paper to write some fun, interesting questions sure to spark discussion during your meals. For example, "What was your favorite family trip?" "What's the first thing you would buy if you won a million dollars and why?" Don't show each other the questions; just put them in the jar and pull that jar out at dinner. Have fun answering them!

CANDLELIGHT DINNER

Romance? Not this time! *But* if you light a candle or two before you gather around the dinner table, it creates a special atmosphere. It establishes a routine, which is great for kids and adults. And it's also calming to the little ones and sets the tone for a more peaceful and less chaotic meal. No one can get up from the table until the candles are blown out. Each night, a different child has the honor of blowing out the candle, officially ending dinnertime—the kitchen is closed! My daughter started doing the candlelight dinner with her family; she also has four children, and they caught on right away. There's always a mad scramble *to* the table on "restaurant nights"!

STORY TIME

I used to do this with my classes when I was a preschool teacher, but it works at dinnertime, too! The person at the head of the table kicks off a story; for example, "Once upon a time there was a princess named Jelly Bean." Then, around the table you go, line by line, each person adding a line to the story. These stories take so many fun, creative, silly turns. As a parent, it's also a good way to gauge your child's mood. Especially if Princess Jelly Bean gets eaten by a dragon. Time for a check-in!

Get Your "Sheet" (Pan) Together Monday

I was my children's alarm clock, which was a difficult job on Mondays. They had to be dragged, literally, out of bed. Nobody started moving willingly. But they just acted the way I felt. Mondays were always the toughest day for me to get through, coming off a weekend that was relatively unstructured and generally more relaxed. Then, all of a sudden, reality bites, and I had to get back on the responsibility train! Kids up, off to school, surprise homework discoveries in backpacks. I couldn't wait for Mondays to be over, and yet, the end of the day always had one last hurdle: dinner!

If you're like me, Monday dinner needs to be a no-brainer. That's because, in all likelihood, you don't have your "sheet" together quite yet. So, I want to make this easy. If you have a sheet pan, you can make dinner. The ease of simple ingredients, all cooked on one pan in your oven, takes the dinner pressure off your plate! Clean-up is a breeze because nobody wants to be in the kitchen, washing multiple pots and pans, on a Monday night.

Let's get our "sheet" together; you may actually start to look forward to Mondays!

ROASTED SAUSAGE, PEPPERS & GNOCCHI

Serves 4

PREP
10 minutes

COOK
35 minutes

My dear friend and surrogate mother, Ida, made the most amazing homemade potato gnocchi I have ever tasted. It required time, but it was out of this world. Today, most of us don't have the kind of time during the week that Ida did back then.

For this recipe, I use packaged potato gnocchi, right off the shelf, roasted alongside Italian sausage and chopped bell peppers and onions. Whereas homemade gnocchi is fluffy, store-bought potato gnocchi has a chewy bite that gets crispy and savory when roasted. Just top this with Parmesan and basil. It's delicious!

---

1   (12- to 18-ounce) package shelf-stable potato gnocchi

2   red, orange, or yellow bell peppers, chopped into 1-inch pieces (about the same size as the gnocchi)

1   yellow onion, coarsely chopped

3   tablespoons extra-virgin olive oil

    Kosher salt and freshly ground black pepper

1   pound sweet or hot Italian sausage

1   tablespoon unsalted butter

    For serving: grated Parmesan, small handful of torn basil leaves

1. Preheat the oven to 450°F.

2. On a sheet pan, toss together the **gnocchi**, **bell peppers**, **onion, olive oil**, **½ teaspoon salt**, and **a few grinds of pepper**. Shake into an even layer. Squeeze roughly **½-inch pieces of sausage** out of the casings onto the sheet pan, all over the gnocchi and vegetables. Roast, stirring halfway through, until the peppers are softened and the sausage is browned and crisp, 30 to 35 minutes.

3. Add the **butter** to the sheet pan and toss until the butter is melted, scraping up browned bits from the pan as you go. Serve topped with **Parmesan** and **basil**.

BABS SAYS

Shelf-stable gnocchi is exactly what it sounds like. You'll find it on the shelves of the pasta aisle. It doesn't need to be boiled before roasting—more time saved!

♥

Cut a bell pepper like a pro! Remove the top and bottom of the pepper, then make a slit from top to bottom, remove the seeds and core, and slice.

♥

For an extra-creamy affair, serve topped with ricotta or burrata.

LEMON-BASIL CHICKEN & COUSCOUS

Serves 4

PREP
10 minutes

COOK
40 minutes

I have to confess, when it comes to chicken, I'm a thigh girl. I know there are those who prefer the all-white meat of a chicken breast. I get it. But if you're looking to deliver a juicy, flavorful bite, it's all in the thighs. Let me introduce you to a recipe that will convert you, if you're not already a believer!

Here, chicken thighs and tomatoes are layered on a sheet pan along with one of my all-time favorites, instant couscous. This tiny, quick-cooking pasta is just right for soaking up all the delicious pan drippings from the chicken thighs, without needing to cook the grain first. It's such a novel way of cooking couscous (you don't even have to boil water!), so the prep couldn't be easier—you'll thank me later.

---

1 or 2 lemons

3 cups chicken broth

¼ cup plus 3 tablespoons extra-virgin olive oil

1 cup chopped fresh basil, plus more for serving

3 garlic cloves, finely chopped or grated

2 teaspoons sweet paprika, plus more for seasoning

1 teaspoon dried thyme

Kosher salt and freshly ground black pepper

1½ cups (about 10 ounces) instant couscous

2 pounds bone-in, skin-on chicken thighs (4 to 6 thighs)

3 zucchini (about 1 pound), halved lengthwise and thinly sliced into half-moons

1 pint (about 10 ounces) cherry tomatoes

Lemon wedges, for serving

1. Arrange a rack in the center of the oven and preheat the oven to 450°F.

2. Grate the zest of 1 **lemon** into a large bowl or liquid measuring cup. Squeeze the lemon(s) to get ⅓ cup juice and add to the bowl. Add the **broth**, **¼ cup of the olive oil**, the **basil**, **garlic**, **paprika**, **thyme**, **1 teaspoon salt**, and **¼ teaspoon pepper** and whisk to combine.

3. Spread the **couscous** on a sheet pan, then nestle the **chicken thighs**, **zucchini**, and **cherry tomatoes** on the couscous. Pour the liquid all over. Season the chicken with ½ teaspoon salt and a sprinkle of paprika. Seal tightly with a piece of aluminum foil, then bake until the couscous has absorbed all the liquid and the chicken is just cooked through, 30 to 35 minutes.

4. Remove the pan from the oven. Set the broiler to high.

5. Uncover the pan and drizzle everything with the remaining 3 tablespoons olive oil. Return the pan to the middle rack, uncovered, and broil until the top is golden brown, checking often, 5 to 6 minutes.

6. Divide the baked mixture among plates. Scatter more basil on top and serve with **lemon wedges** for squeezing.

> **BABS SAYS**
>
> For a little kick and some extra depth, trade the sweet paprika for smoked paprika.

PORK TENDERLOIN
with PEACH GLAZE

Serves 4

PREP
15 minutes

COOK
30 minutes

During the late 1980s, I was in the thick of my child-rearing years, with kids ranging in age from a newborn to a ten-year-old. I was feeding my children so much chicken for dinner, I told them they were going to start clucking! At the time, there was a popular ad campaign for pork, "the other white meat." The idea was to let families know that pork was a delicious, easy alternative to chicken. Healthy, lean, and simple to cook to temperature—call it the original influencer campaign. I wasn't a stranger to pork, of course, but it reminded me I needed to mix up my dinnertime routine and this meal does just that. It's done in under an hour. Make sure to spoon the pan juices over the plates of food before serving.

1 pound green beans, trimmed

2 tablespoons extra-virgin olive oil

   Kosher salt and freshly ground black pepper

3 sweet potatoes (about 1 pound), peeled and cut into 1-inch pieces

¼ cup hoisin sauce

¼ cup peach preserves

2 (1-pound) pork tenderloins, patted dry and any silver skin removed (see page 229)

1 small garlic clove, finely chopped or grated

> **BABS SAYS**
>
> Use precut sweet potato cubes if you need a shortcut.
>
> ♥
>
> If you learn only one cooking tip from this book, let it be this: *double the sauce*. You can always use extra deliciousness. The pan juices here are to die for, but if you want a more traditional sauce, mix some more peach preserves and hoisin sauce in a small saucepan over medium heat, then thin it with a bit of water to the consistency you like.

1. Preheat the oven to 450°F.

2. On a sheet pan, toss the **green beans** with 1 tablespoon of the **olive oil** and ½ **teaspoon each salt and pepper**. Arrange in a single layer on half the pan. On the other half, toss the **sweet potatoes** with the remaining tablespoon olive oil and ½ teaspoon each salt and pepper.

3. In a small bowl, stir together the **hoisin sauce**, **peach preserves**, 2 teaspoons salt, and 1 teaspoon pepper until smooth.

4. Place the **tenderloins** on top of the green beans. With a basting brush or clean hands, coat the tenderloins all over with the hoisin glaze. Roast until the internal temperature reaches 145°F and the vegetables are tender, 25 to 30 minutes.

5. Transfer the pork to a cutting board to rest for 5 minutes before slicing. Stir the **garlic** into the vegetables, scraping to get the browned bits up from the pan. Serve the tenderloin and the pan juices with the vegetables alongside.

MAPLE-LIME SALMON BOWLS
with COCONUT RICE

Serves 4

PREP
10 minutes

COOK
30 minutes

I must admit, I came to the bowl game a little late. For so long, I associated bowls with the kind of fast-casual dining you get at Chipotle, which I like, but I didn't see the infinite possibilities they presented for a busy home cook. Well, call me a convert and use me as an example: you *can* learn new things, even at my age!

This Asian-inspired bowl starts with sweet, floral rice from the coconut, while the salmon is glazed with a wonderfully balanced combination of soy, lime, and maple syrup. The simplicity of cooking the rice right on the sheet pan is a revelation!

---

3   tablespoons liquid coconut oil or neutral oil, such as avocado

2   cups uncooked long-grain white rice

1   (14-ounce) can full-fat coconut milk

Grated zest of 1 lime

Juice of 2 limes

1½ pounds skinless salmon fillets, cut into 1-inch pieces

3   tablespoons pure maple syrup

2   tablespoons soy sauce

Kosher salt and freshly ground black pepper

4   mini cucumbers

2   large avocados

For serving: fresh cilantro leaves and tender stems, lime wedges for squeezing

BABS SAYS

Two time-saving tips: (1) Skip step 2 and use 4 cups of cooked rice, coat it in 2 tablespoons oil, and spread it on the sheet pan. Top with the salmon and broil. (2) You can skip the marinade and use ½ cup teriyaki sauce.

1. Arrange a rack in the upper third of the oven and preheat the oven to 450°F.

2. Grease a sheet pan with **2 tablespoons of the coconut oil**, then add the **rice** and shake it into an even layer. Pour the **coconut milk** over the rice, then fill up the can with water and add that water to the sheet pan, stirring with a fork to combine. Seal tightly with a piece of aluminum foil and bake until the rice is just tender, 20 to 25 minutes.

3. Meanwhile, in a medium bowl, combine the **lime zest** and **half the lime juice**. Add the **salmon**, **maple syrup**, **soy sauce**, remaining 1 tablespoon coconut oil, **1 teaspoon salt**, and ½ **teaspoon pepper** and stir to combine. For the salad, cut the **cucumbers** into bite-size pieces and slice the **avocados**, then transfer to another medium bowl. Stir in the remaining lime juice and ½ teaspoon salt.

4. When the rice is ready, remove the pan from the oven and set the broiler to high. Remove the foil and place the salmon on top of the rice. Broil until the salmon is just cooked through, 3 to 5 minutes. (Check halfway through, and if the rice is burning anywhere, stir it with a fork.)

5. Fluff the rice with a fork, then scoop the rice and salmon into bowls and top with the salad and **cilantro**. Serve with **lime wedges**.

FAMILY FAJITA NIGHT

Serves 4

PREP
10 minutes

COOK
30 minutes

I love Mexican food: traditional, Tex-Mex, and any spin on those delicious flavors. Luckily, not too far from where I raised my children in Connecticut, there was a Mexican restaurant, El Toritos. A celebration at that festive spot was how we ended every birthday week for our children. My standard order was fajitas. I loved getting the piping-hot plate and filling the flour tortillas with the veggies and protein, then piling on toppings like guacamole and pico de gallo.

Here's the best part about fajitas: you can make them at home! They are versatile enough to please any member of the family and are very quick to make. The perfect way to put together an everyday meal is to throw the ingredients onto a sheet pan. Don't wait to go out—have a birthday night *any* night!

---

1 (1½-pound) flank steak

1 tablespoon chili powder, or as desired

1 teaspoon light brown sugar

Kosher salt and freshly ground black pepper

8 (6-inch) flour tortillas

3 bell peppers, any color, cut into ½-inch-thick strips

1 large red onion, cut into ½-inch-thick rounds

3 garlic cloves, thinly sliced

2 tablespoons neutral oil, such as avocado

1 tablespoon fresh lime juice

2 tablespoons chopped fresh cilantro

For serving: sour cream

BABS SAYS

If you want some extra char on your vegetables, take the steak off the sheet pan and set aside to rest. Return the sheet pan of vegetables to the oven under the broiler until you get the level of browning you like best.

1. Preheat the oven to 475°F.

2. Cut the **steak** against the grain into 3 equal pieces. Pat the pieces dry with paper towels, then sprinkle all over with the **chili powder**, **brown sugar**, **2 teaspoons salt**, and **1 teaspoon pepper**.

3. Wrap the **tortillas** together in a piece of aluminum and set aside.

4. On a sheet pan, toss together the **bell peppers**, **onion**, **garlic**, **oil**, 1 teaspoon salt, and 1 teaspoon pepper. Spread into an even layer. Roast until the vegetables are lightly browned around the edges, 10 to 12 minutes.

5. Push the vegetables to one half of the sheet pan. Place the 3 steak strips on the other half, leaving a little space between them. Roast until the vegetables are spotty brown and the meat registers 135°F (for medium), 8 to 12 minutes.

6. Transfer the steak slices to a cutting board to rest for 5 minutes. Place the tortilla packet in the oven, directly on the rack, and heat until the tortillas are warm, about 5 minutes. Meanwhile, toss the roasted vegetables with the **lime juice** and steak drippings.

7. Thinly slice the steak strips against the grain and transfer to the pan with the vegetables. Sprinkle with the **cilantro**. Serve the steak and vegetables with the warm tortillas, plus **sour cream** and **lime wedges**.

OLIVE BAR CHICKEN

Serves 4 to 6

PREP
5 minutes

COOK
40 minutes

One of my favorite sections in the grocery store is the olive bar. It's not *all* olives. There is always a dizzying assortment of marinated vegetables and cheeses to choose from. You could create a whole meal from items at that station alone. Sometimes I do! This chicken is my way of capturing all those delicious flavors. It's so easy; there's virtually no prep—just popping open jars.

The braising mixture makes a flavorful sauce for the chicken, so don't forget you can just pour it from the pan to the plate. It goes so well with pasta, mashed potatoes, or toasted bread. Don't love olives? Don't fret; see Babs Says.

---

1 (7- to 8-ounce) jar oil-packed sun-dried tomatoes, sliced if necessary (about 1 cup)

3 pounds bone-in, skin-on chicken thighs (6 to 8 thighs), patted dry

1 tablespoon brown sugar or pure maple syrup

1 (12- to 14-ounce) jar marinated artichokes, quartered if necessary (about 1½ cups)

1 (12- to 16-ounce) jar roasted red peppers, thinly sliced if necessary (1 to 1½ cups)

1 (6- to 8-ounce) container mixed pitted olives, drained (about 1½ cups)

1. Preheat the oven to 400°F.

2. Dump the entire jar of **sun-dried tomatoes** (and oil) onto a sheet pan. Add the **chicken** and **brown sugar** and toss everything together to coat. Arrange the chicken skin side up.

3. Add the **artichokes** (with their liquid), the **roasted peppers** (with their liquid), and the drained **olives**. Stir to combine with the other ingredients, making sure the chicken stays skin side up. Roast, carefully stirring the olive bar ingredients halfway through, until the chicken is cooked through, 35 to 40 minutes. Serve with the braising liquid poured over the top.

BABS SAYS

If you don't like olives, pick up a jar of marinated mushrooms, pickled peppers, or giardiniera. Anything with a nice briny bite will balance the flavors of the other ingredients in this recipe. Just make sure to drain them first, like you would have done with the olives.

SAMUEL'S CHICKEN SHAWARMA
with ROASTED CAULIFLOWER

Serves 4

PREP
10 minutes (optional:
up to 8 hours
marinating time)

COOK
45 minutes

My grandfather, Samuel Shamon, came to Chicago from Lebanon along with his brother, Abraham. They had a textile business and would travel back and forth from Chicago to Lebanon for work. One of his most beloved dishes was shawarma like this one.

Of course, having a spit to slow-roast lamb or chicken isn't really practical. So, I created a quick sheet-pan version. You'll get all the tang and spice of chicken shawarma without renovating your kitchen to include a spit! Serve in pita, on salad greens, or over rice or couscous.

2	pounds boneless, skinless chicken thighs, each halved crosswise
6	tablespoons extra-virgin olive oil
¼	cup fresh lemon juice (from 2 small lemons)
2	teaspoons garlic powder
2	teaspoons smoked paprika
2	teaspoons ground coriander
2	teaspoons ground cumin
2	teaspoons ground turmeric
¼	teaspoon ground cinnamon
¼	teaspoon cayenne (omit if you don't like heat)
	Kosher salt and freshly ground black pepper
1	(8- to 9-ounce) bag fresh cauliflower florets (about 4 cups), or cut from ½ small head cauliflower
1	red onion, halved and cut into ½-inch-thick wedges
	For serving: pita, thinned Greek yogurt, tahini, feta, olives, chopped cucumbers, chopped tomatoes, lettuce leaves, parsley, and/or mint

1. Preheat the oven to 425°F. Line a sheet pan with aluminum foil.

2. Toss the **chicken** on the sheet pan with **¼ cup of the olive oil**, the **lemon juice**, **garlic powder**, **smoked paprika**, **coriander**, **cumin**, **turmeric**, **cinnamon**, **cayenne** (if using), **2 teaspoons salt**, and **1 teaspoon pepper** until well coated. (Alternatively, you can marinate the chicken in the refridge for up to 8 hours, then bring to room temperature before cooking.)

3. Add the remaining 2 tablespoons oil to the sheet pan along with the **cauliflower**, **onion**, and ½ teaspoon salt and toss with the chicken to coat well. Spread into an even layer and roast until the chicken and cauliflower are golden brown and cooked through, 30 to 40 minutes. (If you'd like more browning, broil for a few minutes.)

4. If serving with **pita**, wrap the pita in aluminum foil; when the chicken's done, set it aside briefly and transfer the pita to the oven to warm for about 5 minutes. Thinly slice the chicken and eat with the cauliflower, onion, and any accompaniments you like.

BABS SAYS

The longer the chicken sits in the marinade, the juicier and more flavorful it will become, so throw the chicken in the marinade in the morning and stick it in the refridge. You'll leave the house feeling like you've accomplished something, even on a Monday!

♥

To cut an onion without tears, place a crumpled wet paper towel next to where you're slicing your onion. It will absorb the gasses that produce those tears!

BAKED SHRIMP
with FETA & TOMATOES

Serves 4

PREP
10 minutes

COOK
25 minutes

Shrimp, in my opinion, is an overlooked protein. It's so easy to keep a bag of frozen shrimp ready to go in your freezer, and it couldn't be simpler to make—especially on a sheet pan.

Sheet-pan dinners don't need to feel heavy; this one is light and fresh but still packed with flavor. Squeeze a few lemon wedges over the finished dish, then close your eyes and imagine yourself in Mykonos with every bite. (I've never been, but it's on my bucket list!) If you want to swap out the bread, try the shrimp with couscous or pasta.

1 (1½-pound) bag peeled and deveined large shrimp (16–20 count), patted dry

3½ tablespoons extra-virgin olive oil

1 tablespoon fresh lemon juice, plus lemon wedges for serving

4 garlic cloves, finely chopped

¾ teaspoon dried oregano

½ teaspoon chopped fresh tarragon

Pinch of red pepper flakes

Kosher salt and freshly ground black pepper

2 pints (about 20 ounces total) cherry or grape tomatoes

8 ounces crumbled feta (about 2 cups)

1 loaf ciabatta bread, wrapped in aluminum foil

¼ cup fresh parsley leaves, chopped

1. Preheat the oven to 450°F.

2. In a large bowl, toss the **shrimp** with **1½ tablespoons of the olive oil**, the **lemon juice**, **half the garlic**, the **oregano**, **tarragon**, **pepper flakes**, **¾ teaspoon salt,** and **½ teaspoon pepper**. Set aside to marinate briefly.

3. On a sheet pan or in a 3-quart baking dish, toss together the **tomatoes**, remaining 2 tablespoons olive oil, the remaining garlic, and a pinch of salt. Spread into an even layer, then sprinkle **two-thirds of the feta** on top. Bake until the tomatoes are bubbling and the feta is beginning to soften, 10 to 15 minutes.

4. Remove the pan from the oven and scatter the shrimp over the top. Sprinkle with the remaining feta. Return the pan to the oven and place the foil-wrapped **loaf of bread** directly on the rack alongside. Bake until the shrimp are opaque and cooked through and the bread is warm inside, 5 to 7 minutes.

5. Slice the bread and sprinkle the shrimp with the **parsley**. Serve immediately with **lemon wedges**.

BABS SAYS

Here is a quick way to thaw and rinse your shrimp. Turn your shrimp bag into a colander! Use a skewer to poke holes in the bottom third of the bag of shrimp. Open the top of the bag and stand it up in your sink. Let cold water run continuously into the bag until the shrimp are thawed, about 5 minutes. This will both defrost and rinse the shrimp as the water drains through the bag.

SNAPPY KIELBASA
with SAUERKRAUT & POTATOES

Serves 4

PREP
10 minutes

COOK
35 minutes

Chicago has the largest concentration of Polish immigrants in the country. Because of that, I was introduced to Polish cuisine at an early age. I loved going to the Polish buffets that were all-you-could-eat for less than three dollars. Sausage, pierogies, cabbage rolls—it was all so crave-worthy.

My favorite was, and still is, kielbasa. I've been making this recipe in my slow cooker for years, but here, I've adapted it to a sheet pan. Roasting the kielbasa gives it an extra-delicious snap.

1½ pounds small new potatoes, halved

2 (1-pound) containers sauerkraut, drained

2 tablespoons extra-virgin olive oil

1½ teaspoons caraway seeds

½ teaspoon smoked paprika

Kosher salt and freshly ground black pepper

2 (12- to 16-ounce) kielbasa

2 teaspoons apple cider vinegar

¼ cup chopped fresh parsley leaves and tender stems

For serving: Dijon mustard and/or sour cream

1. Preheat the oven to 425°F.

2. On a sheet pan, toss together the **potatoes**, **sauerkraut**, **olive oil**, **caraway seeds**, **paprika**, and **½ teaspoon each salt and pepper**. Spread into an even layer. Prick the **kielbasa** all over with a fork and place on top of the potatoes and sauerkraut. Roast, flipping the kielbasa halfway through, until the potatoes are tender and the sausage is heated through, 30 to 35 minutes.

3. Transfer the kielbasa to a cutting board, let it cool for a few minutes, then cut into slices. Drizzle the pan with the **vinegar** and toss to combine, scraping up the browned bits from the bottom. Top the veggies with the **parsley** and season to taste with salt and pepper.

4. Serve the kielbasa slices and potatoes with a dollop of **mustard** and/or **sour cream** for dipping.

BABS SAYS

I like the juicy savoriness you get by cooking the kielbasa whole, but you can slice it before adding to the sheet pan, if you'd like; just watch the cooking time.

♥

Consider serving this with applesauce, in addition to mustard and sour cream.

ZESTY CHILI-LIME SHRIMP & CORN SALAD

Serves 4

PREP
10 minutes

COOK
30 minutes

If you have anyone in your family, like a kiddo, who is more excited about salad mix-ins than an overwhelming base of lettuce, this sheet pan salad (yes you read that correctly!) will bring them pure joy.

There is so much you can add to this salad to make it your own, like scallions, Cotija, or feta just to name a few. Play around with the flavors and don't be afraid to write down what you like right here on this page so you don't forget!

---

6   (6-inch) corn tortillas, sliced into ¼-inch strips

¼   cup plus 1 tablespoon neutral oil, such as avocado

1½ teaspoons chili powder

Kosher salt and freshly ground black pepper

1   (16-ounce) bag frozen corn (no need to thaw)

1½ pounds peeled and deveined large shrimp (16–20 count), patted dry

1   garlic clove, peeled but whole

2   limes, plus more as needed

⅓   cup mayonnaise or Greek yogurt

2   heads romaine lettuce, thinly sliced, or 2 (10-ounce) bags chopped romaine

6   small radishes, trimmed and thinly sliced

1   cup pineapple chunks, fresh or canned

½   cup fresh cilantro leaves and tender stems

1   avocado, thinly sliced

1. Preheat the oven to 425°F.

2. On a sheet pan, toss the **tortillas** with **1 tablespoon of the oil**, the **chili powder**, and **½ teaspoon each salt and pepper** until well coated. Spread into an even layer and roast, stirring halfway through, until golden brown and crisp, 10 to 12 minutes. Transfer to a plate and set aside to cool.

3. Pour the **corn** onto the sheet pan. Top with the **shrimp**, then toss with the remaining ¼ cup oil, 2 teaspoons salt, and ½ teaspoon pepper. Roast until the shrimp are opaque throughout, 8 to 15 minutes. Let cool for 5 minutes.

4. Finely grate the **garlic** and the zest of both **limes** over the sheet pan, then squeeze lime juice over all. Add the **mayonnaise** and stir to coat. Add the **lettuce** and ½ teaspoon salt and toss gently to combine. Season to taste with salt, pepper, and more lime juice. Top with the **radishes**, **pineapple**, **cilantro**, **avocado**, and last but not least, the chips.

BABS SAYS

Here's a great way to "peel" a pineapple: First, cut off the top and bottom of the pineapple. Then stand it upright and cut the rind off, moving from top to bottom and cutting about ¼ inch deep, all the way around the pineapple!

♥

Use store-bought chips to streamline this even more; you can pop them in the oven and just hit them with a bit of chili powder for that added kick.

♥

If you have 2 sheet pans, save 10 minutes by cooking the chips and the shrimp/corn at the same time. Put the shrimp/corn on the upper rack and chips on the lower rack.

PUT-YOUR-KIDS-TO-WORK CRISPY BEAN & CHEESE TACOS

Serves 4

PREP
10 minutes

COOK
10 minutes

My first cookbook when I was a little girl was the 1957 edition of *Betty Crocker's Cookbook for Boys and Girls.* I've gotten the updated version for each one of my grandchildren. Kids don't always love to eat, but they usually love helping you cook. Two of my granddaughters, Grace and Charlotte, have both come over to my home with their cookbooks to make their family dinner (they're sisters). They chose a menu from the book—a drink, an entree, and a dessert—and I helped them make it. The meals were simple: a lemonade, a pasta, and a batch of cookies. When they were done cooking, we bagged it all up and they took it home for their family dinner, so excited and proud!

Here's a recipe that would be perfect for helpers but won't slow down the dinnertime flow. You can switch the beans out for leftover chicken or cooked chorizo if you'd like, but this is also a terrific and fun way to get kids to eat beans! They can layer on the shredded cheese, you stick the tortillas in the oven, and less than 10 minutes later, dinner is ready. Compliments to the chefs!

---

12 (6-inch) flour tortillas (sometimes labeled taco or fajita tortillas)

Nonstick cooking spray or neutral oil, such as avocado

Kosher salt

2 (15-ounce) cans pinto beans, drained and rinsed

1 (1-ounce) packet taco seasoning mix (about 3 tablespoons)

2 cups (8 ounces) shredded Mexican, Monterey Jack, or Cheddar cheese

For serving (optional): salsa, shredded lettuce, sliced scallions, cilantro, chopped white onion, hot sauce, lime wedges, and/or sour cream

1. Preheat the oven to 450°F. Line 2 sheet pans with parchment paper.

2. Arrange the **tortillas** on the sheet pans (it's okay if they overlap). Spray with **cooking spray or brush with oil,** then sprinkle very lightly with **salt** and flip over.

3. In a medium bowl, stir the **beans** and **taco seasoning** to coat. Sprinkle each tortilla with about **1 tablespoon of the cheese**, followed by the beans (scant ¼ cup each), and then the remaining cheese. Bake, rotating the pans halfway through, until the tortillas are crisp underneath and the cheese is melted, 7 to 9 minutes.

4. Working quickly, sprinkle the tortillas with the toppings (if using). Press the tortillas in half with a spatula, then let them cool for a minute or two before serving.

BABS SAYS

If you don't have taco seasoning on hand, use 1½ tablespoon ground cumin and 1½ tablespoon chili powder (or to taste). Or, leave it out entirely for a really simply flavored taco.

♥

If you want to add a veggie, do that before adding the second round of cheese. You could use cauliflower rice, some spinach, or cooked peppers or squash.

CURRIED FISH BITES
with CHICKPEAS & CARROTS

Serves 4

PREP
10 minutes

COOK
20 minutes

To this day, I remember every detail of my friend Lucy's bridal shower. It was held at the home of a fabulously wealthy Lebanese family. The house took up an entire block. I was twenty-three at the time, and I had never seen or experienced anything like it. Dressed to the nines, we were led into the dining room and offered a choice between filet mignon and chicken curry—or both! The perfume of that chicken curry was intoxicating. It was completely new to me. I skipped right over the steak and have loved all things curry ever since— including these amazing curried fish bites.

This is a delicately spiced, almost soothing meal of white fish, carrots, chickpeas, herbs, and a lemon-yogurt sauce. It's truly feel-good food.

---

5   carrots (1 pound), peeled and thinly sliced into coins

1   (15-ounce) can chickpeas, drained, rinsed, and dried well

1   tablespoon finely chopped fresh ginger

5   tablespoons extra-virgin olive oil

3   teaspoons curry powder

     Kosher salt and freshly ground black pepper

1½   pounds skinless cod fillets or other firm fish

¾   cup plain whole-milk Greek yogurt (5-ounce container)

1   lemon

½   cup fresh mint and/or cilantro leaves, torn if large

     For serving: salad greens, rice, cauliflower rice, or naan

1. Preheat the oven to 425°F.

2. On a sheet pan, toss together the **carrots**, **chickpeas**, **ginger**, **3 tablespoons of the olive oil**, **2 teaspoons of the curry powder**, **1½ teaspoons salt**, and **½ teaspoon pepper**. Spread into an even layer and roast for 10 minutes.

3. Meanwhile, cut the **fish fillets** into 1-inch pieces and pat dry. In a medium bowl, combine the fish, remaining 2 tablespoons olive oil, remaining 1 teaspoon curry powder, and 1 teaspoon salt. Toss to combine.

4. In a small bowl, combine the **yogurt** with the **juice of half the lemon** (about 1½ tablespoons) and ½ teaspoon each salt and pepper. Thin with water until saucy, if necessary. Cut the other half of the lemon into wedges for serving.

5. Stir the carrots and chickpeas, spread into an even layer on the pan, then top with the fish. Roast until the fish is cooked through and the carrots are tender, 7 to 9 minutes.

6. Serve the fish and vegetables with a squeeze of lemon, a drizzle of the yogurt sauce, a sprinkle of the **herbs**, and **salad greens**, **rice**, **cauliflower rice**, or **naan**.

SHEET-PAN DUMPLING STIR-FRY

Serves 4

PREP
10 minutes

COOK
20 minutes

When they were first married, my daughter Elizabeth and her husband, Ray, my number-one son-in-love, lived above a Chinese restaurant. They'd just had their first baby, Charlie. There was only one bedroom, so I was sleeping on the sofa while helping Elizabeth navigate being a brand-new mother and allowing her a little rest. Charlie really kept me on my toes, so I was only too happy to fuel those long nights by taking the elevator down a few floors to pick up some delicious steamed pork dumplings. So, I wanted to make sure to bring the ease of a delicious dinnertime dumpling to you, too.

Here is an extremely easy way to make a complete meal of frozen dumplings. On one sheet pan, you get tender dumplings, lots of cooked veggies, and a glazy sauce that coats everything. It's like making a stir-fry without the stirring and frying—plus, the frozen vegetables mean this is a mostly no-prep dinner.

---

3   tablespoons neutral oil, such as avocado

1½ pounds frozen veggie dumplings (no need to thaw), can substitute pork or chicken, just increase bake time by 2 to 4 minutes

¼   cup reduced-sodium soy sauce

2   tablespoons honey

1   tablespoon cornstarch

1   tablespoon unseasoned rice vinegar

2   teaspoons toasted sesame oil

1   teaspoon red pepper flakes (optional)

2   (10-ounce) bags frozen mixed vegetables (no need to thaw), preferably Asian medley with baby corn, snow peas, and/or water chestnuts

2   scallions, thinly sliced

    For serving: toasted sesame seeds (optional)

1. Preheat the oven to 450°F. Grease the sheet pan with **1 tablespoon of the oil**.

2. Add the **dumplings**, the remaining 2 tablespoons oil, and ¼ **cup water** to the sheet pan and toss to combine. Spread into an even layer, leaving a bit of space between the dumplings. Seal with a piece of aluminum foil and bake until the dumplings are just tender, about 10 minutes.

3. In a small bowl, stir together the **soy sauce**, **honey**, **cornstarch**, **rice vinegar**, **sesame oil**, and **red pepper flakes** (if using).

4. After the dumplings have baked for 10 minutes, stir the sauce again, then add the **veggies** and sauce to the dumplings. Gently stir to coat. Return to the oven and bake, uncovered, until the dumplings and veggies are heated through and the sauce is thickened and bubbling, about 10 minutes more.

5. Serve topped with the **scallions** and **sesame seeds** (if using).

BABS SAYS

Although these dumplings are glazed with a stir-fry sauce, you may want a dipping sauce as well. So, make a dipping sauce! Combine ¼ cup soy sauce, 1 tablespoon unseasoned rice vinegar, 2 teaspoons toasted sesame oil, a sliced scallion, and a pinch of red pepper flakes.

♥

If you want to use fresh veggies, go for anything that will roast in 10 minutes: asparagus, corn kernels, baby corn, or sliced bell peppers.

♥

If you want some crispy bits, like pan-fried dumplings, place the sheet pan on the upper rack under the broiler for a few minutes at the end of cooking.

Eat Twice Twosday

Raising a family of four children meant we didn't typically have leftovers. And, boy, as they got bigger and grew into teenagers, did I try to make the recipes stretch! Whether it was for second helpings, lunch, or even for dinner the next week.

I thought of Tuesday as *Twosday* and I challenged myself to batch-cook. Hello, freezer staples! I still had most of the week ahead of me, so instead of one meatloaf, I'd make two: one for dinner, one for the freezer. Meatballs? I'd double the recipe and pop the extras in the refridge. Spaghetti and meatballs or meatball subs? Whatever you're in the mood for, you're ready to go! Crispy fried chicken cutlets can easily do double duty for chicken parm the next night or sandwiches the next day.

It all makes the rest of the week seem a little more manageable, a little more under control. You're already dirtying the dishes, pots, and pans, and you have the ingredients right in front of you. So, just make once and eat twice!

GRAMMIE'S CHICKEN CUTLETS

Serves 4 twice

PREP
30 minutes

COOK
25 minutes

Nonnas are great at having food at the ready—it's a grandma thing. If you were to stop by my house and open my freezer, you would see a stack of these chicken cutlets ready to go. Think of these as your new dinnertime best friend. The recipe, as noted, serves four—twice! But you can make as many of these as you like, and you won't be sorry.

You can use these cutlets for any dinner recipe you can imagine. Slice them into tenders and serve with a side of fries and the dipping sauce of your choice. Make a chicken club sandwich or sub. Pour on your favorite marinara and some mozzarella cheese, and you've got a delicious chicken parm. Go lighter and serve with a simply dressed salad with arugula, tomatoes, and shaved Parmesan, like chicken Milanese.

---

4   boneless, skinless chicken breasts (8 ounces each)

Kosher salt and freshly ground black pepper

½   cup all-purpose flour

1   teaspoon garlic powder

1   teaspoon Italian seasoning

2   large eggs

1¼   cups panko bread crumbs

½   cup (2 ounces) grated Parmesan cheese

Neutral oil, such as avocado, for shallow-frying

1   tablespoon unsalted butter

BABS SAYS

You wouldn't think you could get these as crispy in the oven as with the fry method, but this recipe manages to do just that.

♥

Here's the simple salad recipe. In a large bowl, combine baby arugula and halved cherry tomatoes, then dress with a drizzle of olive oil, fresh lemon juice, grated Parmesan, and salt and pepper.

1. Set one hand on top of a **chicken breast** to hold it in place, then cut horizontally through the middle so you have 2 thinner cutlets. Repeat for all the chicken breasts for a total of 8 cutlets. Pat the chicken dry with paper towels. Season the chicken all over with **2 teaspoons salt**.

2. Prepare 3 shallow dishes or large plates for coating the chicken. In the first dish, combine the **flour**, **garlic powder**, and **Italian seasoning**. Season with ½ teaspoon each salt and **pepper**. In the second dish, beat the **eggs**. In the third dish, combine the **panko** and **Parmesan**, then season with ¼ teaspoon each salt and pepper.

3. One at a time, dip the chicken cutlets in the flour and coat all sides, tapping off the excess. Next, dip in the egg, allowing any excess to drip back into the dish. Finally, coat with the panko mixture, pressing to adhere. Place on a plate as you coat all the cutlets.

ENJOY NOW: In a large cast-iron skillet or heavy-bottomed pot, heat **¼ inch of oil** over medium heat. Once shimmering, add the **butter**, swirling until melted. Carefully add 2 chicken cutlets to the skillet. Fry until golden brown and fully cooked, 2 to 4 minutes per side. Transfer to a clean plate, then immediately sprinkle with a little salt. Repeat with 2 more chicken cutlets. Serve.

ENJOY LATER: Arrange half the cutlets on a plate or sheet pan, cover with plastic wrap, and freeze until solid. Transfer the cutlets to a zipper-top plastic bag and freeze for up to 1 month. While still frozen, bake at 450°F until until cooked through, 20 to 25 minutes.

THE ULTIMATE RED CHIMICHURRI SAUCE with SKIRT STEAK

Serves 4 twice

PREP
10 minutes, plus marinating time

COOK
10 minutes

Skirt steak with chimichurri is one of those meals that is super easy but seems like you put in a ton of effort. This particular cut of meat is perfect for a weeknight, too, because when cooked over very high heat, by the time the outside chars, the inside is a beautiful medium-rare. I use a red chimichurri instead of a green. I like to think of it is like salsa but with peppers instead of tomatoes. You know I love sauce, and this recipe makes enough that you can use the extra sauce in tacos, burritos, salad, or with rice and beans.

STEAK

- 2½ pounds skirt steak, cut into roughly 6-inch pieces, patted dry
- ¼ cup extra-virgin olive oil, plus more for greasing
- 1½ teaspoons smoked paprika
- 1½ teaspoons ground cumin
- 1½ teaspoons garlic powder
- Kosher salt and freshly ground black pepper

RED CHIMICHURRI

- 2 garlic cloves
- 2 (12-ounce) jars roasted red peppers, drained (about 2½ cups)
- 1 teaspoon smoked paprika
- 1 teaspoon ground cumin
- Kosher salt and freshly ground black pepper
- ½ cup extra-virgin olive oil
- ¼ cup red wine vinegar

1. **Marinate the steak:** In a large bowl or resealable container or bag, combine the **steak, olive oil, paprika, cumin, garlic powder, 1 teaspoon salt,** and **½ teaspoon pepper**. Toss to coat, then set aside at room temperature to marinate while you make the chimichurri (or refrigerate overnight or for up to 2 days).

2. **Make the red chimichurri:** Add the **garlic** to a food processor and pulse until coarsely chopped. Add the **roasted red peppers,** paprika, cumin, 2 teaspoons salt, and ½ teaspoon pepper and pulse until combined but still chunky. Stir in the **olive oil** and **vinegar**. Season to taste with additional salt and pepper. (Store in the empty roasted red pepper jars or another large container for up to 5 days in the refridge.)

3. If grilling, clean and grease the grates, then preheat the grill to high. If using the broiler, arrange a rack in the top of the oven and set the broiler to high. Line a sheet pan with aluminum foil.

4. Scrape off most of the marinade from the steak. If grilling, place the steak directly on the preheated grill. If broiling, arrange the steak on the sheet pan under your oven's broiler. In both instances, cook until charred, 2 to 5 minutes per side. Let the steak rest for 5 minutes.

ENJOY NOW: Slice the steak against the grain for the amount you want and serve with the red chimichurri on top.

ENJOY LATER: Refrigerate the extra steak whole for up to 3 days and the sauce for up to 5 to 7 days. To reheat, warm it in the microwave sprinkled with a little water—just enough to not dry it out. Or, eat at room temperature. Slice right before serving and add the chimichurri.

TWO BIRDS, ONE OVEN

Serves 4 twice

PREP
20 minutes

COOK
50 minutes

Roasting a chicken is easy and *very* satisfying. You can find my traditional recipe in the Sunday Supper chapter on page 202, but sometimes you can't wait for Sundays! Spatchcocking (aka butterflying) is your ticket to delicious, juicy meat and crispy skin during the week. It takes much less time, *and* this method leaves room in your oven for *two chickens*. Two birds, one stone . . . or oven.

This recipe features two really different pantry-friendly rubs. The herb rub has the essence of tzatziki and ranch—garlicky and herbaceous. The spice rub is is a simplified version of Lebanese seven-spice, with its warming and grounding spices.

---

2   whole chickens
     (3½ to 4 pounds each)

HERB RUB (FOR 1 CHICKEN)

1   tablespoon dried dill

1   tablespoon garlic powder

2   teaspoons kosher salt

SPICE RUB (FOR 1 CHICKEN)

2   teaspoons sweet paprika

2   teaspoons ground cumin

2   teaspoons kosher salt

1   teaspoon freshly ground
     black pepper

½   teaspoon ground cinnamon

½   teaspoon ground allspice

4   tablespoons extra-virgin olive oil

> **BABS SAYS**
>
> Invest in a really good pair of kitchen shears; they will make spatchcocking the chicken a breeze. Or just ask your friendly butcher at the grocery store.

1. **Spatchcock the chickens:** One at a time, place the **chickens** on a cutting board breast side down. Use sharp kitchen shears to cut along the backbone on both sides. Remove the backbone. Flip the chicken over, then press firmly in the center until you hear a crack. Pat the chickens dry. Transfer the chicken to a sheet pan.

2. **Season the chickens:** In a small bowl, stir together the herb rub, combining the **dill**, **garlic powder**, and **salt**. In another small bowl, stir together the spice rub, combining the **paprika**, **cumin**, salt, **pepper**, **cinnamon**, and **allspice**. Use the herb rub to coat one chicken all over; use the spice rub to coat the other chicken. If time allows, let both chickens sit up to 1 hour at room temperature (or refrigerate uncovered up to overnight), for the seasoning to flavor the birds.

3. When you're ready to cook, preheat the oven to 425°F.

4. Rub the skin of each chicken with **2 tablespoons of the olive oil**. Roast both chickens until a thermometer registers 165°F in the thickest part of the thigh, 40 to 50 minutes. Let rest for 10 minutes.

ENJOY NOW: Carve 1 chicken and serve.

ENJOY LATER: When the chicken is cooled, pull the meat off the bones and shred it for sandwiches, salads, or even soups (like my Lemony Chicken Soup, page 129).

Chicken 4/9

LICK-YOUR-PLATE-CLEAN GREEN GODDESS SALMON

Serves 4 twice

PREP
15 minutes

COOK
20 minutes

Advance warning on this one: you won't be able to stop eating this dressing! In my version, a creamy, herby combination of mayo, yogurt, dill, and basil is whizzed in the blender while the salmon and asparagus roast. Drizzle the green goddess over everything warm—just be sure to save some for later in the week, for dipping, spreading on sandwiches, or spooning over eggs. You can and *should* use this on anything and everything!

If you need an idea for the salmon on day 2, make salmon cakes! Shred the cooked salmon with a couple of forks, then add egg, mayo, diced asparagus, panko, and flour and mix until you can easily form patties. Season to your liking, then fry them up. The best part? You already have a great dipping sauce!

SALMON AND ASPARAGUS

2 to 3 bunches asparagus, trimmed

3   tablespoons extra-virgin olive oil

    Kosher salt and freshly ground black pepper

3   pounds skin-on salmon fillet, preferably center-cut

GREEN GODDESS DRESSING

1   cup mayonnaise

⅔   cup plain whole-milk yogurt

⅔   cup chopped fresh dill, plus more for serving

⅔   cup packed fresh basil, plus more for serving

6   tablespoons fresh lemon juice (from 3 lemons)

    Heaping tablespoon Dijon mustard

1   large garlic clove, peeled but whole

    Kosher salt and freshly ground black pepper

1. Arrange racks in the upper and lower thirds of the oven and preheat the oven to 450°F. Line 2 sheet pans with parchment paper.

2. **Prepare the salmon and asparagus:** Place the **asparagus** on one sheet pan, drizzle with **2 tablespoons of the olive oil**, and sprinkle with ½ **teaspoon salt** and some **pepper**; shake the pan to coat the asparagus. Place the **salmon** on the other sheet pan. Brush the top of the fish with the remaining tablespoon olive oil and season with ½ teaspoon salt and some pepper.

3. Place both sheet pans in the oven and roast until the salmon is cooked through and the asparagus is crisp-tender, 15 to 17 minutes.

4. **Make the dressing:** In a blender, combine the **mayonnaise**, **yogurt**, **dill**, **basil**, **lemon juice**, **mustard**, **garlic**, 1 teaspoon salt, and ½ teaspoon pepper. Process until smooth. (Makes about 2 cups.)

ENJOY NOW: Transfer half the salmon and asparagus to a serving platter, leaving the fish skin behind (it slips off easily). Drizzle with some of the dressing and sprinkle with more dill. Serve some of the dressing alongside.

ENJOY LATER: The remaining salmon will keep, refrigerated, in an airtight container for 3 days; the remaining asparagus and dressing will keep, refrigerated, in airtight containers for up to 4 days. See the headnote for suggestions on using the remaining salmon.

BOURBON-GLAZED PORK CHOPS

Serves 4 twice

PREP
10 minutes, plus
marinating time

COOK
15 minutes

When I was in my twenties, my go-to drink was bourbon and ginger ale with a twist of lime. It was so refreshing! Now that I'm in my seventies, I find I like my bourbon *best* when I use it to cook. It has just a touch of subtle sweetness that pairs well with so many things, especially pork, like in these glazed pork chops. This works especially well during the summer because it's a grilling recipe, but you can get the same charred effect with a grill pan or in your oven (see Babs Says). Since the alcohol burns off in the cooking process, these are family friendly, too. Pour the sauce over the pork chops and serve with mashed potatoes or your favorite veggies.

⅓   cup firmly packed light brown sugar

3   tablespoons Dijon mustard

3   tablespoons reduced-sodium soy sauce

3   tablespoons bourbon

    Kosher salt and freshly ground black pepper

8   bone-in, 1-inch-thick pork chops (about 6 pounds total), patted dry

    Neutral oil, for greasing, such as avocado

BABS SAYS

Too cold outside to grill? No problem! Preheat the oven to 400°F. Heat 1 tablespoon oil in a large cast-iron skillet over high heat. Scrape off the marinade from the pork chops and add half the chops to the skillet. Sear until browned, 1 to 3 minutes per side. Transfer to a sheet pan and repeat with the remaining pork chops and more oil. (Reserve the marinade and don't wash the skillet.) Transfer the sheet pan to the oven and roast until the internal temperature of the pork registers 145°F, 7 to 12 minutes. Wipe up the burnt bits from the skillet, then pour the marinade into the skillet and continue with the last step.

1. In a large zip-top plastic bag, stir together the **brown sugar**, **mustard**, **soy sauce**, **bourbon**, **1 teaspoon salt**, and **¼ teaspoon pepper.** Add the **pork chops** and turn to coat well. Seal and chill for at least 30 minutes or up to overnight.w

2. Grease your grill with **oil** and heat it to medium-high heat. (Alternatively, see Babs Says for oven roasting.) Pull out and shake the pork chops to remove any marinade, then add the chops to the grill. (Reserve the remaining marinade.) Cover and cook, turning once, until the internal temperature reaches 145°F, 10 to 12 minutes. Transfer the pork chops to a plate to rest.

ENJOY NOW: Pour the reserved marinade into a medium saucepan. Bring to a boil over medium-high heat, then reduce the heat to medium-low and simmer until the sauce resembles maple syrup, 2 to 3 minutes. Spoon half the sauce over half the pork chops and serve.

ENJOY LATER: Refrigerate the remaining pork chops along with their resting juices and the remaining half of the glaze for up to 3 days. To reheat, place in a baking dish, spoon over a little of the juices and/or glaze, and warm in a 350°F oven for 20 to 30 minutes. Also, any leftovers are great cut off the bone and added to a sandwich or stirred into fried rice, cut up into a salad (like the one on page 75), or served with mashed potatoes and vegetables.

MOM'S MEATLOAF

Serves 4 twice

PREP
15 minutes

COOK
1 hour

Kresge's was one of those classic dime stores in Chicago, similar to Woolworth's. The kind of place that had a lunch counter where shoppers and non-shoppers alike could have an inexpensive, hearty meal. I remember going with my mom and ordering the special of the day, the all-American meatloaf. The ultimate comfort food. Back in the day, meatloaf was a weeknight staple for many families, and every family had its own special recipe. *This* one is mine. Not only is it mouthwatering and yummy, but it can also be a life preserver for those days when you can't even think of making dinner. I use ketchup for the glaze here because meatloaf glaze is made of tomato, sugar, vinegar, and spices—just like ketchup.

This recipe makes two loaves, one for the same night you make it and one for the freezer. That extra meatloaf will serve you well. Just take it out of the freezer the night before you see a day on the calendar that looks a little exhausting and, presto, dinner awaits you!

---

2 tablespoons extra-virgin olive oil

2 yellow onions, finely chopped

4 garlic cloves, finely chopped or grated

4 large eggs

½ cup whole milk or water

2 sleeves Ritz crackers (about 60 crackers total), finely crushed (2 cups)

2 pounds ground beef (80% lean)

2 pounds ground pork

1½ cups ketchup

2 tablespoons Worcestershire sauce

⅓ cup finely chopped fresh parsley, or 2 tablespoons dried

Kosher salt and freshly ground black pepper

1. Preheat the oven to 375°F. Line a sheet pan with parchment paper or aluminum foil.

2. In a medium skillet, heat the **olive oil** over medium-high heat. Add the **onions** and cook, stirring occasionally, until lightly browned and tender, 3 to 5 minutes. Add the **garlic** and cook until fragrant, about 1 minute more. Set aside to cool.

3. In a large bowl, beat the **eggs** with a fork until homogenous. Stir in the **milk** and **cracker crumbs**. Let sit for 5 minutes, then add the onion mixture, the **ground beef** and **pork**, ½ cup of the **ketchup**, the **Worcestershire sauce**, **parsley**, **2½ teaspoons salt**, and **1 teaspoon pepper**. Knead until combined but try not to overmix.

4. Using damp hands, form the meat mixture into 2 loaves and place on the sheet pan. (Alternatively, divide the meat between two 9 × 5-inch loaf pans.) Use a spoon to glaze the top and sides of the loaves with the remaining 1 cup ketchup. Bake until the internal temperature is 160°F and the glaze is bubbling and slightly browned, 50 minutes to 1 hour. (Broil for a few minutes if you want the glaze more browned.) Let the loaves rest for 10 minutes on the sheet pan.

(recipe continues)

ENJOY NOW: Transfer one of the loaves to a cutting board and slice to serve while still warm.

ENJOY LATER: Cover and refrigerate the other baked meatloaf for a day or two. To freeze, wrap the loaf in plastic and then in freezer paper. When ready to use, allow to thaw in the refridge overnight. Reheat the whole loaf in a preheated 350°F oven for 20 minutes; if in slices, simply microwave for 1 to 2 minutes per slice. Better yet, brown the slices in an olive oil–greased skillet for crispy bits!

FINALLY, I NAILED FALAFEL
with TZATZIKI SLAW

Serves 4 twice

PREP
30 minutes

COOK
20 minutes

It's confession time: I've tried to re-create falafel at home so many times and failed (until now!). I'd bake the falafel instead of frying the traditional way, not just because it's healthier but also because when you're trying to get dinner on the table, who has time to heat up a pot of oil? Not me! But they never came out crispy enough and were always too dry inside.

Finally, I figured out how to make the perfect baked falafel! Forget the balls and make it a patty! Think of this as the most delicious veggie burger you've ever had, and the easiest falafel you've ever made, all rolled into one. Make this double batch and serve them on the slaw or other salad, in grain bowls, in pita, between burger buns, or however else you'd eat a veggie burger.

FALAFEL

1½   large bunches fresh cilantro

1   small red onion, coarsely chopped

2   garlic cloves, smashed

2   teaspoons ground cumin

2   teaspoons baking powder

      Kosher salt and freshly ground black pepper

4   (15-ounce) cans chickpeas, drained and rinsed

2   tablespoons all-purpose flour, or more as needed

¼   cup extra-virgin olive oil

1. Arrange a rack in the bottom third of the oven and preheat the oven to 425°F.

2. **Prepare the falafel:** Hold on to the stem ends of the **cilantro** and thinly slice the tops until you get to the thicker stems. Discard the thicker stems. Place the chopped leaves and tender stems in the food processor. Pulse to coarsely chop. Add the **onion**, **garlic**, **cumin**, **baking powder**, **1½ teaspoons salt**, and **½ teaspoon pepper** and pulse until finely chopped but not pureed. Add the **chickpeas** and pulse again, scraping down the sides of the bowl a few times, until well combined and slightly pasty but not yet smooth like hummus.

3. Transfer the mixture to a large bowl and sprinkle evenly with the **flour**, then use a silicone spatula to fold in the flour until no streaks remain. The mixture should be moist and hold together easily if you scoop a handful of it. (Think meatball mixture.) If it is too wet, add more flour 1 tablespoon at a time; if it is too dry, add water 1 tablespoon at a time.

4. Brush a sheet pan with **2 tablespoons of the olive oil**. Shape the falafel mixture into 8 patties about 1 inch thick and 3½ inches in diameter. Press firmly to pack the mixture together. Place the patties on the sheet pan and brush the remaining 2 tablespoons olive oil all over the tops and sides of the patties.

(recipe continues)

TZATZIKI SLAW

1	English hothouse cucumber, halved lengthwise and sliced ¼ inch thick
	Kosher salt
3	(10-ounce) bags coleslaw mix, or 12 cups shredded green or red cabbage
¼	cup fresh lemon juice (from 2 lemons)
¾	cup plain whole-milk Greek yogurt (5-ounce container)
¼	cup extra-virgin olive oil
	Freshly ground black pepper
½	cup chopped fresh dill

For serving: toasted pita or burger buns, Tahini Dressing (from Refridge-Friendly Sheet-Pan Farro & Kale Salad, page 75)

5. Bake until the patties are crisp and browned on the bottom, about 10 minutes. Very carefully flip the patties. (They'll be a bit delicate at this point; don't worry too much if a piece breaks off while you're flipping. Just gently press the patty back together.) Return the patties to the oven to bake until crisp and golden all over, 10 minutes more. Sprinkle with salt and let rest for 5 minutes to firm up.

6. **While the falafel bake, make the slaw:** In a colander, toss the **cucumber** with ½ teaspoon salt. Set in the sink to drain for 10 to 15 minutes. In a large bowl, combine the **coleslaw mix**, **lemon juice**, and 1½ teaspoons salt. Add the **yogurt**, olive oil, and ½ teaspoon pepper and stir until coated. Stir in the cucumber and the **dill**, then season to taste with salt and pepper.

ENJOY NOW: Serve half the falafel hot with the tzatziki slaw on the side (or sandwich both in a pita or burger bun, if using). Drizzle the falafel with tahini dressing to take it over the top and around the block!

ENJOY LATER: The remaining falafel will keep well in the refridge for up to 4 days. To reheat, toast the patties in a skillet over medium heat until crisp on the bottom, about 2 minutes. Flip, add a tablespoon of water to the pan, reduce the heat to low, cover, and cook for 2 to 3 minutes to heat through. The falafel can also be frozen for future use. Freeze the patties on a sheet pan, then transfer to a zip-top bag and freeze for up to 2 months. To reheat, place the frozen patties on a sheet pan and bake at 350°F until hot all the way through, 20 to 25 minutes.

BREAKFAST-FOR-DINNER SANDWICHES

Serves 6 twice
(12 sandwiches)

PREP
15 minutes

COOK
30 minutes

There's always that one night when Murphy's law kicks in big time, when anything that can go wrong does go wrong. Maybe you get stuck at work, or you get a call from the school to pick up your sick child, or—worse yet—one of the kids slipped at gymnastics and you're off to the ER. Those are the days you'll be so happy to have these sandwiches in your freezer. They are incredibly easy to make and to freeze, and are quite simply your sanity saviors.

When you need one, into the microwave it goes and later you have a hot and melty egg and cheese that rivals the iconic McMuffin. They're so convenient . . . and, let me tell you, *so delicious*. Make sure to prepare even more than you think you'll need, because they'll be gobbled up on non-emergency days, too!

SHEET-PAN EGGS

Nonstick cooking spray

18   large eggs

⅓   cup whole milk

Kosher salt and freshly ground black pepper

1   cup (4 ounces) shredded Cheddar cheese

1   cup cooked veggies, such as bell peppers or spinach (optional)

ASSEMBLY

12   slices bacon, sausage patties, ham, or Canadian bacon

12   English muffins

3   tablespoons unsalted butter

12   slices Cheddar or other cheese

1. **Make the eggs:** Preheat the oven to 350°F. Grease an 11 × 17-inch rimmed sheet pan with **cooking spray**, line with parchment paper, then spray again.

2. In a blender, puree the **eggs**, **milk**, **2 teaspoons salt**, and **½ teaspoon pepper** until smooth. Pour the egg mixture onto the sheet pan and top with the **shredded cheese** (and **veggies**, if using). Bake until the eggs are set, 15 to 18 minutes. Allow the eggs to cool for a few minutes, then use a drinking glass the size of an English muffin to cut out 12 rounds.

3. **Begin the assembly:** While the eggs are cooking, in a large skillet, cook the **meat** over medium-high heat until browned, 2 to 5 minutes per side depending on the meat. Transfer to a plate.

4. Split the **English muffins** and place on a sheet pan. Bake until toasted, 3 to 5 minutes. Right out of the oven, spread them with the **butter**.

5. For each sandwich, place the bottom of an English muffin on a square of parchment and top with a piece of meat, a slice of cheese, and a round of egg, then add the top of the English muffin. Wrap and secure with tape. Repeat with the remaining muffins.

ENJOY NOW: Pop a wrapped sandwich in the microwave for 30 seconds and you're good to go.

ENJOY LATER: Refrigerate the remaining sandwiches for up to 4 days or freeze for up to 1 month. (You can even store the sandwiches right in the bags the muffins came in!) To reheat from either the refridge or freezer, microwave the sandwich in its parchment for 30 seconds to 2 minutes, or heat in a 350°F oven or toaster oven for 10 to 15 minutes.

VINCENZA'S "SCAROLE" SOUP
with SAUSAGE & WHITE BEANS

Serves 4 twice

PREP
10 minutes

COOK
30 minutes

My grandmother made an amazing white bean and escarole soup. We called the soup "scarole." Escarole is a green leafy vegetable that's hearty enough for soups yet tender enough for salads. The irony here is that *scarole* is also Italian American slang for "money"! We didn't have a lot of that, which is why we had so much *actual escarole*. Besides being economical and full of nutrients, it's also delicious! My grandmother's classic soup gets a kick here from no-fuss sausage meatballs and all their flavorful juices.

2	pounds sweet Italian sausage, casings removed
1	tablespoon extra-virgin olive oil, or more as needed
8	garlic cloves, smashed
2	sprigs fresh rosemary
½	teaspoon red pepper flakes, plus more for serving
2	bunches escarole (about 2 pounds), cleaned and roughly chopped
	Kosher salt and freshly ground black pepper
2	quarts chicken broth, preferably bone broth
4	(15-ounce) cans white beans, drained but not rinsed
¼	cup (1 ounce) finely grated Parmesan cheese, plus more for serving
	Lemon wedges (optional)

> **BABS SAYS**
>
> If you don't want to use "scarole," feel free to switch up the greens. If you're using spinach, don't add it until the very end of the cooking time.

1. Use a tablespoon measuring spoon or a 1-inch cookie scoop to form meatballs from the **sausage meat**. Add a single layer of the balls to a heavy-bottomed large pot, add the **olive oil**, set the pot over medium-high heat, and cook until browned on two sides, 5 to 8 minutes. Transfer to a plate and repeat with the remaining sausage.

2. Reduce the heat to low and add the **garlic** and **rosemary**. Stir until the garlic is lightly golden, 1 to 2 minutes. Stir in the **pepper flakes**, then stir in half the **escarole** and add **¼ teaspoon salt**. Increase the heat to high and stir until wilted, scraping up any browned bits. Add the remaining escarole and another ¼ teaspoon salt to the pot and stir until the full batch is wilted. This will take about a minute.

3. Add the **broth** and **beans** and bring to a simmer over high heat. Smash some of the beans against the side of the pot to thicken the broth and simmer the liquid until flavorful, 2 to 3 minutes. Reduce the heat to medium, add the meatballs and any juices from the plate, and simmer until the soup is flavorful and the meat is cooked through, 5 to 7 minutes.

4. Remove the rosemary sprigs from the pot. Stir in the **Parmesan**, then season to taste with salt and **pepper**.

ENJOY NOW: Serve topped with more Parmesan, more pepper flakes, and a **squeeze of lemon** (if using).

ENJOY LATER: The remaining soup will keep in the refridge for up to 4 days. To freeze it, let the soup cool completely, then divide it among zip-top freezer bags. Press out all the air and seal. (Don't fill the bags all the way, as liquid expands when frozen.) Lay the bags flat on a sheet pan and freeze until firm, then remove the bags from the pan and store them in the freezer for up to 3 months.

MINNIE'S MEATBALLS

Serves 6 twice
(makes 50 meatballs)

PREP
20 minutes, plus
30 minutes
refrigeration time

COOK
20 minutes

It seems like only yesterday that my mother and grandmother were making meatballs in my grandmother's kitchen, speaking Italian a mile a minute, while my grandfather was at the kitchen table grating cheese and listening to Italian opera on his radio. He was so moved by the music, tears would roll down his cheeks (not into the cheese). What I wouldn't give to be back in that kitchen!

This is the traditional way my Neapolitan grandmother made her meatballs, but with a few modern updates to save time. Make a *big* batch, then pop half in the freezer to have on hand for anything you're in the mood for: on pasta or on sandwiches.

---

4   large eggs

2   cups unseasoned bread crumbs

2   cups whole milk

1   cup packed fresh parsley leaves, finely chopped

6   garlic cloves, finely chopped or grated

1   cup (4 ounces) freshly grated Pecorino Romano cheese

Kosher salt and freshly ground black pepper

3   pounds ground beef (80% lean)

1   pound ground pork

> **BABS SAYS**
>
> These are also a great way to sneak in veggies; just grate ¼ cup of zucchini or carrots into the mixture.

1. In a large bowl, beat the **eggs** until smooth. Stir in the **bread crumbs** and **milk** and let sit until a smooth paste forms, 5 to 10 minutes.

2. To the bowl with the eggs, add the **parsley**, **garlic**, **cheese**, **2 teaspoons salt**, and **1 teaspoon pepper**. Add the **beef** and **pork** and, with clean hands, mix everything until combined, but try not to overwork. Cover and transfer to the refridge for 30 minutes.

3. Arrange racks in the upper and lower thirds of the oven and preheat the oven to 425°F.

4. Mix the meatball mixture again lightly with damp hands. Use a 1½-inch ice cream scoop to scoop the meat into balls and transfer to 2 sheet pans. You'll have about 50 (2½-tablespoon) balls.

5. Bake both sheets of meatballs until sizzling and no longer pink, 10 to 12 minutes. Switch the oven to broil and broil the top pan until beginning to brown on top, 2 to 4 minutes. Remove to rest, then move the second pan to the top rack and broil until beginning to brown on top, 2 to 4 minutes. Let the meatballs rest on the sheet pans for 5 minutes.

ENJOY NOW: Serve half the meatballs using any of my above suggestions (see the headnote).

ENJOY LATER: Freeze the remaining meatballs. Let them cool completely, then arrange them on a parchment-lined sheet pan and freeze until solid. Transfer the meatballs to a zip-top freezer bag and freeze for up to 2 months. To reheat, thaw overnight in the refrigerate or place the frozen meatballs in simmering sauce for 10 to 15 minutes, or reheat them in a 350°F oven for 10 to 15 minutes (note that the sauce method will keep the meatballs from becoming dry).

This salad is totally customizable: Swap out the farro for 3 cups of any cooked grain. Add 1½ cups of beans or diced chicken for additional protein. Toss in fresh apples or pears, parsley or mint.

♥

The dressing may thicken while it sits in the refridge, so when you're ready to use it, thin it with a bit of water and brighten it with a squeeze of lemon and more salt, if needed.

♥

This salad also pairs well with the Green Goddess Dressing from Lick-Your-Plate-Clean Green Goddess Salmon (page 58).

REFRIDGE-FRIENDLY SHEET-PAN FARRO & KALE SALAD

Serves 4 twice

PREP
15 minutes

COOK
35 minutes

Sometimes you're just in the mood for a big salad. The problem with salads, I find, is they can be sneaky about how much time it takes to make them because of all the chopping and assembling. And then? They're gone in a flash. You can't really save leftovers because they wilt.

This salad is going to change all that for you. Make this once and have salad for a week. No wilting! It will still have the same delicious freshness. This recipe makes a lot, so you'll have this ready to go as a healthy dinner, lunch, a side—whatever you choose!

ROASTED VEGETABLES

6	cups (1-inch cubes) butternut squash (about 2 pounds)
1	large red onion, cut into ½-inch wedges
3	tablespoons extra-virgin olive oil
1	teaspoon ground allspice
	Kosher salt and freshly ground black pepper
⅓	cup pepitas or any nut on hand

FARRO

	Kosher salt
1½	cups pearl farro or barley

TAHINI DRESSING

½	cup well-stirred tahini
¼	cup fresh lemon juice (from 2 small lemons)
	Kosher salt and freshly ground black pepper

ASSEMBLY

4	cups thinly sliced Tuscan kale leaves (1 large bunch)
	Kosher salt and freshly ground black pepper
½	cup dried cranberries or cherries
6	ounces goat cheese or feta, crumbled (optional)

1. Preheat the oven to 425°F.

2. **Roast the vegetables:** On a sheet pan, toss together the **squash** cubes, **onion**, **olive oil**, **allspice**, **1½ teaspoons salt**, and **½ teaspoon pepper**. Roast for 25 minutes. Add the **pepitas** and continue to roast until the squash is tender and the pepitas are toasted, another 5 to 10 minutes.

3. **While the vegetables roast, make the farro:** Bring a medium saucepan of salted water to a boil. Add the **farro** and simmer over medium heat until tender but still chewy, 15 to 20 minutes. Drain and rinse under cold water. Shake dry.

4. **Make the tahini dressing:** In a jar or other resealable container, stir together the **tahini**, **lemon juice**, and ½ teaspoon salt. Whisk in **¼ cup cold water** until you have a dressing consistency. Season to taste with more salt and some pepper.

5. **Assemble the salad:** Let the squash sit for 5 minutes (cooling the squash helps keep it from breaking while stirring), then add the **kale**, a pinch of salt and pepper, the farro, and the **dried cranberries** to the sheet pan. Stir gently to combine.

ENJOY NOW: Divide half the salad among 4 bowls and top with half the **cheese** (if using). Toss with enough dressing to coat and season to taste with salt and pepper.

ENJOY LATER: Place the remaining salad in a resealable container, top with the other half of the cheese (if using), and refrigerate for up to 5 days. Serve with the dressing; the dressing will keep, refrigerated, for up to 5 days.

SESAME CHICKEN NOODLE SALAD

Serves 4 twice

PREP
15 minutes

COOK
25 minutes

There is so much to love about this sesame chicken noodle salad. It's a satisfying blend of texture and flavor; it's delicious at *any* temperature plus, it saves beautifully. What I love most, though, is that it uses poached chicken. Not only will you have a second batch of this delicious salad, but you may also want to poach extra breasts to have on hand for tacos, salads, wraps—or whatever! If you've been reluctant in the past to try whole wheat pasta, it works great here! But feel free to swap the noodles if you like, and the protein and vegetables, too. The possibilities are endless.

CHICKEN

Kosher salt

2 pounds boneless, skinless chicken breasts

SESAME PEANUT SAUCE

½ cup creamy peanut butter

¼ cup hoisin sauce

3 tablespoons unseasoned rice vinegar

1 tablespoon soy sauce

1 tablespoon chili crisp

2 teaspoons toasted sesame oil

Kosher salt and freshly ground black pepper

3 tablespoons toasted sesame seeds

NOODLE SALAD

1 pound whole wheat spaghetti

6 cups thinly sliced raw veggies, such as bell peppers, slaw blend, carrots, cucumbers, radishes, snap or snow peas, and/or celery

For serving: toasted sesame seeds, lime wedges

1. **Prepare the chicken:** Fill a large pot with **salted water**. Add the **chicken** and bring to a boil over medium-high heat. Skim off any foam that has floated to the top, then cover the pot and turn off the heat. Let the chicken sit until cooked through and it registers 160°F internally, 5 to 15 minutes, depending on breast size. Transfer to a cutting board to cool, leaving the water in the pot. When the chicken is cool enough to handle, cut or shred the breasts into bite-size pieces.

2. **While the chicken is cooking, make the sesame peanut sauce:** In a large jar, stir together the **peanut butter**, **hoisin**, **rice vinegar**, **soy sauce**, **chili crisp**, and **sesame oil**. Add water until you have a saucy consistency. Season to taste with **salt** and **pepper** and stir in the **sesame seeds**.

3. **Prepare the noodle salad:** Return the water in the pot to a boil. Add the **spaghetti** (or whatever noodle you're using) and cook until al dente according to the package directions. Drain and shake very dry.

4. Return the noodles to the pot and toss with ¼ cup of the sauce until evenly coated.

   ENJOY NOW: Add half the chicken and **veggies** to the noodles in the pot and toss to combine. Add more sauce until everything is well coated, then transfer the salad to plates. Sprinkle with some **sesame seeds**, season to taste with salt, and add a **squeeze of lime**.

   ENJOY LATER: If storing for later, divide the noodles, chicken, and veggies among containers, then sprinkle with scallions and sesame seeds. When ready to eat, shake the dressing, then toss with enough dressing to coat and season to taste with salt.

One and Only Wednesday

Four children. Four different directions. On any given day, I had to be at soccer and football practices, after-school academics, Scout meetings—the list goes on and on. Whether you have four kids, two kids, or no kids, by Wednesday you're in the thick of it all. Schedules need to be juggled, errands accomplished, or maybe there are extra work responsibilities that need attention. "Life gets in the way," as they say—but I say, it should never get in the way of a good meal!

When you're managing dinner with everything else going on, dinner has to be simplified. That's where a single pot or skillet can save the day. Whether it's pastas, stews, or stir-fries, it's surprising how much variety you can get from just one pot or skillet, and also you won't have much to clean! Think Kids' Favorite Broccoli Pasta (page 95; my grandchildren love this!), Skillet Orange-Sesame Beef (page 84), Minivan Pepperoni Pizza Chicken with Garlic Bread (page 83), or the Easiest Chicken Pot Pie (page 91). Let these dishes hang out on the stove for individual hands to grab and go, or enjoy them as sit-down family meals. They're a midweek lifeline! Whatever your schedule allows, know everyone is eating a delicious meal that is also convenient and easy on the cook.

FULLY LOADED CHEESEBURGER SOUP

Serves 4 to 6

PREP
15 minutes

COOK
50 minutes

You know that saying "Don't knock it till you've tried it"? It's perfect for this soup. You'll be truly bowled over (no pun intended) by how much it tastes just like a mouthwatering, juicy cheeseburger—only better!

The soup is hearty and creamy, with a bit of tang from a few pickles sprinkled on top. It's all the things you love about a burger: beef, bacon, and cheese, enveloped in a velvety soup and topped with toasted sesame croutons that stand in for the classic bun. Like its inspiration, it's a delight in every bite!

4   slices bacon, halved crosswise

1   large white onion, finely chopped

2   carrots, peeled and coarsely chopped

2   small potatoes, peeled and coarsely chopped

1   celery stalk, thinly sliced

Kosher salt and freshly ground black pepper

1   pound ground beef (90% lean)

3   cups chicken broth

2   teaspoons garlic powder

2   sesame burger buns, cut into 1-inch cubes

1   tablespoon extra-virgin olive oil

2   cups (8 ounces) shredded yellow Cheddar cheese

2   teaspoons Dijon mustard

For serving: ½ cup dill pickle chips (halved if large), sour cream (optional)

> **BABS SAYS**
>
> All the veggies can be prepped ahead of time. Just make sure to cover your potatoes in cold water and pop them in the refrigere to slow any browning.

1. Preheat the oven to 350°F.

2. Add the **bacon** to a large pot or Dutch oven. Cook over medium-high heat, flipping halfway through, until browned and crisp, 5 to 7 minutes. Transfer the bacon to a paper towel–lined plate, leaving the drippings in the pot.

3. Measure out **2 tablespoons of the onion** and set aside for garnish. Add the remaining onion to the pot along with the **carrots**, **potatoes**, and **celery**. Add a pinch of **salt** and cook, scraping up the browned bits and stirring just once or twice, until the vegetables are browned in spots, 3 to 5 minutes. Add the **ground beef** and 1 teaspoon each salt and **pepper**. Stir to combine with the vegetables, then press into an even layer that fills the pot (like one big patty!). Cook, undisturbed, until browned underneath, 6 to 8 minutes.

4. Break up the beef into small pieces. Add the **broth** and **garlic powder**. Bring to a simmer over medium heat and cook, stirring occasionally, until the flavors have developed and the vegetables are tender, 20 to 25 minutes.

5. While the soup simmers, toss the **cubed buns** with the **olive oil** on a sheet pan. Bake until the croutons are crisp and golden brown, 5 to 7 minutes.

6. Remove the soup from the heat. Measure out ½ **cup of the Cheddar** and set aside for garnish. Stir the remaining 1½ cups cheese and all the **mustard** into the soup. Season to taste with salt and pepper.

7. Crumble the bacon. Serve the soup topped with the bacon bits, reserved onion, reserved Cheddar, croutons, **pickles**, and **sour cream** (if using).

MINIVAN PEPPERONI PIZZA CHICKEN
with GARLIC BREAD

Serves 4

PREP
10 minutes

COOK
25 minutes

My Plymouth Voyager got a workout most days. Carting my children back and forth was especially taxing by midweek, with four of them in the back drawing imaginary "DO NOT CROSS" lines on the seats, yelling at whomever dared test those boundaries. Such a treat! When I promised to make pepperoni pizza chicken, one of their favorites, for dinner, that would calm things down for a second. It was a lifeline—I grabbed it, and it was worth it—for everyone.

You gotta have a good sauce for a stand-out pepperoni pizza chicken. This is my go-to pizza sauce, and it takes only 30 seconds to make. You can even get your kids to help—they can crush the tomatoes with their (clean) hands.

PIZZA SAUCE

1	(28-ounce) can best-quality peeled whole tomatoes
1	teaspoon dried oregano
	Kosher salt
1	garlic clove, peeled but whole

CHICKEN

1	tablespoon extra-virgin olive oil, plus more for drizzling
2	pounds boneless, skinless chicken thighs, patted dry and cut into 1-inch pieces
1	teaspoon dried oregano
	Kosher salt and freshly ground black pepper
4	slices crusty bread or ciabatta
1	garlic clove, peeled but whole
1	cup (4 ounces) shredded mozzarella cheese
¼	cup (1 ounce) finely grated Parmesan cheese
¼	cup pepperoni slices

1. Arrange a rack in the upper third of the oven and set the broiler to high.

2. **Make the pizza sauce:** In a large bowl, combine the **tomatoes**, **oregano**, and **1 teaspoon salt**. Finely grate the **garlic** into the bowl. Squeeze with clean hands until the tomatoes are in bite-size pieces. Taste and if it doesn't taste like the best tomato sauce you've ever had, add another ¼ teaspoon to ½ teaspoon salt (the quantity of salt in canned tomatoes varies by brand).

3. **Cook the chicken:** In a large ovenproof skillet, heat the **olive oil** over medium-high heat. Add the **chicken** and sprinkle with the **oregano**, 1 teaspoon salt, and ½ **teaspoon pepper**. Cook, undisturbed, until browned underneath, 5 to 7 minutes. Reduce the heat to medium, stir the chicken, and carefully pour in the pizza sauce. Simmer, stirring occasionally, until the chicken is cooked through and the sauce is thickened slightly, 7 to 10 minutes.

4. Meanwhile, arrange the **bread** on a sheet pan and drizzle with some olive oil. Broil until toasted, 1 to 2 minutes per side (watch closely). Right out of the oven, rub the bread with the garlic clove until you smell garlic. Season with a pinch of salt. Set aside.

5. Top the chicken with the **mozzarella**, **Parmesan**, and **pepperoni**. Transfer the skillet to the oven (if the skillet is full, place on a sheet pan) and broil until the cheese is melted and browned in spots, 1 to 3 minutes. Transfer to plates and serve with the bread alongside for dipping.

SKILLET ORANGE-SESAME BEEF

Serves 6

PREP
25 minutes,
plus up to 8 hours
refrigeration time

COOK
15 minutes

There are so many things to love about where I live in Connecticut. The closeness to my grandchildren, community I've built, and the New England quaintness. But sadly, it doesn't have *everything*. Like the endless takeout options we used to enjoy when we lived in Chicago. There was an amazing Chinese restaurant in the Loop called Jimmy Wong's, where Bill and I would pick up dinner. My absolute favorite was an orange beef dish: sweet, savory, salty, spooned over rice—a dream! I missed it a lot when we moved to the East Coast, so I re-created a version of it. And you know what? It's just as quick to make as it was placing an order and going to pick it up!

1½ pounds boneless beef sirloin, thinly sliced against the grain

1 tablespoon soy sauce

1 tablespoon toasted sesame oil

TERIYAKI SAUCE

1 cup fresh orange juice (about 2 oranges; save the zest)

5 tablespoons soy sauce

2 tablespoons toasted sesame oil

2 tablespoons unseasoned rice vinegar

2 tablespoons cornstarch

2 tablespoons honey

2 teaspoons chili-garlic sauce (optional)

TO FINISH

4 tablespoons neutral oil, such as avocado

4 scallions, thinly sliced, greens and whites separated

4 garlic cloves, finely chopped

5 cups (12 ounces) broccoli florets (from 1 large head)

1 red bell pepper, thinly sliced

For serving: toasted sesame seeds, cooked rice

1. In a medium bowl, toss the **meat** with the **soy sauce** and **sesame oil**. Cover and set aside at room temperature or refrigerate for up to 8 hours.

2. **Make the teriyaki sauce:** In a small bowl, whisk together the **orange juice**, soy sauce, sesame oil, **vinegar**, **cornstarch**, **honey**, and **chili-garlic sauce** (if using) until smooth.

3. **To finish:** In a very large skillet, heat 3 tablespoons of the **oil** over high heat. Add half the beef in a single layer and sear until browned underneath, 2 to 3 minutes. Push to the side of the skillet. Add the remaining beef and repeat.

4. Reduce the heat to medium-high. Pile the beef to one side of the skillet and add the remaining 1 tablespoon oil, the **reserved orange zest**, **scallion whites**, and **garlic** and cook until fragrant, just a minute. Add the **broccoli**, **bell pepper**, and **¼ cup water**. Cover and cook until the broccoli turns bright green, 2 to 3 minutes.

5. Pour the teriyaki sauce into the skillet and stir until the mixture is glazy, 2 to 4 minutes. Remove and discard the orange peels. Divide among bowls, sprinkle with **sesame seeds** and the scallion greens, and serve with **rice**.

BABS SAYS

You can make an even faster version by swapping out the ingredients for the sauce in step 2 for store-bought teriyaki and orange juice. You can also use a bag of fresh broccoli florets.

♥

Get ahead by doing steps 1 and 2 in the morning.

♥

If you're having trouble slicing the beef, freeze it for 15 minutes to firm it up. You could also use shaved steak, if your store sells it.

CHICKEN with ORZO, CORN & GOAT CHEESE

Serves 4

PREP
10 minutes

COOK
40 minutes

Orzo pasta is often confused with rice because it looks like extra-large rice grains. Whenever I make this recipe for my grandchildren, the littlest ones call it "chicken with the big rice." Orzo is good, but orzo cooked in rendered chicken fat and chicken broth is better. Here, each bite of orzo is sweet and spicy from the corn and red pepper flakes. A crumble of goat cheese on top provides salty and gooey bites. I know it may seem like a lot of chicken broth, but you'll need it to make the orzo saucy and brothy for soft, cozy bites.

2	pounds bone-in, skin-on chicken thighs (4 to 6 thighs), patted dry
	Kosher salt
1	tablespoon extra-virgin olive oil
1	cup (8 ounces) orzo
2	shallots, finely chopped
3	garlic cloves, finely chopped or grated
2	pinches of red pepper flakes
2	cups chicken broth
1	(10-ounce) bag frozen corn (no need to thaw)
1	pint fresh cherry tomatoes, halved
4	ounces herbed goat cheese, crumbled (about 1 cup)
¼	cup thinly sliced fresh basil

1. Preheat the oven to 400°F.

2. Season the **chicken thighs** all over with **1 teaspoon salt**. Drizzle the **olive oil** into a large ovenproof skillet, then add the thighs, skin side down, and set over medium-high heat. Once sizzling, cook the thighs until golden and the pieces release easily from the skillet, 4 to 10 minutes per side (the first side will take longer). Transfer the chicken to a plate skin side up (it won't be cooked through yet).

3. Reduce the heat to medium and pour off all but 2 tablespoons of the chicken fat. Add the **orzo**, **shallots**, **garlic**, **1 pinch of the pepper flakes**, and 1 teaspoon salt. Stir until the orzo is golden, 1 to 2 minutes. Stir in the **broth** and **corn**, scraping up any browned bits on the bottom. Once simmering, nestle the chicken on top, skin side up. Transfer to the oven and bake until the orzo is tender and the chicken is cooked through, 13 to 17 minutes.

4. Meanwhile, in a medium bowl, stir the **tomatoes** with 1 teaspoon salt and the remaining pinch of pepper flakes. When the chicken is done, top with the tomatoes and crumble on the **goat cheese**. Let sit for a few minutes, then sprinkle with the **basil** and serve.

BABS SAYS

Frozen corn is consistently delicious because it is flash-frozen and packaged at peak of season. It's actually better to use frozen in this recipe than fresh because the extra moisture makes the dish saucier! Plus, frozen couldn't be easier.

♥

Chicken broth stays good in the refridge for only a couple of days after being opened, so pop it in the freezer if you're not planning on using it right away.

SALSA VERDE FISH TOSTADAS

Serves 4

PREP
10 minutes

COOK
40 minutes

I was never skittish at the thought of cooking fish at home. I completely sympathize with those who are. Here is a simple dish that uses mild but firm white fish and is easy to prepare. It's tender, flaky, and not at all "fishy." Baking it with a lot of salsa verde on top is a surefire method for making flavorful tacos, burrito bowls, salads, and, of course, tostadas.

Tostadas are like giant tortilla chips. You can top your tostadas with whatever you like, but a faux crema helps keep everything in place and provides tang. Tostadas are great for this, but if you want something without the crunch, soft warm tortillas work well, too. These elements create a wonderful combination of flavors and textures that will definitely get you over the fish-cooking hurdle!

---

1 (1½-pound) white fish fillet, such as cod, haddock, or halibut

Kosher salt and freshly ground black pepper

1 (16-ounce) jar salsa verde

1 cup sour cream or whole-milk Greek yogurt

2 tablespoons fresh lime juice, plus more if needed

¼ cup chopped fresh cilantro, plus more for serving

2 large avocados (optional)

12 tostadas

1 large head romaine lettuce, thinly sliced

Lime wedges, for squeezing

BABS SAYS

If your store doesn't have tostadas, you can make your own by coating corn tortillas with a neutral oil and baking at 400°F for 5 to 7 minutes per side, until golden and crisp.

1. Preheat the oven to 350°F.

2. Place the **fish** in a large baking dish, such as a 9 × 13-inch pan, and season all over with **1 teaspoon salt** and a few grinds of **pepper**. Pour the **salsa verde** over the fish. Bake until the fish flakes easily with a fork, 25 to 35 minutes.

3. Meanwhile, stir together the **sour cream**, **lime juice**, **cilantro**, and a pinch of salt. If using the **avocados**, pit and thinly slice them. Squeeze with a little lime juice (to keep them from browning) and season with a pinch of salt.

4. When the fish is done, warm the **tostadas** on a sheet pan or directly on the oven rack for 2 to 4 minutes.

5. Transfer the tostadas to plates and spread with the sour cream mixture. Top with **lettuce**, a few small pieces of the fish, avocado (if using), a spoonful of the salsa verde from the pan, cilantro, and a squeeze of lime. Enjoy!

EASIEST CHICKEN POT PIE

Serves 6

PREP
20 minutes

COOK
1 hour

I don't know if *you* remember your first bite of chicken pot pie, but I do. It was at the Walnut Room, the restaurant in the iconic Marshall Field's department store in Chicago. After a morning of shopping along State Street, I headed there for lunch. It was a brisk day, so the thought of a pot pie warming me up was definitely appealing.

Their pot pie had a flaky, buttery crust and a warm, velvety center filled with peas, carrots, celery, and—of course—chicken. This version is much more streamlined. I make it with rotisserie chicken, frozen veggies, and puff pastry. It's just as delicious as my first, but easy and quick enough to make on a weeknight. Just remember to thaw the puff pastry and vegetables in the refridge overnight.

---

4   tablespoons (½ stick) unsalted butter

2   large celery stalks, coarsely chopped

1   small yellow onion, coarsely chopped

Kosher salt and freshly ground black pepper

3   garlic cloves, finely chopped

2   teaspoons chopped fresh thyme, or 1 teaspoon dried thyme

⅓   cup all-purpose flour, plus more for dusting

3   cups chicken broth

3   cups shredded cooked chicken (from 1 rotisserie chicken)

2   cups frozen mixed peas and carrots (10-ounce package), thawed in the refridge overnight

1   sheet frozen puff pastry dough, thawed in the refridge overnight

1   large egg, lightly beaten

Celery salt or flaky sea salt, for sprinkling (optional)

1. Arrange a rack in the center of the oven and preheat the oven to 425°F. Line a sheet pan with parchment paper.

2. In a medium (10-inch) ovenproof skillet, melt 2 tablespoons of the **butter** over medium-high heat. Stir in the **celery**, **onion**, and **¼ teaspoon each salt and pepper**. Cook, stirring occasionally, until slightly softened, 3 to 5 minutes. Stir in the **garlic** and **thyme** and cook until fragrant, just 1 minute.

3. Add the remaining 2 tablespoons butter and stir until melted. Add the **flour** and cook, stirring, until golden, 1 to 2 minutes. Pour in the **broth**. Bring to a simmer, scraping the bottom of the pan to loosen any browned bits. Cook until slightly thickened, 2 to 3 minutes. Turn off the heat and add in the **chicken**, **peas and carrots**, 1 teaspoon salt, and ¼ teaspoon pepper. Season to taste with more salt and pepper.

4. On a lightly floured work surface, use a lightly floured rolling pin to roll out the **puff pastry** and trim it into a 12-inch round. If it contracts when you roll, wait a few minutes before trying again.

5. Transfer the skillet to the sheet pan. Lay the puff pastry over the skillet so there's an even 1-inch overhang all around. (Trim if there is more than 1 inch.) Brush the puff pastry with the beaten **egg** and sprinkle with **celery salt or flaky salt** (if using). Use a sharp paring knife to cut 4 large slits in the top of the pastry. Bake until puffed and lightly golden brown, 10 to 15 minutes. Reduce the oven temperature to 375°F and bake until the pastry is cooked through and the filling is bubbling up, 30 to 35 minutes more. (If the pastry is getting too dark, cover with aluminum foil.) Let cool for a few minutes before diving in.

HOISIN TURKEY LETTUCE CUPS

Serves 4

PREP
5 minutes

COOK
15 minutes

I have a secret. Whenever my lifelong girlfriend Joanne and I would get together for lunch, we wouldn't head to a fancy café or a trendy restaurant. Instead, we would go to one of two places, the Cheesecake Factory or P.F. Chang's. These two places have something in common other than their mass appeal: chicken lettuce wraps on their menus. I would order them every time we'd go. I love the idea of having a warm, wonderfully spiced protein—chicken in this case—balanced by the cool, crisp lettuce and, of course, the sauce! I could eat an entire plate.

Naturally, I had to make an at-home version to serve up any day. This recipe uses ground turkey, which gives it more flavor, and it has some sneaky cauliflower rice, which contributes moisture to the lean turkey. In less than 30 minutes, you'll be enjoying this finger-licking dish.

---

3   tablespoons neutral oil, such as avocado

1   (10- to 12-ounce) package cauliflower rice, fresh or frozen (no need to thaw)

1   pound ground turkey

Kosher salt and freshly ground black pepper

4   scallions, thinly sliced

1   (8-ounce) can water chestnuts, drained and thinly sliced

⅓   cup hoisin sauce

3   tablespoons soy sauce, or more to taste

For serving: large lettuce leaves, like butter or iceberg

1. In a large cast-iron skillet, heat **2 tablespoons of the oil** over high heat. Add the **cauliflower rice** and cook, stirring occasionally, until golden and the liquid has evaporated, 5 to 7 minutes. Add the remaining tablespoon oil, the **turkey**, and ½ **teaspoon each salt and pepper**. Cook, breaking up the turkey into small pieces, until cooked through and the liquid has evaporated, 5 to 8 minutes.

2. Remove the skillet from the heat, then add half the **scallions**, the **water chestnuts**, **hoisin**, and **soy sauce**. Stir until everything is coated in sauce. Serve in **lettuce cups** with the remaining scallions sprinkled on top.

BABS SAYS

Other things you could add to this mix include shredded carrots, cilantro, sesame seeds, peanuts, Sriracha, and regular rice. If you feel like ginger or garlic, add a bit, either finely chopped or grated, to the turkey mixture as it cooks.

This makes a heap (4 cups) of filling, so keep leftovers for the next day. It's good at room temperature or warmed up.

KIDS' FAVORITE BROCCOLI PASTA

Serves 4 to 6

PREP
10 minutes

COOK
15 minutes

All of my nine grandchildren have, at one time or another, been picky about dinner. While some have had more limited ranges than others, I'm used to the whole spectrum. Nobody wants to be a short-order cook at home, so I've got the perfect recipe. It's one that everyone will enjoy, no matter where they may fall in the range of picky eaters (children *or* adults!). The ingredient list is short, there is virtually no prep, and, of course, there's only one pot. The gateway ingredient here is cheese! Lots of Parmesan (or Pecorino Romano) mixed with your pasta and veggies—and who wouldn't love that? The broccoli florets are added to the boiling pasta pot toward the end, making the process extra-streamlined. Don't forget to save a cup of the starchy cooking water to help create a silky, flavorful sauce!

Kosher salt

1 pound short pasta, such as bow ties

3 cups broccoli florets (about 8 ounces)

2 lemons

⅓ cup extra-virgin olive oil

5 garlic cloves, thinly sliced

¼ teaspoon red pepper flakes, plus more for serving

1¼ cups (5 ounces) finely grated Parmesan cheese, plus more for serving

BABS SAYS

To get more juice from your lemons, pop them in the microwave for 15 seconds before squeezing.

1. Fill a large pot halfway with generously **salted water** and bring to a boil over high heat. Add the **pasta** and cook to al dente according to the package directions. During the last 2 minutes of cooking, add the **broccoli** and cook briefly. Scoop out and reserve 1 cup of the pasta water, then drain the pasta and broccoli.

2. Meanwhile, **zest 1 of the lemons**, then halve both lemons and squeeze to have ¼ cup juice.

3. In the same pot as you cooked the pasta, heat the **olive oil** over medium heat. Add the **garlic** and **pepper flakes** and stir until golden and fragrant, about 3 minutes. Add the pasta and broccoli, ¾ cup of the reserved cooking water, lemon zest, and lemon juice. Stir in the **Parmesan** and cook, stirring, until the pasta is slightly creamy, about 2 minutes. Add more of the pasta water as needed until the pasta is glossed with sauce. Season with salt, if needed.

4. Divide the pasta among bowls and top with more Parmesan and pepper flakes.

WARM HUG BACON PASTA

Serves 4 to 6

PREP
10 minutes

COOK
35 minutes

When Bill and I were first married and finishing school, he drove a cab for a short time and I waited tables a longer time. In those days, suburban cab drivers weren't permitted to pick up and drop off fares in Chicago. Well, Bill got a call from his dispatcher to pick up a fare at O'Hare and drop off in the city, and he did it. The Chicago PD did not let him slide! He was arrested. He spent only a few hours in jail, until the cab company sprang him. What does that have to do with food, you ask? Well, I felt so sorry that he went through that. Being Italian, I immediately wanted to comfort him with food, and the most comforting food for us is *pasta*! I made a simple but classic plate of spaghetti with a slow-simmered sauce, which, I have to say, made him feel so much better, especially after a hot shower.

That simple recipe evolved into an amazing pasta dish based on traditional Amatriciana. It's a classic sauce made from guanciale (cured pork jowl), tomatoes, pepper, and pecorino. This version uses bacon, which is easier to find than guanciale and adds smokiness to the dish. The pasta is also cooked *in* the sauce. No boiling, no draining! Especially good for nights when you need a big, warm hug. Channel that energy into something with a little spice and lots of comfort!

---

8   slices bacon (not thick cut), chopped into small pieces

1   red onion, halved and thinly sliced

     Kosher salt and freshly ground black pepper

¼   teaspoon red pepper flakes, plus more for serving

1   (28-ounce) can crushed tomatoes

1   pound spaghetti or bucatini

½   cup (2 ounces) grated Pecorino Romano or Parmesan cheese, plus more for serving

> **BABS SAYS**
>
> You can use any pasta that boils in 10 minutes. Spaghetti is traditional.

1. Add the **bacon** and **onion** to a large deep skillet (at least 12 inches wide) or Dutch oven wide enough to fit the whole spaghetti lying down. Season with ½ **teaspoon salt**. Set over medium heat and cook, stirring often, until the onion has softened and the bacon is golden, 7 to 10 minutes. Add the **pepper flakes** and ¼ **teaspoon pepper** and stir until fragrant, about 1 minute.

2. Carefully pour in the **tomatoes**, scraping up any browned bits from the pan, and simmer until slightly thickened, 2 to 4 minutes. Fill the tomato can up with water (about 3 cups) and add that to the skillet along with the **pasta** and ½ teaspoon salt. Simmer over medium heat, stirring often to keep the pasta from sticking, until al dente, 12 to 15 minutes. (It may take longer than the package directions.) If the sauce is looking dry, add another ½ cup water. Turn off the heat and stir in the **cheese** until melted. Season to taste with salt and pepper.

3. Serve the pasta topped with more cheese and pepper flakes.

DON'T KNOCK IT 'TIL YOU TRY IT STUFFED CABBAGE SOUP

Serves 6 to 8
(makes 12 cups)

PREP
10 minutes

COOK
35 minutes

Cabbage is completely underrated. My mom and I would make the best stuffed cabbage rolls. They are the ultimate in old-world comfort, but they take a lot of time. We'd spend a good part of the day just rolling up those tight little packets of yumminess filled with beef, rice, and the sweet acidity of tomatoes. This soup combines all the delicious flavors of a traditional cabbage roll, but without the hours of work. It makes a satisfying, soul-warming soup that's also packed with nutrients. You'll want to share it with your kids; I promise you, they'll gobble it up. You'll make this, you'll love it, and you'll think of cabbage in a whole new way!

1½ pounds ground beef (80% lean)

1 large yellow onion, finely chopped

4 garlic cloves, finely chopped

Kosher salt and freshly ground black pepper

2 teaspoons dried thyme

1 teaspoon ground allspice (less if you like it mild)

8 cups thinly sliced green cabbage (from 1 small head), or use coleslaw mix

4 cups low-sodium beef broth, plus more as needed

1 (28-ounce) can diced tomatoes

1 (8-ounce) can tomato sauce

½ cup long-grain white rice

2 tablespoons balsamic vinegar

½ cup chopped fresh parsley

For serving: sour cream

1. In a large Dutch oven or heavy-bottomed pot, break up the **ground beef** into small pieces and cook over medium-high heat until sizzling. Add the **onion, garlic,** and **½ teaspoon each salt and pepper** and cook, stirring occasionally, until the beef is no longer pink and the vegetables are tender, 6 to 8 minutes. Add the **thyme** and **allspice** and stir until fragrant.

2. Add the **cabbage** in batches, stirring until wilted, before adding the next batch. Season with ½ teaspoon salt and cook until just tender, 4 to 5 minutes. Add **1½ cups water,** the **broth, diced tomatoes, tomato sauce, rice, balsamic vinegar,** 1½ teaspoons salt, and 1 teaspoon pepper. Bring to a boil over high heat, then reduce the heat to medium-low. Simmer, stirring occasionally, until the rice is tender and the soup has thickened, 15 to 20 minutes.

3. Stir in the **parsley,** reserving a little for garnish, if you like. Transfer to serving bowls and top with **sour cream.**

PICKY-EATER PASTA
with SAUSAGE & PEAS

Serves 4

PREP
5 minutes

COOK
25 minutes

Of all my kids, Shawn was my pickiest eater. He reserved a special dislike for anything green, especially peas. But he *loved* anything with meat or pasta. Who doesn't? Eventually, at the end of my mom-rope, I combined two of his favorites—sausage and pasta—and I slipped in a handful of peas, hoping he wouldn't notice or try to pick them out. Of course, he noticed! But after some probably not-so-gentle encouragement, he took a bite. He was a big fan of the pasta, the savory spice of the sausage, and the yummy salty cheesiness of the Parmesan. Also . . . peas! They add just a hint of freshness here, complemented by a little lemon zest. I can say with confidence backed by experience that this delicious pasta with sausage and peas is a crowd pleaser. It will convert even the pickiest eater into a pea-liever!

1   pound sweet Italian sausage, casings removed

3   shallots, coarsely chopped

2   garlic cloves, coarsely chopped

Kosher salt and freshly ground black pepper

Pinch of red pepper flakes (optional)

4   cups chicken broth

1   pound orecchiette or other small pasta

2   cups (10-ounce package) frozen peas (no need to thaw)

½   cup (2 ounces) grated Parmesan cheese, plus more for serving

2   teaspoons grated lemon zest

1   tablespoon fresh lemon juice

1. Add the **sausage**, **shallots**, **garlic**, **¾ teaspoon salt**, **¼ teaspoon pepper**, and the **pepper flakes** (if using) to a large Dutch oven. Set over medium-high heat and use a wooden spoon to break the sausage into small pieces. Cook until the sausage is lightly browned and dark brown bits have formed on the bottom of the pot, 10 to 12 minutes.

2. Add ½ cup of the **chicken broth** and scrape up the browned bits from the bottom of the pot. Cook until the liquid has mostly evaporated, about 2 minutes. Stir in the **pasta** and the remaining 3½ cups broth. Once simmering, cover and reduce the heat to medium-low. Cook, stirring halfway through, until the pasta is tender, 10 to 12 minutes.

3. Add the **peas**, **Parmesan**, **lemon zest**, and **lemon juice** to the pot and stir to combine. Turn off the heat, cover, and let sit for 5 minutes to allow the peas to warm through and the sauce to thicken slightly.

4. Transfer to plates and sprinkle the portions with more Parmesan cheese and black pepper.

> **BABS SAYS**
>
> Always save your Parmesan rinds! I put mine in a zip-top bag in my freezer. They add a really wonderful umami to soups and sauces; just drop a rind into the simmering liquid and remove when done.

HONEY MUSTARD SALMON
with **BRUSSELS SPROUTS**

Serves 4

PREP
10 minutes

COOK
15 minutes

My son Bill caught on to balanced eating earlier than my other children—they waited until adulthood. Bill was always more open to having veggies or trying new things, and he was the first of my kids to explore cooking fish at home. Salmon was an easy place for him to start. This is a version of the recipe I gave him to practice his skills.

This recipe enjoys the benefits of the delightful and classic combination of honey mustard—a little sweet and a little spicy. The Brussels sprouts are charred on the outside and crisp yet tender inside, so they have a good bite and aren't mushy. The salmon spends most of its time cooking on its skin side, so it is hard to overcook, plus you get a nice crisp skin. This is perfect to serve with rice pilaf, boiled potatoes, roasted carrots, or orzo. Balanced eating at its finest, this one is definitely Bill-approved!

---

4   skin-on salmon fillets
      (6 ounces each), patted dry

      Kosher salt and freshly ground
      black pepper

1   tablespoon honey mustard

2   teaspoons whole-grain mustard

3   tablespoons neutral oil, such as
      avocado

1   pound Brussels sprouts, trimmed
      and halved

2   tablespoons sliced fresh chives or
      scallion

> **BABS SAYS**
>
> Instead of Brussels sprouts, use any other vegetable that you can stir-fry, like snap peas, broccoli, or sliced bell peppers.
>
> ♥
>
> If you don't have honey mustard, use equal parts honey and Dijon mustard, and make your own!

1. Preheat the oven to 425°F.

2. Season the **salmon** all over with **1 teaspoon salt** and **½ teaspoon pepper**. Arrange skin side down on a plate and spread the top with the **honey mustard** and **whole-grain mustard**.

3. In a large ovenproof skillet, such as cast-iron, over medium-high heat, warm the **oil** until shimmering. Add the **Brussels sprouts**, cut sides down, in a single layer, and season with ½ teaspoon salt and a few grinds of pepper. Cook, undisturbed, until browned underneath, 3 to 5 minutes. Turn off the heat and push the Brussels sprouts to one side of the skillet. Add the salmon skin side down to the skillet, then arrange the Brussels sprouts around the fish (they will be piled up and that's okay). Transfer the skillet to the oven and roast until the salmon easily flakes with a fork and the Brussels sprouts are crisp-tender, 5 to 10 minutes.

4. Divide the fish among plates, slipping off the skin. Sprinkle with the **chives** and serve.

CHEATER'S CHEESY PASTA BAKE

Serves 4 to 6

PREP
10 minutes

COOK
55 minutes

There are some nights you don't even have time to just boil a pot of water. I remember nights like that as if it were yesterday. In running my own preschool, my days were filled with three- and four-year-old children, while my afternoons were back-to-back being a Taxi-Bab driver for my own kids. Whether you work in the home or out of it, it's a juggling act.

This recipe is perfect for one of those nights. This pasta bake involves zero boiling of water and zero chopping. It feels like cheating because you still get the gooey, saucy, baked pasta exactly how you want it. And it calls for your favorite jarred sauce, so it's even less work!

---

2   (24-ounce) jars good marinara sauce (I like Rao's)

1   teaspoon Italian seasoning (optional)

1   pound tubular pasta, such as penne or ziti

8   ounces fresh mozzarella cheese, torn into bite-size pieces

1   (15- to 16-ounce) container whole-milk ricotta

½   cup (2 ounces) finely grated Parmesan cheese

Nonstick cooking spray or olive oil, for greasing

Kosher salt and freshly ground black pepper

BABS SAYS

This dish makes a lovely "pop by" meal. You can bring it over fresh or frozen to a neighbor or friend as a thank-you or just a kind gesture. New moms especially appreciate having something yummy they can pull out of the freezer. Bake, cool completely, then freeze. The night before serving, refrigerate. Bake covered at 350°F until warm in the center, about 30 minutes.

1. Arrange a rack in the upper third of the oven and preheat the oven to 400°F.

2. Pour the **marinara** into a 9 × 13-inch or 3-quart baking dish. Pour **1 cup water** and the **Italian seasoning** (if using) into one of the jars, close the lid, and shake to get all the sauce in the jar. Pour that into the other jar, close the lid, shake, then pour the saucy water into the baking dish. Add the **pasta** and half the **mozzarella** and stir until combined. Spread into an even layer. Dollop the **ricotta** in spoonfuls on top, then sprinkle with the remaining mozzarella and the **Parmesan**. Coat a piece of aluminum foil with **cooking spray** or olive oil, then use it to cover the pan tightly, coated side down.

3. Bake until the pasta is al dente and the sauce is bubbling, 30 to 35 minutes. Uncover and cook until the pasta is tender and the sauce is thickened, 10 to 15 minutes. Move the pan to the top rack, set the broiler to high, and broil until browned in spots, 2 to 3 minutes. Let cool for 10 to 15 minutes.

4. Spoon the servings onto plates and season to taste with **salt** and **pepper**.

SPINACH-ARTICHOKE RICE & BEAN BAKE

Serves 4

PREP
10 minutes

COOK
1 hour 30 minutes

Who says you can't have a dip for dinner? My favorite indulgent party dip is, without rival, spinach-artichoke dip. Not only is it delicious and melty, but I also get to tell myself I'm getting some greens. Spinach and artichokes are both packed with nutrients. While you certainly can't have that dip *every* day, you *could* have this dinnertime spin on that classic appetizer.

This easy meal gives you all the yummy flavor of that savory snack. It includes rice and beans, which along with the spinach create a complete meal. Jarred marinated artichokes are easy to find in the supermarket. They're packed with herbs, garlic, and vinegar, so using the brine in the bake is an easy way to incorporate even more flavor. And don't get me started on those crispy onions! We all need more reasons to use them beyond holiday casseroles.

1   (12- to 14-ounce) jar marinated artichokes

1   (15-ounce) can cannellini beans, drained and rinsed

1   (10-ounce) package frozen chopped spinach, thawed and squeezed dry

1   cup long-grain white rice

1   cup heavy cream

1   garlic clove, finely grated

1   teaspoon onion powder

     Kosher salt and freshly ground black pepper

4   ounces cream cheese

¼   cup (1 ounce) grated Parmesan cheese

¾   cup French's fried onions

> **BABS SAYS**
>
> For added freshness, sprinkle with some chopped dill or a squeeze of lemon. It is also great with an added ¼ teaspoon cayenne in step 3 for some heat.

1. Arrange a rack in the upper third of the oven and preheat the oven to 350°F.

2. Place the **artichokes** on a cutting board and pour the liquid from the jar into a liquid measuring cup. Add enough water to the measuring cup to reach 1½ cups. Quarter the artichokes, if large.

3. In a 2-quart baking dish, stir together the artichokes and the brine mixture, the **beans**, **spinach**, **rice**, **cream**, **garlic**, **onion powder**, **1½ teaspoons salt**, and **½ teaspoon pepper**. Spread into an even layer, then dollop tablespoon-size scoops of **cream cheese** over the top. Cover tightly with aluminum foil and place the baking dish on a sheet pan to catch any spills. Bake until the rice is tender, stirring halfway through, 1 hour to 1 hour 30 minutes.

4. Remove the baking dish and switch the oven to the broiler setting. Sprinkle the baking dish with the **Parmesan** and broil until golden brown on top, 3 to 5 minutes.

5. To serve, transfer to plates, top with the **fried onions**, and add another sprinkle of pepper.

Thrifty Thursday

Does anyone else feel like by the time you've gotten to Thursday, you've been eaten out of house and home? I remember many times staring into a once fully stocked refridge wondering, *Where did all that food go?* I get it. I've been there, and that's when I had to lean on pantry staples a little more. I had to be thrifty. But guess what? You don't have to sacrifice deliciousness for thrifty.

Every week, my mom would go through the newspaper looking for sale flyers. After she decided what she and my grandma needed, they mapped out a plan to visit multiple stores to save money. The quest to get the best prices and stretch the food budget sometimes required many stops. Needless to say, I got my thrifty gene from my mom. Being resourceful, especially in the kitchen, will help stretch your food budget in ways you could never have imagined.

In this chapter, you'll find stellar dishes that inspire you to make good use of ingredients you may already have on hand, like my mom's tuna noodle casserole (a cherished favorite of mine; see page 134), Clean-Your-Refridge Frittata (page 130), and Shake-It-Up Garlic Knot Drumsticks (page 113).

So, think of this chapter as permission to take that shortcut and shop your pantry! Rice, canned beans, dried pastas, frozen veggies—they're all-star ingredients here that save time and money. We're all doing the best we can, after all, and basic pantry staples will get you out of a dinner jam every time, no matter your budget.

DAD'S AWAY SAUSAGE, EGG & CHEESE SKILLET

Serves 4 to 6

PREP
15 minutes

COOK
50 minutes

Bill worked in sales. Sometimes that required a car . . . sometimes a plane. Either way, it occasionally involved an overnight stay somewhere other than home. Those were the nights we could have breakfast for dinner! Alone with four little ones, I had to make dinner easy and a little special, so BFD (breakfast for dinner) checked all the boxes. One thing I knew would send my children into fits of joy was Tater Tots, a favorite at school, in regular cafeteria rotation. So, I combined these two joyful food experiences into *one* exceptional "Dad's Away" dinner! Crispy Tator Tots top a creamy sausage, egg, and cheese base—and it's even better as leftovers.

1 tablespoon extra-virgin olive oil, or more as needed

1 yellow onion, finely chopped

1 bell pepper (any color), finely chopped

12 ounces bulk breakfast sausage (not links)

6 large eggs

¾ cup whole milk, half-and-half, or heavy cream (whatever you've got!)

1 teaspoon dry mustard

Kosher salt and freshly ground black pepper

1½ cups (6 ounces) finely shredded sharp Cheddar cheese, or for a kick, use pepperjack cheese instead

1 (16-ounce) package frozen Tater Tots, preferably seasoned (no need to thaw)

2 scallions, thinly sliced

For serving: ketchup and hot sauce

1. Preheat the oven to 375°F.

2. In a large ovenproof skillet, heat the **oil** over medium-high heat. Add the **onion** and **bell pepper** and cook, stirring occasionally, until the onion is translucent and softened, about 5 minutes. Add the **sausage** and cook, breaking up any large pieces with a spoon, until browned and cooked through, about 5 minutes more. Turn off the heat and let cool slightly for 5 minutes.

3. In a large bowl, whisk together the **eggs**, **milk**, **mustard**, **1 teaspoon salt**, and **½ teaspoon pepper** until no streaks remain. Stir in **half the cheese**. To make sure your casserole won't stick to the skillet, rub the sides with a little oil or coat with cooking spray. Pour the eggs over the cooled sausage mixture. Top with a single layer of **Tater Tots**, press them gently into the egg mixture, then sprinkle with the remaining cheese.

4. Bake until the eggs are set and the Tater Tots are golden brown and crisp, 35 to 40 minutes. Let sit for 5 minutes, then serve topped with the **scallions**, more black pepper, and a squiggle of **ketchup** and/or **hot sauce**.

BABS SAYS

Feel free to use whatever fresh pork sausage you have on hand (or is on sale at the store): chorizo, Italian, and the like.

SHAKE-IT-UP GARLIC KNOT DRUMSTICKS

Serves 4

PREP
10 minutes

COOK
30 minutes

Kid favorite alert! There aren't too many cuts of meat less expensive than a chicken drumstick and even fewer that are as fun to eat—they have a built-in handle, after all! These garlic knot drumsticks are my way of pairing two of my grandchildren's dinnertime favorites: chicken legs and their top pizza parlor appetizer.

The breading on the chicken is inspired by the garlic knots: garlic, Parmesan cheese, and parsley (in the seasoned bread crumbs). Dip these garlicky breaded drumsticks in pizza sauce just like you would a traditional garlic knot!

---

5   garlic cloves, peeled

4   tablespoons extra-virgin olive oil

Kosher salt and freshly ground black pepper

½   cup seasoned bread crumbs

Heaping ¼ cup (1 ounce) grated Parmesan cheese, plus more for serving

3   pounds chicken drumsticks (8 to 10), patted dry

1   (12-ounce) package fresh broccoli florets (about 5 cups)

Pizza sauce or marinara sauce, for dipping

BABS SAYS

To keep this thrifty, I use olive oil in the breading since that's what we're cooking with, but you could use the same amount of melted butter and really pay tribute to the delicious garlic knot!

♥

If you don't have broccoli, you could roast another vegetable that cooks in 15 minutes, such as carrots. Or skip it and just make the chicken!

1. Preheat the oven to 450°F.

2. Finely grate the **garlic** into a large zip-top bag. Add 2 tablespoons of the **olive oil** and **½ teaspoon each salt and pepper**, then squeeze to combine. Add the **bread crumbs** and **Parmesan** and squeeze until the crumbs are evenly coated with the oil.

3. On a sheet pan, toss the **drumsticks** with 1 tablespoon of the olive oil and 1 teaspoon salt until coated. Add the drumsticks to the bread crumbs in the bag, close the bag, and shake to coat. Return the drumsticks to the sheet pan and roast for 15 minutes.

4. Carefully flip the drumsticks and move them to one half of the sheet pan. On the empty side, add the **broccoli**, the remaining tablespoon olive oil, and ½ teaspoon each salt and pepper. Toss to coat, then spread in an even layer. Roast until the chicken is cooked through and the broccoli is tender, 10 to 15 minutes.

5. Shower the sheet pan with more Parmesan, then serve with a small bowl of **pizza sauce** for dipping.

BETH'S SLOPPY JOE CASSEROLE

Serves 8

PREP
10 minutes

COOK
1 hour

Adult children always have that *one* dish they request over and over whenever they come home to their parents. It's a slice of nostalgia, the comfort of a simpler time. My niece Beth has three grown children who are spread out all over the world. When they are able to make it back home, they always ask her to make this sloppy Joe casserole. Who would have thought, of all the quintessentially "American" dishes, this is the one they'd long for the most. But trust me, it's worth longing for. Savory, saucy (and just a touch sweet) ground beef is layered with melty Cheddar cheese and is topped with a golden crescent-roll crust. It has all the flavors of a traditional sloppy Joe, but since you eat this with a fork, it's a lot less sloppy! I like to serve it with bread and butter pickles. Yum!

2   pounds ground beef (90% lean) or turkey

1   yellow onion, finely chopped

1   bell pepper (any color), finely chopped

     Kosher salt and freshly ground black pepper

1½   cups ketchup

1   tablespoon brown sugar

1   tablespoon Worcestershire sauce

1   tablespoon yellow mustard

2   teaspoons garlic powder

2   (8-ounce) cans refrigerated crescent roll pastry sheets

2   cups (8 ounces) shredded Cheddar cheese

2   teaspoons white sesame seeds

> **BABS SAYS**
>
> My gluten-free friends can substitute gluten-free pizza dough for the crescent rolls. Feel free to do that even if you're *not* gluten-free!

1. Preheat the oven to 350°F.

2. In a large nonstick skillet, press the **beef** into an even layer to fill the skillet. Set over medium-high heat and sprinkle with the **onion** and **bell pepper**. Cook, undisturbed, until the beef is deeply browned underneath, 6 to 8 minutes (the meat won't be fully cooked). Season with **1½ teaspoons salt** and **1 teaspoon pepper**, then break up the meat and cook until no longer pink and the onion and pepper are tender, 2 to 4 minutes.

3. Reduce the heat to medium and add **¼ cup water**, the **ketchup**, **brown sugar**, **Worcestershire sauce**, **mustard**, and **garlic powder**. Scrape the browned bits up from the bottom of the skillet and simmer until the liquid is reduced to a thick gravy, 10 to 15 minutes. Turn off the heat and season to taste with salt and pepper.

4. Unroll the dough from one can of **crescent rolls** in the bottom of an ungreased 9 × 13-inch baking dish, preferably glass. Pinch the seams together to make one big sheet. Spread the beef mixture on top of the dough in an even layer, then sprinkle with the **cheese**. Unroll the dough from the second can on top of the cheese. Sprinkle with the **sesame seeds**. Bake until the top is browned, 25 to 30 minutes. Let cool slightly and serve.

BETTER THAN BOXED MAC & CHEESE

Serves 4 kids
or 2 grown-ups

PREP
10 minutes

COOK
30 minutes

My kids grew up eating from the blue box. You know what I'm talking about here. With all its convenience and powdered-cheese goodness, I would even make an extra box just so I could have some, too. What can I say, I'm a kid at heart!

Now my grandkids love mac and cheese for dinner, but they request my homemade version every time. And guess what? It's just as easy and as ooey and gooey as the boxed stuff, with lots of real cheese flavor. The key to success here is in the texture. I use evaporated milk, which ensures the sauce won't scorch, and American cheese, heroically meltable. With both in play, the sauce stays smooth and creamy. If you want, you can fancy it up with garlic powder, black pepper, hot sauce, and/or mustard, but I like the original!

Kosher salt

8   ounces elbow macaroni

1   cup evaporated milk

1   cup (4 ounces) shredded sharp yellow Cheddar cheese

4   slices yellow American cheese

2   tablespoons unsalted butter

BABS SAYS

Evaporated milk is a shelf-stable product that won't go bad on you, like milk. It's simply fresh milk that has been heated until the water content evaporates! Just check the expiration date on the can to make sure it hasn't been in the pantry too long.

♥

For a full meal, you can add veggies. Just reduce the quantity of pasta to 6 ounces; add about 1 cup of frozen peas, cauliflower rice, or broccoli florets in the last 3 minutes of boiling the pasta.

1. Bring a medium pot of **salted water** to a boil. Add the **macaroni** and cook until tender according to the package directions, then drain.

2. In the same pot, warm the **evaporated milk** over medium-high heat. When bubbling around the edges, reduce the heat to low. One at a time, stir in the **Cheddar cheese**, **American cheese**, and **butter** until melted and smooth. Stir in the macaroni and season to taste with salt. Serve right away. The sauce will thicken as it cools, but you can add a little warm water to thin if necessary.

COOK'S SECRET WEEKNIGHT BEEF STEW

Serves 4

PREP
15 minutes

COOK
40 minutes

Even on a weeknight, my mother would make a beef stew. It was a dinnertime staple in our home. But it would take hours on the stove to get those cuts of beef tender enough to enjoy and the flavors bubbling together in happy harmony. I don't know how my mother did it, honestly, especially during the work week.

If you're craving those flavors but *not* the time involved, this is my quick take on her beef stew that anyone in your family will devour. My shortcut version uses ground beef and the combination of savory heavy hitters (Worcestershire sauce, tomato paste, and wine) to create a deep stewy flavor in less time. Just like a traditional beef stew, this is best served with crusty bread, buttered egg noodles, or mashed potatoes. It will fool everyone into thinking you were working over that stove for hours. Don't give away your secret!

1	pound ground beef (80% lean)
1	yellow onion, coarsely chopped
2	tablespoons tomato paste
	Kosher salt and freshly ground black pepper
1	tablespoon all-purpose flour
1	cup dry red wine
2½	cups beef broth
2	carrots, peeled and thinly sliced
4	small Yukon Gold potatoes (8 ounces total), halved (no need to peel)
1	tablespoon Worcestershire sauce
4	sprigs fresh thyme
1	cup frozen peas (no need to thaw)

BABS SAYS

The quickest and easiest way to brown ground beef is to press the beef into an even layer in the bottom of your pan and leave it alone! It will have a terrific crunchy brown exterior and is easily stirred and broken up into the small pieces you need later.

1. In a large heavy-bottomed pot or Dutch oven, press the **beef** into an even layer to fill the pot. Set over medium-high heat and sprinkle with the **onion** and **tomato paste**. Cook, undisturbed, until the beef is deeply browned underneath, 6 to 8 minutes (the meat won't be fully cooked).

2. Season the meat with **1 teaspoon each salt and pepper** and break up the beef into small pieces. Continue to cook, stirring often, until the onion is softened and the tomato paste is well combined, 1 to 2 minutes. Add the **flour** and stir for 1 minute. Add the **wine** and simmer, scraping up the browned bits, until thick like gravy, 2 to 4 minutes.

3. Add the **broth**, **carrots**, **potatoes**, **Worcestershire sauce**, and **thyme sprigs** and bring back to a boil. Once boiling, reduce the heat to medium. Simmer, stirring occasionally, until the potatoes are tender and the stew is thickened, 15 to 20 minutes. Add the **peas** and simmer until bright green, about 5 minutes. Remove the thyme sprigs and season to taste with salt and pepper. Serve immediately.

TAKEOUT LOVERS' STICKY CHICKEN FRIED RICE

Serves 4

PREP
10 minutes

COOK
35 minutes

I love really good Chinese food. Especially takeout. Who doesn't? It's convenient, quick, and *always* yummy. What if I told you it's possible to get that same satisfaction without having to pull out of the driveway to pick it up?

Getting great ingredients to make quick, satisfying, better-than-takeout Chinese food is not hard. Everything you need for my chicken fried rice is likely in your freezer, refridge, or pantry right now. Think of this as the Chinese takeout you need but homemade, thrifty, and customizable. This is also another opportunity to clear out your refridge: use 3 cups of leftover cooked rice or 2 cups of any cooked vegetables, and you'll save time too!

---

1 cup basmati or jasmine rice

Kosher salt

3 tablespoons neutral oil, such as avocado

1 shallot, finely chopped

1½ pounds boneless, skinless chicken thighs, trimmed and cut into 1-inch pieces

⅓ cup reduced-sodium soy sauce

⅓ cup honey

2 tablespoons unseasoned rice vinegar

1 tablespoon grated fresh ginger

1 (10-ounce) package frozen mixed vegetables (no need to thaw)

2 teaspoons toasted sesame oil

2 large eggs, beaten with a pinch of salt

> **BABS SAYS**
>
> For a bit of nutty crunch, add toasted sesame seeds or chopped cashews to the top.

1. In a large nonstick skillet with a lid, combine the **rice**, **2 cups water**, and **1 teaspoon salt**. Bring to a boil over medium-high heat. Reduce the heat to low, cover, and cook until the water is absorbed and the rice is tender, about 17 minutes. Set aside, covered.

2. In a second large skillet, heat **1 tablespoon of the oil** over medium-high heat. Add the **shallot** and cook until softened, 2 to 3 minutes. Add the **chicken**, **soy sauce**, **honey**, **rice vinegar**, and **ginger**. Increase the heat to high and cook, stirring often, until the chicken is cooked through and glazed with the sauce, 10 to 12 minutes.

3. While the chicken is simmering, add the **mixed vegetables** and remaining 2 tablespoons oil to the skillet with the rice. Set over medium-high heat and cook, stirring occasionally, until the vegetables are heated through and the rice is crisp in spots, 7 to 10 minutes.

4. Push the rice mixture to one side of the skillet. To the empty side, add the **sesame oil** and **eggs**. Once the eggs set around the edges, stir until scrambled, 1 to 2 minutes. Stir the eggs into the rice mixture and top with the chicken. Serve immediately.

PASTA "FAZOOL"

Serves 6

PREP
10 minutes

COOK
40 minutes

Pasta e fagioli or, in my house, "pasta fazool," was one of our Friday standards. This classic Italian pasta and bean soup brings back as many memories for me as there are possibilities with the soup itself. It's the very definition of a "use what you have" dish. I like ditalini pasta, but you could use elbow macaroni. Use crushed or whole peeled tomatoes instead of diced, if that's what you have in your pantry. Or, make it meat-free by skipping the pancetta—just like my mother did on Fridays.

---

2 tablespoons extra-virgin olive oil, plus more for serving

4 ounces pancetta (optional), chopped

1 large yellow onion, coarsely chopped

1 large carrot, peeled and finely chopped

2 celery stalks, finely chopped

4 large garlic cloves, coarsely chopped

1 teaspoon Italian seasoning, or ½ teaspoon dried rosemary plus ½ teaspoon dried thyme

Kosher salt and freshly ground black pepper

1 (28-ounce) can whole tomatoes, undrained

2 (15-ounce) cans cannellini beans, undrained

Grated Parmesan or Pecorino Romano cheese, for serving, plus a piece of rind if you have one

8 ounces ditalini or other small pasta

1 teaspoon red wine vinegar, or more to taste

1. In a heavy-bottomed large pot or Dutch oven, add the **olive oil**, **pancetta** (if using), **onion**, **carrot**, **celery**, **garlic**, **Italian seasoning**, **1 teaspoon salt**, and **½ teaspoon pepper**. Set over medium heat and cook, stirring often, until the onion is translucent and fragrant, 7 to 9 minutes.

2. Stir in the **tomatoes** and **4 cups water** (pour some of the water into the tomato can first to get all the tomato). Add the **beans**, including their liquid. If you have a **cheese rind**, add that to the pot as well. Bring the mixture to a simmer over medium-high heat. Reduce the heat to medium, partially cover, and gently simmer, stirring occasionally, until slightly thickened, 8 to 10 minutes.

3. Add the **pasta** to the pot and stir well to combine. Simmer, uncovered, stirring often to keep the pasta from sticking, until the pasta is tender, 10 to 12 minutes. If the soup is too thick before the pasta is cooked, add about ½ cup additional water.

4. Remove the cheese rind, if using. Stir in the **vinegar**. Season to taste with salt, pepper, and vinegar if needed. Spoon into bowls, drizzle with a little olive oil, and sprinkle with grated cheese. (Any leftovers can be frozen for up to 3 months.)

CHICKEN & RICE CASSEROLE FOR THE SOUL

Serves 4

PREP
10 minutes

COOK
1 hour 10 minutes

Every cook has their workhorse. The meal you can make with your eyes closed will be ready quickly, and you know with certainty that your family will eat it. For me, that was chicken and rice casserole.

There are so many flavor directions you can take a chicken and rice casserole. But this one tastes like broccoli Cheddar soup *and* sour cream—and onion dip jumped into the dish, too. It's like a mash-up of three retro classics. The Cheddar and sour cream both add creaminess and tang to this comforting dish. This is a dump-and-bake casserole; no stovetop stirring tonight!

2½ cups chicken broth

½ cup sour cream

1 (2-ounce) package dried onion soup mix

½ teaspoon fresh or dried thyme leaves

Kosher salt and freshly ground black pepper

1 cup long-grain white rice

1 to 1½ pounds boneless, skinless chicken breasts, cubed

1 broccoli crown, cut into florets (about 4 cups)

1¾ cups (7 ounces) shredded sharp Cheddar cheese

1 sleeve (32) Ritz crackers, crushed by hand (about 2 cups)

BABS SAYS

If you buy shredded cheese and broccoli florets, the only thing you need to do is cut the chicken. This is a great place to use chicken tenderloins, because you can just use scissors to snip them into cubes.

1. Preheat the oven to 350°F.

2. In a 9 × 13-inch or other 3-quart baking dish, whisk together the **chicken broth**, **sour cream**, **onion soup mix**, **thyme**, **½ teaspoon salt**, and a **few grinds of pepper** until smooth. Stir in the **rice** and **chicken**. Seal the dish tightly with aluminum foil and bake until the rice is al dente, 35 to 40 minutes.

3. Stir in the **broccoli** and 1 cup of the **cheese**. Cover and bake until the rice is tender, another 10 to 20 minutes. Sprinkle with the remaining ¾ cup cheese and the **cracker crumbs**. Bake, uncovered, until the crumb crust is lightly golden and the cheese is melted, 4 to 6 minutes. Let cool for a few minutes, then serve.

FOOD TRUCK TAMALE PIE

Serves 4

PREP
5 minutes

COOK
35 minutes

I remember as a kid in Chicago, there was a food truck parked on the corner of North Avenue and Natoma, about a block from my house, every summer night. He sold only three things: hot dogs, pop, and tamales. On nights when the adults would allow us to get a late snack, my friends and I would run to the corner and I would get one of each. And boy, do I remember those tamales! They were stuffed with a mouthwatering spicy meat, bean, and cheese mixture. This recipe reminds me of those carefree days from my childhood.

Tamale pie is a retro, Tex-Mex spin on the traditional Mexican dish. It is much less labor intensive than the classic and is both vegetarian *and* pantry friendly, since we use beans instead of beef. You won't miss the meat, as this bean mixture is smoky and savory from the enchilada sauce, chili powder, and garlic powder. The cornbread topping is crisp and cheesy outside and tender within.

---

6 tablespoons unsalted butter

1 (8.5-ounce) box Jiffy corn muffin mix

1 large egg

¼ cup sour cream, plus more for serving

Kosher salt and freshly ground black pepper

1 tablespoon chili powder

1 tablespoon ground cumin

1 tablespoon garlic powder

2 (15-ounce) cans black, kidney, or pinto beans, drained but not rinsed

1 bunch scallions, chopped (optional)

3 (10-ounce) cans mild red enchilada sauce

2 cups (8 ounces) shredded Cheddar cheese

For serving (optional): avocado, cilantro, and/or hot sauce

1. Preheat the oven to 425°F. Line a sheet pan with parchment paper.

2. In an ovenproof 10-inch skillet, melt **4 tablespoons of the butter** over medium-high heat. Once the butter is melted, stir constantly until the foam subsides and the butter turns light brown and smells nutty, 1 to 3 minutes. Scrape the brown butter into a medium bowl. Stir in the **corn muffin mix**, **egg**, **sour cream**, **½ teaspoon salt**, and **½ teaspoon pepper**. Set the cornbread mixture aside.

3. In the same skillet, melt the remaining 2 tablespoons butter over medium-high heat. Add the **chili powder**, **cumin**, and **garlic powder** and stir until fragrant, about 2 minutes. Add the **beans**, half of the **scallions** (if using), and the **enchilada sauce**. Bring the mixture to a simmer and cook until slightly thickened, 7 to 10 minutes.

4. Remove the skillet from the heat and dollop the cornbread topping over the bean mixture. (Don't worry about covering the entire top.) Sprinkle **half the cheese** over the top. Place the skillet on the sheet pan and bake until the cornbread is just firm to the touch and lightly browned and the sauce is bubbling, 12 to 15 minutes.

5. Let the tamale pie sit for 10 minutes. Serve topped with the remaining cheese, some sour cream, and if you'd like, the remaining scallions, **avocado**, **cilantro**, and/or **hot sauce**.

LEMONY CHICKEN SOUP

Serves 4

PREP
10 minutes

COOK
40 minutes

Years ago, as newlyweds, Bill and I would go to Greektown in Chicago and enjoy delicacies like spanakopita and pastitsio, along with a bottle of Roditis. I had always liked Greek food, but these experiences with my new husband made me *really* fall in love. So, I wanted to capture some of that love for you! This recipe is reminiscent of the classic Greek soup avgolemono.

The creaminess of this dish comes from the egg; the result is silky, but much lighter than a heavy cream-based soup. Plus, you don't have to fuss with cooking the chicken; you could easily shred a rotisserie chicken or use some of your leftover spatchcocked chicken from page 56.

2	tablespoons extra-virgin olive oil
3	large carrots, peeled and finely chopped
4	celery stalks, finely chopped
6	scallions, thinly sliced, plus more for serving
	Kosher salt
2	garlic cloves, finely chopped or grated
8	cups chicken broth
2	dried bay leaves
1	cup long-grain rice, such as basmati or jasmine
2	large eggs
½	cup fresh lemon juice (from 3 lemons)
3	cups shredded cooked chicken (from 2 breasts)
	Freshly ground black pepper

1. In a large heavy-bottomed pot or Dutch oven, heat the **olive oil** over medium-high heat. Add the **carrots**, **celery**, **scallions**, and **½ teaspoon salt** and sauté until softened but not browned, 5 to 7 minutes. Add the **garlic** and stir until fragrant, about 1 minute.

2. Add the **broth** and **bay leaves** and bring to a simmer. Add the **rice** and reduce the heat to medium-low. Simmer, stirring occasionally, until the rice is tender, 15 to 20 minutes.

3. Meanwhile, in a liquid measuring cup, whisk together the **eggs** and **lemon juice** until smooth. Pour ½ cup of the hot broth into the egg mixture and whisk to combine.

4. Stir the soup with one hand while slowly pouring in the egg mixture. Add the **chicken** and stir until the soup has thickened and the chicken is warm, 2 to 4 minutes. Remove and discard the bay leaves. Season to taste with salt and **pepper**, then top with more scallions. Serve.

> **BABS SAYS**
>
> The key to not curdling the egg is to temper it, meaning to add some hot broth to the egg so the temperature difference between the soup and the egg is not too wide.

CLEAN-YOUR-REFRIDGE FRITTATA

Serves 4

PREP
10 minutes

COOK
25 minutes

My grandmother was the original environmentalist. In the morning, she would take an old milk carton, set it on the counter, and add all the food scraps from the day—potato peels, onion skins, anything you could compost. There was hardly any waste in her kitchen. Even now, the thought of tossing away food makes me a little anxious. So, I do my best to use what I have, especially toward the end of the week, when the clock starts ticking on fresh veggies.

This recipe is a perfect vehicle for any vegetable or protein you need to use up! Eggs are magical; they go with *everything*. Bacon and Cheddar, chicken and feta, or veggies, and a little mozzarella—mix any of those combinations into a fluffy warm frittata not only for breakfast or lunch but dinner, too! This frittata freezes exceptionally well, so you can portion it out for future meals. Who wouldn't love a meal that is as easy and practical as it is tasty!

8 large eggs

½ cup heavy cream

½ teaspoon dried basil, dill, or Italian seasoning

   Kosher salt and freshly ground black pepper

1 cup (4 ounces) shredded Gruyère or other hard cheese, or ½ cup crumbled soft cheese, such as goat cheese or feta

4 tablespoons (½ stick) unsalted butter

4 ounces boneless ham steak (or other cooked protein, like bacon!), coarsely chopped (about ½ cup)

1 yellow onion, finely chopped

½ bunch asparagus, thinly sliced, or 1 cup other thinly sliced vegetable

1 cup frozen peas (no need to thaw)

1. Arrange a rack in the center of the oven and preheat the oven to 375°F.

2. In a medium bowl, whisk the **eggs** until just mixed (don't beat until fluffy). Whisk in the **cream**, **dried herbs**, **1¼ teaspoons salt**, and **¼ teaspoon pepper** until well blended. Stir in the **shredded cheese**. (If using soft cheese, you'll mix it in later.) Set aside.

3. In a large cast-iron skillet, melt **2 tablespoons of the butter** over medium-high heat. Add the **ham**, **onion**, and **asparagus** and sauté until the vegetables are softened, 3 to 5 minutes. Add the **peas** and cook, stirring occasionally, until bright green, 2 to 3 minutes. Season with salt and pepper, if needed. Add the remaining 2 tablespoons butter, stir until melted, then spread the filling in an even layer. Turn off the heat and pour in the egg mixture. If using soft cheese, crumble or scatter it on top now.

4. Transfer the skillet to the oven and bake until the eggs are just set in the middle, 10 to 12 minutes. Let cool slightly, then remove the frittata from the pan and slice into wedges. Serve immediately.

BABS SAYS

The only way to make bacon is in a cold oven. After you place the bacon on a sheet pan, put it in an oven set to 400°F for 15 to 17 minutes, depending on the thickness of the bacon. You'll have crisp and perfect bacon every time!

AUNT MIMI'S MUJADDARA

Serves 4 to 6

PREP
20 minutes

COOK
40 minutes

My aunt Mimi was the matriarch of the Shamon family, the Lebanese side of my family. If you visited her home on any weekday, you would be guaranteed a serving of her scrumptious mujaddara, a classic Lebanese dish of rice, lentils, and crispy onions. And let me tell you, I *love* onions. She would fry her onions in oil to get them nice and crisp, but for this, we make it easy.

This recipe is streamlined so you cook the rice with the lentils and the onions crisp themselves in the oven. It's important that these are crispy, browned, nearing burnt onions—not soft and jammy, like caramelized onions.

Mujaddara makes excellent leftovers, too. Top it with an egg or chopped leftover protein, toss it into salad greens and add dressing, fold it into a taco or burrito, or use it as the base for a grain bowl. It's a staple dish for a reason!

---

5 cups low-sodium chicken or vegetable stock, or water

1 cup brown or green lentils

1 teaspoon ground cumin

½ teaspoon ground allspice

½ teaspoon ground coriander

Kosher salt and freshly ground black pepper

3 yellow onions, thinly sliced

¼ cup extra-virgin olive oil

1 cup basmati rice, well rinsed

¾ cup plain whole-milk Greek yogurt (5-ounce container)

⅓ cup chopped fresh cilantro or parsley (optional)

1. Arrange a rack in the bottom third of the oven. Place a sheet pan on the rack and then preheat the oven to 400°F.

2. In a large pot, bring the **stock** to a boil over high heat. Add the **lentils**, **cumin**, **allspice**, **coriander**, **1½ teaspoons salt**, and **½ teaspoon pepper**. Reduce the heat to medium, cover, and cook until the lentils are softened but al dente (not fully cooked yet), 8 to 10 minutes.

3. While the lentils are cooking, remove the hot sheet pan from the oven. Combine the **onions**, **olive oil**, and ½ teaspoon salt on the pan. Return the pan to the oven and roast, stirring the onions with a fork every 10 minutes, until browned and crisp, with some charred ends, 30 to 40 minutes.

4. When the lentils are al dente, stir in the **rice**. Cover and reduce the heat to low. Cook, undisturbed, until the lentils and rice are tender, 17 to 20 minutes. Turn off the heat and let rest, covered, for 10 minutes.

5. Stir half the crispy onions into the rice and lentils. Serve the rice and lentils with a dollop of **yogurt**, the remaining onions, and the **chopped herbs** (if using).

BABS SAYS

The trick to getting anything fabulously crispy—in this case, the onions—is to place the sheet pan in a cold oven so it can preheat along with the oven.

♥

If you are using water instead of stock, double the amount of salt.

♥

If you don't have allspice, cumin, and coriander, you could use turmeric, ¼ teaspoon cinnamon, or skip the spices.

THE CLASSIC TUNA NOODLE CASSEROLE

Serves 4 to 6

PREP
15 minutes

COOK
45 minutes

If I didn't include this recipe, I would expect a warrant to be issued by the cookbook police. As a mother and grandmother writing a book filled with everyday family fare, I'm pretty sure a tuna noodle casserole recipe is required by law. The dish is iconic for a reason. My mother made it, my mother-in-love, Hazel, made it, and I make it—and I know, from now on, *you* will make it, too! I know we're in the Thursday chapter, but when I was growing up, this was our go-to Friday-night dinner, especially during Lent.

I've said not to knock canned goods; they are there for you when you need them, and this comforting, cheesy, homey casserole is the best example. This is a total dump dinner, apart from parcooking your noodles. The best part? The crunchy potato-chip topping. It's another good spot to introduce your little ones to cooking—they will be thrilled to bits at being asked to crumble the chips for you!

1	tablespoon unsalted butter
12	ounces wide egg noodles
1	(10-ounce) can cream of mushroom soup
1	(10-ounce) can cream of celery soup
⅔	cup sour cream
⅔	cup whole milk
1½	teaspoons onion powder
	Kosher salt and freshly ground black pepper
3	(5-ounce) cans water-packed tuna, drained
1	cup frozen peas (no need to thaw)
1	(4-ounce) jar sliced pimientos, drained
¾	cup (3 ounces) grated Cheddar cheese
¾	cup (3 ounces) grated pepper Jack cheese
1½	cups crushed potato chips

1. Preheat the oven to 350°F. Grease a 9 × 13-inch or other 3-quart baking dish with the **butter**.

2. Bring a large pot of water to a boil over high heat. Add the **noodles** and cook until just shy of al dente, 3 to 5 minutes. Drain.

3. In the same large pot (off the heat), combine the **soups**, **sour cream**, **milk**, **onion powder**, and ½ **teaspoon each salt and pepper**. Vigorously stir in the **tuna**, **peas**, **pimientos**, ½ **cup of the Cheddar**, and ½ **cup of the pepper Jack cheese**. Add the noodles and gently fold in until well blended. Season to taste with salt and pepper, then pour the mixture into the baking dish. Sprinkle with the remaining cheese and top with the **crushed potato chips**. Place in the oven and bake until bubbly, about 30 minutes. Let rest for 5 minutes before serving.

> **BABS SAYS**
>
> No need to heat up any leftovers; this is one of those recipes you can eat straight from the refrigerator, like a classic tuna salad.

Fri-Yay!

It's Friday, yay! You've made it to the end of the week. So, now I have two words for you: TV. Trays. Those two words certainly defined Friday nights in the Costello home. When my family was young, I had some little folding tables we could set up in front of us on the couch to eat meals. They came out only when the kids were sick *or* it was time for movie night and a fun dinner. Fridays!

All kids aren't going to eat all things, even those things in a family-friendly cookbook. But this is a chapter I have intentionally geared toward "kid-friendly" recipes, like a fun Giant Crunchy Taco Wrap (see page 154), the ultimate! Back in my TV tray days, we'd watch *Back to the Future* while enjoying English muffin pizzas (as a preschool teacher, this is how I taught my kids about circles—muffin, pepperoni, olives, all were circles!). I've since evolved that tradition into a comforting "grandma pie" that my grandchildren love. My grandchildren *also* love sushi, so I've included an easy sushi bake that adults will eat up, too.

Fridays are for taking a load off. The work week and school week are behind you. So, have a movie night, gather around a board game, take your TV trays and plates into the living room, and have fun—or make yourself a drink and relax!

SPICY TUNA SUSHI BAKE

Serves 6 to 8

PREP
15 minutes

COOK
45 minutes

My grandchildren eat more sushi than I do, even the little ones. I'm talking about my seven-, five-, and three-year-old grandsons. They absolutely love it. And not just the California rolls or the spicy tuna rolls I usually stick with. They get it all. So, I have to say, this dish is one I'm particularly proud of. Sushi beginners and pros have equally raved about it.

A sushi bake is simply sushi flavors in casserole form. The fish isn't raw here, so anyone who might usually yuck sushi will yum this. The mayo and cream cheese make it a rich and creamy dish you can serve with a load of fresh toppings, like avocado, cucumber, or pickled ginger and let people build hand rolls with small squares of nori (dried seaweed). Leftovers are great cold, right out of the refridge.

Toasted sesame oil

2 cups sushi rice, well rinsed

2 tablespoons unseasoned rice vinegar

1 tablespoon plus 1 teaspoon sugar

Kosher salt

4 ounces cream cheese, at room temperature

6 (5-ounce) cans tuna, drained

½ cup mayonnaise, plus more for serving

2 tablespoons Sriracha, plus more for serving

2 tablespoons soy sauce

6 scallions, thinly sliced

¼ cup furikake seasoning, plus more for serving

For serving: small nori sheets, sliced cucumber, sliced avocado, and sushi ginger

1. Preheat the oven to 400°F. Lightly grease the bottom and sides of a 9 × 13-inch baking dish with the **sesame oil**.

2. In a large saucepan, combine **2 cups water**, the **rice**, **vinegar**, **1 tablespoon of the sugar**, and **1 teaspoon salt**. Bring to a boil over high heat, cover, reduce the heat to low, and cook until the rice is tender, 18 to 20 minutes.

3. Meanwhile, place the **cream cheese** in a large bowl and add the **tuna**, **mayonnaise**, **Sriracha**, **soy sauce**, remaining 1 teaspoon sugar, and **half the scallions**. Stir to combine.

4. Add the rice to the baking dish and press it into an even layer. Sprinkle with half the **furikake**, then add the spicy tuna and press into an even layer atop the rice. Sprinkle with the remaining furikake. Bake until sizzling and the edges are lightly golden, 15 to 20 minutes.

5. Top the sushi bake with the remaining scallions, another drizzle of Sriracha, some mayo, and more furikake. Serve spooned into the **nori sheets** and top with the **cucumber**, **avocado**, **sushi ginger**, and more furikake.

BABS SAYS

This homemade Russian dressing is a snap to make and is delicious, but feel free to take a shortcut by using your favorite bottled brand.

♥

Use your imagination with the fillings! Anything gooey and saucy could be a pastry pocket filling, from pizza toppings to a Philly cheesesteak.

REUBEN PASTRY POCKETS

Makes 12 turnovers

PREP
15 minutes

COOK
30 minutes

Reubens are my favorite way to eat corned beef. I make corned beef once a year, on St. Patrick's Day, of course, but I eat Reubens year-round. It's my deli go-to. But they are a messy affair. I have a really good Reuben casserole in *Celebrate,* but for *Every Day,* I've made the classic Reuben extra fun, and less messy, for Friday. Here you'll use a tender, flaky puff pastry dough and layer on the homemade Russian dressing, thin corned beef slices from the deli, and Swiss cheese that melts beautifully, plus zesty sauerkraut. You'll have leftover sauce for dipping, of course!

This is another great opportunity to have the kiddos help. They can crimp the edges of the pockets!

RUSSIAN DRESSING

½   cup sour cream

½   cup mayonnaise

¼   cup ketchup

¼   cup sweet relish

1   tablespoon spicy brown or Dijon mustard

½   teaspoon Worcestershire sauce

Kosher salt and freshly ground black pepper

PASTRY POCKETS

2   large eggs

Kosher salt and freshly ground black pepper

2   (17.3-ounce) boxes frozen puff pastry (4 sheets), thawed overnight in the refridge

8   ounces sliced corned beef

1   (16-ounce) container sauerkraut, drained and squeezed dry

12   slices Swiss cheese (about 10 ounces)

2   teaspoons caraway seeds

1. Arrange racks in the upper and lower thirds of the oven and preheat the oven to 400°F. Line 2 sheet pans with parchment paper.

2. **Make the Russian dressing:** In a medium bowl, stir together the **sour cream**, **mayonnaise**, **ketchup**, **relish**, **mustard**, and **Worcestershire sauce**. Season to taste with **salt** and **pepper**.

3. **Make the pastry pockets:** In a small bowl, beat the **eggs** with ¼ teaspoon salt. On a work surface, unfold 2 sheets of **puff pastry** and cut each into 3 equal strips (for 6 strips total). In the bottom half of the pastry strips, spoon 1 teaspoon of the Russian dressing in the center. Divide half the **corned beef** slices among the pastry strips, folding them to fit on half the pastry. Top each with **1 tablespoon sauerkraut** and **1 slice of cheese** folded in half. Make sure to leave a ¼- to ½-inch border on all sides.

4. Brush the 3 edges surrounding the filling with some of the egg wash and fold the top halves of the strips over the filling, gently stretching each to reach the edges. Using a fork, crimp and seal around the edges.

5. Transfer the crimped pastries to the sheet pans. Using a sharp knife or scissors, make 3 evenly spaced cuts in the tops of each pastry. Brush the pastries with egg wash and sprinkle with the **caraway seeds** and salt and pepper. Refrigerate while you make the remaining pockets.

6. Place the sheet pans in the oven and bake, rotating the pans top to bottom halfway through, until browned, 25 to 30 minutes. Let the pastries rest for 5 minutes. Serve the Reuben turnovers with the remaining dressing for dipping.

SHEET-PAN SHRIMP BOIL

Serves 4 to 6

PREP
25 minutes

COOK
35 minutes

When we lived in Virginia, we would vacation on the Outer Banks in North Carolina. One of the local beach places made a terrific shrimp boil, and it was always our "big meal" of the vacation. The combination of sweet shrimp and corn with spicy sausage and tender potatoes hit the spot after a long day of relaxing—or more accurately, running after kids on a beach. At home, I make this streamlined version. The biggest benefit of roasting this in the oven is that all the ingredients get browned and crisped, adding an additional layer of flavor and texture. This is my invitation to you to enjoy a good shrimp boil—year-round!

⅓ cup extra-virgin olive oil

1 tablespoon Old Bay seasoning

Kosher salt

18 small red potatoes (about 1½ pounds), halved

12 ounces andouille sausage (or kielbasa), cut into 1½-inch lengths

6 ears of yellow corn, shucked and snapped in half

1½ pounds extra-large shrimp (10–12 count), peeled and deveined, tails on

Grated zest of 1 lemon

HERBED BUTTER

1 stick (4 ounces) unsalted butter, at room temperature

4 garlic cloves, finely grated

¼ cup chopped fresh parsley

¼ cup chopped fresh chives

1 teaspoon Old Bay seasoning

1 teaspoon smoked paprika

For serving: chopped chives, chopped parsley, lemon wedges

> **BABS SAYS**
>
> To making shucking corn a breeze, run water over each ear, then microwave for 2 minutes and the husks will slip right off.

1. Arrange a rack in the upper third of the oven and preheat the oven to 425°F. Line a sheet pan with parchment paper.

2. In a small bowl, stir together the **olive oil**, **Old Bay seasoning**, and **1½ teaspoons salt**.

3. Add the **potatoes**, **sausage**, and **corn** to your sheet pan. Add 3 tablespoons of the Old Bay oil and toss with your hands and combine, then spread in an even layer in the pan. Roast until the potatoes are tender, 20 to 25 minutes.

4. Meanwhile, in a medium bowl, add the **shrimp** and remaining Old Bay oil and stir in the **lemon zest**. Refrigerate until ready to use.

5. **Make the herbed butter:** In a medium bowl, stir together the **butter**, **garlic**, **parsley**, **chives**, Old Bay seasoning, and **smoked paprika**. Mash with a fork until combined and set aside.

6. When the vegetables are ready, arrange the shrimp on top and continue to roast until the shrimp are pink and opaque, 5 to 7 minutes more.

7. Right out of the oven, spread some of the herbed butter on the shrimp boil, then return to the oven for a minute or two to melt the butter. Serve sprinkled with chives and parsley, the remaining herbed butter for spreading, and **lemon wedges** for squeezing. (Any extra butter will keep for 1 week refrigerated; spread it on seafood, steak, or chicken.)

CHICAGO DOGS with FRIES

Serves 4

PREP
10 minutes,
plus 30 minutes
soaking time

COOK
25 minutes

Way back when, my mom, aunt, sister, and I bought a restaurant together in Chicago and named it Mrs. Murphy's Italian Cousins. We called it that because, prior to us, it had been simply "Mrs. Murphy's," and we couldn't afford to change the neon sign. So, instead we tacked on "Italian Cousins." My mother was the head chef and she made everything from scratch. On special days, she'd put her manicotti on the menu, but we served all sorts of Italian American and Chicago classics: pepper and eggs, Italian beef, sub sandwiches of all kinds, chicken parm, eggplant parm, and of course, Chicago dogs with fries.

There is nothing like a true Chicago dog, and this is the classic recipe. I've added a few helpful tips so you can make a version even outside of Chicago. By the way, I still have my old Mrs. Murphy's Italian Cousins T-shirt, but after so many years and Chicago dogs later, it doesn't quite fit the way it used to!

FRIES

2   pounds russet potatoes (about 4 large)

Neutral oil, such as avocado, or beef tallow, for deep-frying

Kosher salt

HOT DOGS

4   all-beef hot dogs, preferably Vienna

4   hot dog buns

½   tablespoon unsalted butter, melted

1   teaspoon poppy seeds

Yellow mustard

¼   cup sweet pickle relish, preferably Vienna relish

1   small white onion, finely chopped

1   Roma (plum) tomato, cut into 8 wedges

4   dill pickle spears

4   sport peppers (or pepperoncini)

For serving: celery salt

1. **Make the fries:** Peel the **potatoes** and cut off one short, rounded end. Stand upright on the cut side, then slice ¼ inch thick. Slice the other way into ¼-inch-thick fries. Place the potatoes in a bowl of cold water and refrigerate for 30 minutes or up to overnight.

2. Pour 3 inches of **oil** into a Dutch oven and heat the oil over medium heat to 325°F. Line a sheet pan with paper towels.

3. Drain the potatoes and pat them dry. Add half the fries to the hot oil and cook, stirring occasionally, until blond, 4 to 6 minutes. Transfer to the sheet pan and continue with the rest of the potatoes. Let the fries rest for 10 minutes while you cook the **hot dogs** (or you can leave them out at room temperature for up to 2 hours). Keep the oil hot over medium heat.

4. **Cook the hot dogs:** Fill a medium pot halfway with water and bring to a boil. Reduce the heat to medium-low and drop in the hot dogs to cook until warmed and slightly curved, about 5 minutes.

(recipe continues)

There is no spin on a Chicago dog. You boil Vienna all-beef franks; you steam the S. Rosen's Mary Ann brand poppyseed buns; you use yellow mustard (*never* ketchup), sweet green pickle relish, chopped white onions, tomato wedges, a pickle spear, sport peppers, and a dash of celery salt (phew!). This is all stuff you can get in Chicago. Outside the Chicago area, we're going to get as close as we can!

♥

What the heck is a sport pepper? It's a Chicago thing. They are small, green, pickled hot peppers, which look a little like a tabasco pepper. Depending on where you live, these might be tough to find also, so again, I grant you special Chicago-native permission to use pepperoncini if they are more available!

♥

To save time, you can use frozen fries.

5. Place a steamer basket or colander into the pot, then add the **buns**, cover the pot, and steam until warm and soft, just 1 minute. Turn off the heat, transfer the buns to a plate, brush the outsides of them with the melted **butter**, and sprinkle with the **poppy seeds**. Set aside to let dry.

6. **Finish the fries:** Adjust the oil heat to between 375° and 400°F. Add the once-fried potatoes to the oil and cook, stirring occasionally, until golden brown and puffed, 2 to 4 minutes. While the potatoes fry, change the paper towels on the sheet pan. Transfer the twice-fried potatoes to the fresh paper towels and sprinkle with **1 teaspoon salt**.

7. Add the hot dogs to the buns, then zigzag the hot dogs with **mustard**. Sprinkle with the **relish** and **onion**. On one side of each hot dog, place 2 wedges of **tomato**. On the other side, nestle in a **pickle spear**. Top each hot dog with **sport peppers** and a sprinkle of **celery salt**. Serve with the fries.

GRANDMA'S GRANDMA PIE

Serves 4 to 6

PREP
30 minutes

COOK
20 minutes

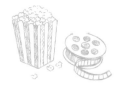

Once a week, my grandmother would get up at four thirty in the morning to bake bread for the week. I wasn't always there, of course, but when I was, what a truly amazing treat it was to wake up to the smell of freshly baked bread! Once a month, she'd add her famous pizza to that mix. She didn't have a pizza stone, so she'd make hers on a sheet pan. A delicious, crispy-on-the-bottom, very simple pizza with some fresh tomato sauce, mozzarella, and homemade sausage.

A "grandma pie" is actually a New York–style pizza. It's traditionally square, thinner than a Sicilian pie, and named such because it was meant to be made at home, not in the 900°F ovens of pizza restaurants. So, all this time, my grandmother was making a traditional New York delicacy. Having no toppings is traditional, too, but go ahead and top this with whatever you like, just like my grandma did!

¼ cup extra-virgin olive oil

2 (1-pound) balls pizza dough, at room temperature

2½ cups (10 ounces) shredded low-moisture mozzarella cheese

¼ cup (1 ounce) grated Pecorino Romano cheese

1 (12- to 14-ounce) jar pizza sauce

Kosher salt

1. Arrange a rack in the bottom third of the oven and preheat the oven as high as it will go (usually around 500°F).

2. Coat a sheet pan with the **olive oil**, then add the **pizza dough**. Pinch the balls together to form one big piece, turn to coat in the oil, then gently stretch and dimple until the dough fills the pan. (If the dough springs back, cover with plastic wrap and rest at room temperature for 10 minutes, then try again.) Use a gentle hand to avoid toughening the crust.

3. Sprinkle the dough with the **mozzarella** and **pecorino**, leaving a ½-inch border at the edges. Dollop spoonfuls of the **pizza sauce** all over (the pizza won't be covered in sauce). Sprinkle with **salt**. Bake on the lower rack, rotating the pan halfway through, until the crust is browned and the mozzarella is browned in spots, 15 to 17 minutes. Let cool for a few minutes, then cut into squares and serve.

BABS SAYS

Coat your sheet pan generously with oil and put the cheese on the dough *before* the sauce, as is traditional. That leaves the dough lovely and crispy with a nice bite, without getting soggy.

♥

Here, I've adapted my grandma's recipe, but you don't have to get up early to make it. Most pizzerias will sell their pizza dough at a reasonable price, and your grocery store will have it, too.

PIMENTO CHEESE PATTY MELTS

Serves 4

PREP
10 minutes

COOK
30 minutes

It's hard to improve on a classic patty melt. So, naturally I've tried! Instead of topping them with Swiss cheese, I've added a pimento cheese spread inspired by my favorite poolside dip. Pimento cheese is a creamy southern spread that combines Cheddar cheese, sweet pimiento peppers, mayo and/or cream cheese, and something spicy like hot sauce. Warmed up in a grilled cheese sandwich, pimento cheese is gooey, sharp, and even more irresistible.

And if you want to save even more time, you can easily use store-bought pimento cheese!

PIMENTO CHEESE

½ cup (2 ounces) shredded sharp yellow Cheddar cheese

½ cup (2 ounces) shredded sharp white Cheddar cheese

¼ cup mayonnaise

2 tablespoons chopped drained pimientos (half a 4-ounce jar)

2 teaspoons drained prepared horseradish

1 teaspoon hot sauce, or to taste

   Kosher salt and freshly ground black pepper

PATTY MELTS

8 slices sourdough bread, lightly toasted

1½ pounds ground beef (80% lean)

4 tablespoons (½ stick) unsalted butter

   Kosher salt and freshly ground black pepper

2 yellow onions, halved and thinly sliced

2 teaspoons Worcestershire sauce

1. **Make the pimento cheese:** In a medium bowl, stir together both **Cheddars**, the **mayonnaise**, **pimientos**, **horseradish**, **hot sauce**, and a pinch of **salt** and **pepper**.

2. **Make the patty melts:** On a work surface, spread each slice of **bread** with 2 tablespoons of the pimento cheese.

3. Divide the **beef** into 4 equal portions. Place the patties between 2 pieces of parchment paper and press down to create very thin patties about ¼ inch larger than the bread slices.

4. Heat a large cast-iron skillet over medium-high heat until just smoking. Add **1 tablespoon of the butter** and swirl until melted. Add 2 of the patties and season generously with salt and pepper. Cook until browned and crusty underneath, 1 to 2 minutes, reducing the heat if the butter is burning. Flip, season with salt and pepper, and cook until browned on the other side, 1 to 2 minutes more. Transfer to 2 of the bread slices, then repeat with the remaining 2 patties and butter.

5. Without wiping out the skillet, reduce the heat to medium. Add the **onions** and ½ teaspoon salt, then slowly add **¼ cup water**. Scrape up the browned bits in the pan and cook, stirring, until golden and tender, 5 to 7 minutes. Add another 2 tablespoons water and the **Worcestershire sauce** and cook, until the liquid is evaporated.

6. Spoon the onions onto the burger patties and top with the remaining 4 slices of bread, pimento cheese side down.

7. Set the skillet over medium heat and add 1 tablespoon of the butter. Working in batches, add the sandwiches and cook, until golden brown on both sides, 3 to 5 minutes. Reduce the heat if the bread is burning. Transfer to plates and sprinkle with salt. Serve right away.

THE ULTIMATE GRILLED CHEESE TOMATO SOUP

Serves 4 to 6

PREP
5 minutes

COOK
20 minutes

Even for those who don't consider themselves "soup people," it's hard to resist a steamy bowl of creamy tomato soup. Especially when it's paired with a melty grilled cheese that you can dunk right in that soup. Like peanut butter and jelly, bacon and eggs, or spaghetti and meatballs, tomato soup and grilled cheese just go together. And you'd be surprised how easy it is to make a luscious tomato soup right at home.

With this tomato soup, I've made it even better by incorporating the grilled cheese part of this iconic duo as a topping rather than as a sidekick (think of the cheesy slice of bread on top of a French onion soup).

- 2 (28-ounce) cans crushed tomatoes, undrained
- 1 cup chicken or vegetable broth
- 1 yellow onion, quartered
- 1 carrot, peeled and coarsely chopped
- 2 tablespoons unsalted butter
  Kosher salt and freshly ground black pepper
  Pinch of red pepper flakes (optional)
- ½ cup heavy cream
- 4 to 6 (¾-inch-thick) slices sourdough or other good-quality bread, toasted and cut in half
- 1 cup (4 ounces) shredded sharp Cheddar cheese

BABS SAYS

If you want to take this soup over the top and around the block, stir 1 cup (4 ounces) of grated Cheddar cheese into the pureed soup along with the cream for a Grilled *Extra* Cheesy Tomato Soup.

1. In a broiler-safe medium pot, combine the **tomatoes** with their juices, the **broth**, **onion**, **carrot**, **butter**, **1 teaspoon salt**, and the **pepper flakes** (if using). Bring to a simmer over medium-high heat, then reduce the heat to medium-low. Cover and cook until slightly thickened and flavorful, 15 to 20 minutes.

2. Using an immersion blender (or working in batches in a stand blender), puree the soup until smooth. Stir in the **cream** and season to taste with salt and **pepper**.

3. While the soup is simmering, arrange an oven rack in the upper third of the oven and set the broiler to high. Fit the **toasted bread** on the surface of the soup in an even layer, cutting the pieces as needed to cover the entire surface (some overlap is okay). Sprinkle the bread with the **cheese**, then place the pot under the broiler. Broil until the cheese is melted and browned in spots, 2 to 4 minutes. Serve right away.

"WE HAVE FOOD AT HOME" GIANT CRUNCHY TACO WRAP

Serves 4 to 6

PREP
15 minutes

COOK
55 minutes

"We have food at home!" I don't know how many times I uttered that phrase with varying degrees of exasperation. So, believe me when I tell you, I've been there. I see you busy moms whose children yell for the immediate gratification of a drive-thru. I am here to rescue you, because the next time you say, "We have food at home," they will applaud you! Okay, maybe not, but they won't be disappointed. Especially when you make this giant crunchy taco wrap that's crispy, cheesy, and full of wonderful flavorful beef.

Neutral oil, such as avocado

2 pounds ground beef (90% lean)

1 (15-ounce) can black beans, undrained

1 (4-ounce) can diced green chiles

2 (1-ounce) packets taco seasoning

10 (10-inch) burrito-size flour tortillas

6 tostadas

1 (15-ounce) can diced fire-roasted tomatoes, drained

2 cups (8 ounces) shredded Mexican cheese blend

For serving: guacamole, pico de gallo or salsa, hot sauce, nacho sauce, and/or shredded lettuce (optional)

1. Preheat the oven to 425°F. Generously grease a sheet pan with **oil**.

2. In a 12-inch skillet, press the **beef** into an even layer to fill the bottom. Cook over high heat, undisturbed, until the meat is deeply browned underneath, 6 to 8 minutes. Break up the meat into small pieces. Cook, stirring occasionally, until the meat is cooked through and the liquid has evaporated, 4 to 5 minutes. Add the **beans** and their liquid, the **green chiles**, and **taco seasoning**. Cook, stirring, until the liquid has evaporated, 2 to 3 minutes. Turn off the heat.

3. Arrange 6 of the **tortillas** along the sides of the sheet pan, allowing half the tortilla to hang over the side (the center of the pan will not be covered). Layer 2 more tortillas overlapping in the center to cover the bottom of the pan. Spread the ground beef over the tortillas. Top with the **tostadas**, pushing them gently to nestle into the beef. Top with the **tomatoes** and **shredded cheese**. Place the remaining 2 tortillas overlapping in the center. Fold the overhanging tortillas in toward the center of the pan to cover the filling, making sure to tuck in any corner pieces.

4. Drizzle the top of the tortillas with more oil, then place another sheet pan on top to weigh it down. Bake for 20 minutes, then remove the top sheet pan and continue baking until golden brown, 10 to 15 minutes.

5. Let cool for 5 to 10 minutes. Then carefully slide it onto a cutting board. Using a serrated knife, cut into squares and serve with your desired **toppings**.

"REVENGE" BIG ITALIAN SUB SALAD

Serves 6 to 8

PREP
15 minutes

COOK
10 minutes

One day, when I was working the counter at my family's restaurant, Mrs. Murphy's Italian Cousins, a man came in and ordered an Italian sub. We sold a lot of those! I made it, packing it with all the meats and cheeses, pickles, and tomatoes, and drizzling on the exact amount of vinaigrette. I put a ton of lettuce on top because it looked fabulous and was going to add the right amount of crunch. It was picture perfect. When I handed it over, he looked at me, got huffy, and said, "What is this? A lettuce sandwich?"

Well, think of this as my revenge salad! If you were to wave a magic wand over an Italian sub and turn it into a salad, this would be it. This makes a whole lotta salad, but it will disappear!

CROUTONS

1	hoagie roll, cut into 1-inch pieces (about 6 cups)
2	tablespoons extra-virgin olive oil
1	teaspoon dried oregano
1	teaspoon garlic powder
	Kosher salt and freshly ground black pepper

SALAD

¼	cup red wine vinegar
1	tablespoon dried oregano
2	small garlic cloves, finely grated
1	small red onion, thinly sliced and rinsed under cold water
	Kosher salt and freshly ground black pepper
½	cup extra-virgin olive oil
½	cup sliced pickled pepperoncini or banana peppers
6	ounces cured meats (one or more, such as salami, mortadella, soppressata, ham), thinly sliced into strips
4	ounces provolone cheese, thinly sliced into strips
1	large head iceberg lettuce (about 1½ pounds), thinly sliced
1	pint cherry tomatoes, halved

1. **Make the croutons:** Preheat the oven to 400°F.

2. On a sheet pan, toss together the **bread cubes**, **olive oil**, **oregano**, **garlic powder**, and **½ teaspoon each salt and pepper**. Bake, tossing halfway through, until golden and crisp, 7 to 10 minutes. (Croutons can be made up to 2 days ahead; keep in an airtight container at room temperature.)

3. **Make the salad:** In a very large bowl, stir together the **vinegar**, oregano, **garlic**, **onion**, and ½ teaspoon each salt and pepper. Add the olive oil, **pepperoncini**, **cured meats**, and **provolone** and toss to combine. Add the **lettuce** and **tomatoes** and sprinkle with 1 teaspoon salt. Toss to combine, then add the croutons. Season to taste with more salt and pepper.

BABS SAYS

Try a twist on this by adding some fresh mozzarella, like the small ciliegine balls.

♥

You can use store-bought croutons for speed.

♥

I know this has fabulous croutons already, but pairing this salad with a bit of garlic bread or toast would be to die for!

♥

To add a little extra protein to the salad, stir a 15-ounce can of chickpeas (drained) into the mix.

JALAPEÑO POPPER TAQUITOS

Serves 4 to 6

PREP
30 minutes

COOK
35 minutes

Decades ago I traded in my old kitchen set (which had seen better days) for a brand-new one. It was beautiful. A dark pine table with lovely Windsor chairs. I owe it all to my husband buying a square in his Super Bowl office pool.

The San Francisco 49ers were playing that year, and we were all gathered around the TV. Our TV trays in place, we had all the yummy foods that accompany Super Bowl viewing: tacos, jalapeño poppers, chips and dip, beer for the adults and soft drinks for the kids. Bill's boss called him at the end of the game to let him know he'd won the pool. I don't know which I remember more fondly, the win or the food, but I know I got that kitchen set with the winnings.

Fun food can bring back happy memories, but it can also create them. These taquitos are crispy-crunchy, just like the tacos we devoured and stuffed with a creamy, smoky, tangy, jalapeño popper–inspired filling. I don't know if these taquitos will bring you a new kitchen set, but I know that you'll have your own memories to share over a plate!

---

8   slices bacon (not thick cut), chopped into small pieces

2   poblano chiles, seeded and finely chopped

2   (8-ounce) packages cream cheese, at room temperature

1   cup (4 ounces) shredded sharp Cheddar cheese

¼   cup coarsely chopped pickled jalapeños, plus some sliced for serving

Kosher salt and freshly ground black pepper

12   (6-inch) corn or flour tortillas

Neutral oil, such as avocado

For serving: sour cream, chopped fresh cilantro

> **BABS SAYS**
>
> The heat from jalapeños can stay on your hands long after you've chopped them; to fix that, rinse your hands with lemon juice or vinegar.

1. Preheat the oven to 425°F. Line a sheet pan with parchment paper.

2. Place the **bacon** in a large pot and set over medium-high heat. Once sizzling, cook, stirring often, until golden and crisp, 5 to 7 minutes. Use a slotted spoon to transfer the bacon to a small bowl. Pour off all but 1 tablespoon of the bacon fat.

3. To the pot, add the **chiles** and cook over medium-high heat until tender and browned in spots, 3 to 5 minutes.

4. Transfer the chiles to a medium bowl and add the **cream cheese**, **Cheddar**, **pickled jalapeños**, and **½ teaspoon each salt and pepper**. Set aside a tablespoon or two of the bacon for serving and add the rest to the bowl. Stir to combine and season to taste with salt and pepper.

5. Wrap the **tortillas** in a damp paper towel and microwave on high until soft and bendable, 30 seconds to 1 minute. On one side of each tortilla, spoon 2 heaping tablespoons of the filling in a line, stopping ½ inch from the edges and roll up tightly. Place seam side down on the sheet pan.

6. Brush the tops and sides of the taquitos generously with **oil** (or the extra bacon fat, if you're really celebrating Fri-Yay). Place the sheet pan in the oven and bake until the taquitos are crisp and golden brown, 14 to 18 minutes. Serve hot, topped with **sour cream**, the reserved bacon, the sliced pickled jalapeños, and the **cilantro**.

OVEN-FRIED CHICKEN & WAFFLES

Serves 4

PREP
15 minutes, plus
2 hours or more
marinating time

COOK
1 hour

Frozen waffles are a busy mom's best friend. I found this to be especially true when my kids reached middle and high school age. Those were the years when they barely made it out in time for the bus. So, my kids' favorite grab-and-go breakfast was Eggos! They could pop one in the toaster, then grab it and run for the bus. Frozen waffles have come a long way since then, and the good news is, you don't just have to have them for breakfast. You can have them for lunch and dinner, too. Waffles, after all, have a savory soulmate . . . fried chicken!

These chicken and waffles are a classic combination for a reason, balancing sweet and salty with a delightful crunch. There is no deep-frying involved and no waffle maker you need to drag out of storage. Since the chicken coating here is cornflakes, it's another breakfast-for-dinner appearance—times two!

---

1 cup well-shaken buttermilk

1 large egg

1 tablespoon plus 1 teaspoon sweet paprika

1 tablespoon plus 1 teaspoon garlic powder

1 tablespoon plus 1 teaspoon onion powder

1 tablespoon hot sauce, plus more for serving

Kosher salt and freshly ground black pepper

3½ to 4 pounds bone-in chicken pieces, breasts halved crosswise, skin removed

6 cups cornflakes

6 tablespoons neutral oil, such as avocado

1 stick (4 ounces) unsalted butter

½ cup pure maple syrup

1 (12-ounce) box frozen waffles (no need to thaw)

1. In a large bowl or resealable container, whisk together the **buttermilk**, **egg**, 1 tablespoon each of the **paprika**, **garlic powder**, and **onion powder**, the **hot sauce**, **2 teaspoons salt**, and **1 teaspoon pepper**. Add the **chicken** and toss well to coat. Cover and refrigerate for 2 hours (and up to 24 hours).

2. Preheat the oven to 425°F. Line a sheet pan with parchment paper, then place an ovenproof wire rack on the sheet pan.

3. Pulse the **cornflakes** in a food processor (or crush in a plastic bag) until they resemble bread crumbs (you should have 2 cups). Transfer to a shallow dish or large plate and stir in 4 tablespoons of the **oil**, the remaining 1 teaspoon each of paprika, garlic powder, and onion powder, 1 teaspoon black pepper, and ½ teaspoon salt. Stir with your fingers until the cereal is coated in oil. Working one piece at a time, shake the excess marinade off the chicken, then add to the cornflake mixture and press to coat all over. Repeat with the remaining chicken.

4. Transfer the chicken to the wire rack bone side up. Bake for 20 minutes, then carefully flip the pieces over and continue to bake until cooked through (an internal thermometer should register 155°F for breasts and 165°F for thighs), 20 to 25 minutes.

(recipe continues)

Using clean hands or kitchen shears, remove the skin from the chicken as best you can; this keeps the breading crispy.

♥

If you already have a favorite homemade waffle recipe, batch-make and freeze them! That is, make double the amount you ordinarily would, put the extras in a zip-top freezer bag, and freeze for up to 1 month (they won't last that long!). When you or your kids have a hankering for a waffle, they can go right into the toaster, just like the store brands.

5. When the chicken is just about done, in a medium saucepan, melt the **butter** and **maple syrup** over medium heat. Turn off the heat and season with ½ teaspoon salt and some hot sauce.

6. Transfer the chicken to a platter, sprinkle with some salt, and let rest. (Reserve the sheet pan.) Increase the oven temperature to 450°F. Dip one side of each **waffle** into the maple butter, then place on the sheet pan, buttered side up. Bake until golden brown and crisp, 8 to 10 minutes.

7. Serve the chicken and waffles drizzled with additional maple butter and more hot sauce, as you like.

NOT A PHILLY CHEESESTEAK–STUFFED BREAD

Serves 6

PREP
10 minutes

COOK
30 minutes

My daughter Erin is a dedicated and gifted athlete. There is no better testament to that than when she ran the Philadelphia Marathon. Anyone who is able to make a commitment to the grueling training and endurance involved in running a marathon, as well as possessing the mental strength to do so, is a star in my book. The trip to Philly to cheer her on also involved cheesesteaks (Bill and I weren't running!). Erin, wearing the number 3015, finished the race and we finished our cheesesteaks. Reason to celebrate all around!

In many ways, this recipe was inspired by that day. It combines the flavors of a Philly cheesesteak, although I cannot emphasize this enough for the loyalists out there: it is *not* a traditional Philly cheesesteak! It *is* thinly sliced rib eye, provolone, mushrooms, onion, and bell pepper stuffed inside a loaf of sourdough, like a big warm hug. As with Erin running that race, this is a big YAY!

---

1   (8- to 9-inch) round loaf sourdough or ciabatta bread

3   tablespoons unsalted butter

1   teaspoon garlic powder

Kosher salt and freshly ground black pepper

1   pound boneless rib eye steak, briefly chilled in the freezer, or shaved steak

2   tablespoons neutral oil, such as avocado

8   ounces sliced fresh button mushrooms

1   small yellow onion, thinly sliced

1   red bell pepper, thinly sliced

6   slices provolone cheese

Hot sauce (optional)

> **BABS SAYS**
>
> Use the bread you scoop out of the loaf to make croutons for a salad or bread crumbs, or add some grated Parmesan and olive oil to make a crispy topping for some pasta.

1. Preheat the oven to 400°F. Line a sheet pan with parchment paper.

2. Using a serrated knife, slice off the top third of the loaf of **bread**. Pull out the inside from the top and bottom of the loaf, leaving a ¾-inch border around the edges. Transfer the hollowed-out loaf to the sheet pan. (Save the inside of the bread for another use; see Babs Says.)

3. In a small microwave-safe bowl, microwave **2 tablespoons of the butter** until melted, 30 to 45 seconds. Stir in ½ teaspoon of the **garlic powder** and ½ **teaspoon salt**. Brush the garlic butter on both sides of the interior of the bread.

4. Trim any large pieces of fat from the **steak**. If using rib eye, very thinly slice it against the grain (if using shaved steak, this is done for you!). Sprinkle the slices with ½ teaspoon each salt and **pepper** and toss to coat.

5. In a large cast-iron skillet, heat **1 tablespoon of the oil** over high heat until just smoking. Add the steak slices in a single layer and cook, undisturbed, until browned underneath, 1 to 2 minutes. Transfer to a plate (it will be rare still).

(recipe continues)

6. Reduce the heat to medium-high and add the remaining tablespoon oil, remaining tablespoon of butter, the **mushrooms**, **onion**, and **bell pepper**. Sprinkle with ½ teaspoon each salt and pepper. Cook, stirring occasionally, until softened and slightly caramelized, 6 to 8 minutes.

7. Add the beef and any juices to the skillet, then the remaining ½ teaspoon garlic powder and stir, scraping up the browned bits, and cook until the steak is medium-rare, 1 to 2 minutes more.

8. Arrange 2 slices of **provolone** on the bottom of the loaf to cover the surface (it's okay if the cheese overlaps). Add half the meat and veggies (about 1½ cups), then add 2 more slices of provolone. Add the remaining meat and veggies, followed by the remaining 2 slices of provolone. Press down to fit snugly, though it's okay if some filling comes above the rim of the bread. Add the top of the bread and press down tightly to close.

9. Bake until the bread is warm and the cheese is melted, 5 to 7 minutes. Let cool slightly. Slice into 6 wedges with a serrated knife and serve. Pass **hot sauce** (if using) alongside.

CHIPOTLE CHICKEN NACHOS

Serves 4

PREP
20 minutes

COOK
15 minutes

Friday in our house was a combination of excitement and exhaustion. Exhaustion for me and Bill; excitement for our four children, who didn't have to think about school and got to stay up just a bit later than usual. So, dinner had to be simple but fun, and maybe something for which we could take out the trusty TV trays or put away the forks and knives for a game night uninterrupted by cutlery!

If there were ever a night to turn nachos into dinner, Friday would be it. I've streamlined the chicken component: you can simply stir cooked chicken into chipotle salsa, which is flavorful right from the jar. Just layer and bake! Gathering around a table getting a pull of chips and cheese and all these ingredients is great for both the exhausted *and* the excited.

---

3 cups shredded cooked chicken (from 1 rotisserie chicken)

1 (15-ounce) can black beans, drained and rinsed

2 cups (16-ounce jar) chipotle salsa

1 (8- to 10-ounce) bag sturdy tortilla chips

2 to 3 cups (8 to 12 ounces) shredded pepper Jack or Colby Jack cheese

1 lime

1 small red onion, finely chopped (about ½ cup)

1 avocado, cubed

Sugar

Kosher salt and freshly ground black pepper

½ cup sour cream

For serving: toppings such as shredded lettuce, cilantro leaves, black olives, sliced radishes, and/or corn salsa

1. Preheat the oven to 375°F. Line a sheet pan with aluminum foil.

2. In a medium bowl, stir together the **chicken**, **beans**, and **half the salsa**. Spread **half the chips** on the sheet pan in an even layer. Top with half each of the chicken mixture and the **cheese**. Repeat with the remaining chips, chicken, and cheese. Bake until the cheese is just melted and the chicken and chips are warm, 10 to 15 minutes.

3. Meanwhile, in the same medium bowl, **juice the lime**. Add the **onion**, **avocado**, ½ **teaspoon each sugar and salt**, and a few grinds of **pepper**. Stir gently to combine, then set aside to briefly marinate.

4. Garnish the nachos with the remaining salsa, the **sour cream**, onion/avocado mix, and toppings of choice (the more the merrier!). Serve directly from the sheet pan.

BABS SAYS

Mixing the pickled onions and the avocado prevents the avocados from browning (it's the lime juice), so not only does it taste great but it looks great, too!

♥

If you want the nachos less spicy, use Colby Jack and milder salsa.

THE BEST FISH & CHIPS

Serves 4 to 6

PREP
45 minutes

COOK
25 minutes

When I was a college student in Wisconsin, fish fries were always on the menu as Friday night specials at local bars, and I *always* ordered them. Cracking the crust of a freshly fried piece of white fish to get to that steamy, perfectly cooked center was music to my ears! I've been making this recipe for my family for decades. Cut the fish into 1-inch strips to make it finger friendly for little hands, like a fish stick!

Frozen fries cut down on the cooking time, and since they're already parcooked in the bag, they'll end up nice and crisp, like a good double fry. But if you prefer homemade fries, use the recipe from the Chicago Dogs (page 145).

TARTAR SAUCE

½ cup mayonnaise

3 tablespoons coarsely chopped white onion

3 tablespoons coarsely chopped cornichon or dill pickles, plus ½ teaspoon brine

1 tablespoon drained capers, coarsely chopped if large

1 tablespoon chopped fresh parsley

2 teaspoons fresh lemon juice

1 teaspoon Dijon mustard

1 teaspoon distilled white vinegar

½ teaspoon Worcestershire sauce

Dash of hot sauce

Freshly ground black pepper

1. **Make the tartar sauce:** At least 1 hour before serving, in a medium bowl, mix together the **mayonnaise, onion, pickles, capers, parsley, lemon juice, mustard, vinegar, Worcestershire sauce, hot sauce,** and **pepper** to taste. Refrigerate until ready to serve. (Makes 1 cup sauce.)

2. **Prepare the fish:** In a medium bowl, whisk together the **flour, cornstarch, baking powder,** and **paprika.** Place the flour mixture in the freezer until cold, about 20 minutes.

3. Preheat the oven to 250°F. Arrange a wire rack on each of 2 sheet pans.

4. Pour 3 inches of **oil** into a Dutch oven and heat the oil over medium heat until a thermometer registers 350°F.

5. Pat the **fish** dry and season with **2 teaspoons salt** and **1 teaspoon pepper.** Lightly coat the fish strips all over with the flour mixture. Add the **beer** and **hot sauce** to the remaining flour mixture and stir to combine. Thin with a tablespoon or two of water if stiff; you want it like a thick pancake batter but not too heavy to stir. Dip the fish strips one at a time into the batter, then transfer the battered fish to one of the wire racks for a few minutes to let the excess batter drip off.

6. When the oil is ready, and working in batches, fry the fish strips until golden brown and cooked through, 3 to 5 minutes. Transfer the fried fish to the other wire rack (do not use paper towels or newspaper, as the fish will steam). Place the sheet pan with the fish in the oven to keep warm.

(recipe continues)

FISH & CHIPS

2 cups all-purpose flour

⅓ cup cornstarch

1 tablespoon baking powder

1 teaspoon sweet paprika

Neutral oil, such as canola or avocado, for deep-frying

2 pounds cod fillets, cut into 1-inch-thick strips

Kosher salt and freshly ground black pepper

1 (12-ounce) bottle lager or pilsner beer

Dash of hot sauce

1 (20-ounce) bag frozen french fries

For serving: lemon wedges and malt vinegar

BABS SAYS

If you don't have a deep-fry/candy thermometer, you can use my wooden spoon trick. Take the handle of a wooden spoon and dip it into your hot oil; if it bubbles rapidly around the handle, the oil is hot enough to fry.

♥

If you want to go the extra mile, here's a great suggestion for you meat lovers. Grease your sheet pan with beef tallow. Just smear the sheet pan with 2 tablespoons of beef tallow and bake the fries as usual. It makes a world of difference!

7. Return the oil to 350°F and add the **fries** in batches. Cook, stirring occasionally, until golden brown, 3 to 5 minutes. (If splattering, cover with a lid.) Transfer the fried potatoes, as finished, to the wire rack with the fried fish to keep warm.

8. Spread the fish and fries on a serving platter and sprinkle with salt. Serve right away with the tartar sauce, **lemon wedges**, and **malt vinegar**.

Low and Slow Saturday

Saturdays are still busy, but it's a different kind of busy and it's not always relaxing. There might not be school or work, but you may be up and out early, with a lot going on. There are errands to run, a house to clean, maybe kids to get to their activities—you get the picture. Bill and I would often need to divide and conquer. Someone had a football game, while someone else had to be at a soccer game or a playdate. Then maybe it was time to squeeze in a haircut for someone else, or we needed to throw in a load of laundry so the kids didn't show up to school the next week in dirty clothes! Depending on the chapter of life you find yourself in, Saturday may look very different. Maybe you're stuck inside taking care of little ones . . . or yourself! That's not exactly "downtime," either.

So, on days like this, dinner should be something you can prepare in the morning and forget about until you're ready to eat. Keep it slow and low! This chapter includes recipes you can prep in the morning, throw into a slow cooker, and have dinner whenever you're ready for it! If you don't have a slow cooker, or you find yourself at home and want to hurry the process along a bit, I've included directions on how to make each recipe in a regular pot or in the oven, instead, so you have that option as well.

Either way, a hearty, delicious meal will be waiting for you when *you* want it!

NOT-TO-BE-MISSED MOROCCAN CHICKPEA APRICOT STEW

Serves 4 to 6

PREP
30 minutes

COOK
6 to 8 hours

The first time I had tagine served in its traditional earthenware pot, steaming with a cornucopia of veggies and aromatic spices, was at a little hole-in-the-wall neighborhood café in Marrakech. My daughter Erin and I took a girls' trip to Morocco many years ago, and it was fabulous. I remember the vibrant colors, the smell of spit-roasted meats drifting out from restaurants and roadside carts. When we popped inside one of those little cafés and tucked into that comforting tagine, I knew I wanted to recapture the experience. This stew has the perfect balance of sweet, spice, and heat, and is full of nature's bounty.

4	garlic cloves
¼	cup extra-virgin olive oil
2	teaspoons sweet paprika
1½	teaspoons ground cumin
1	teaspoon garam masala
½	teaspoon ground ginger
¼	teaspoon cayenne (optional)
	Kosher salt and freshly ground black pepper
2	cups vegetable or chicken broth, or water
2	(15-ounce) cans chickpeas, drained but not rinsed
4	cups (1-inch) cubed peeled butternut squash (from a 1½-pound squash)
1	large red onion, finely chopped
1	pint cherry tomatoes
½	cup dried apricots, quartered
½	bunch fresh cilantro, stems finely chopped and leaves coarsely chopped
¾	cup chili sauce
¼	cup fresh orange juice (from 1 orange)
	For serving: toasted almond slices, pomegranate seeds, and couscous or pita

1. Finely grate the **garlic** into a small skillet. Add the **olive oil**, **paprika**, **cumin**, **garam masala**, **ginger**, **cayenne** (if using), and **½ teaspoon each salt and pepper**. Set over medium heat and stir until fragrant, 1 to 2 minutes. Scrape into a 5- to 8-quart slow cooker. Add the **broth**, **chickpeas**, **squash**, **onion**, **tomatoes**, **apricots**, **cilantro stems**, **chili sauce**, **orange juice**, and 1½ teaspoons salt. Stir to combine.

2. Cover and cook on low until the stew has thickened slightly and the squash is tender, 6 to 7 hours. (If you'd like a thicker stew, increase the temperature to high and cook uncovered until the stew has thickened, 45 minutes to 1 hour.)

3. Stir in half the cilantro leaves and season to taste with salt and pepper. Serve the stew with **toasted almonds**, the remaining cilantro leaves, **pomegranate seeds**, and **couscous** or **pita** as you like.

MAKE IT IN A DUTCH OVEN

Complete step 1 in a Dutch oven, then add all the other ingredients, cover, and cook in a preheated 325°F oven for 3 to 4 hours.

BABS SAYS

If you don't have, or can't find, garam masala, use ½ teaspoon each ground cinnamon and cardamom and ¼ teaspoon ground cloves.

MATT'S FAVORITE FINGER LICKIN' GOOD SWEET & SOUR RIBS

Serves 4 to 6

PREP
15 minutes

COOK
6 hours 30 minutes to
7 hours 30 minutes

Ribs present one of the greatest effort-to-reward ratios I know! They are so fun to eat, and you have to do so little to prep them. Steaming the ribs with sauce in the slow cooker for 6 to 7 hours ensures they're super tender. Then a quick trip under the broiler gives them the perfect char. These have a sweet-and-sour, Asian-inspired glaze of sweet chili sauce, brown sugar, soy sauce, rice vinegar, and ginger.

½ cup Thai sweet chili sauce

¼ cup packed brown sugar

¼ cup soy sauce

3 tablespoons unseasoned rice vinegar

1 tablespoon grated fresh ginger

4 to 5 pounds St. Louis–style pork spareribs, cut into individual ribs

Kosher salt and freshly ground black pepper

For serving: fresh cilantro leaves, thinly sliced scallions, and/or toasted sesame seeds, and steamed jasmine or sushi rice

BABS SAYS

I love to serve this with a super-quick pickled cucumber salad. Dice your cucumbers, stir in a little rice wine vinegar, a pinch of salt, a pinch of sugar, a little toasted sesame oil, and some sesame seeds.

1. In a 5- to 8-quart slow cooker, combine the **chili sauce**, **brown sugar**, **soy sauce**, **vinegar**, and **ginger**.

2. Season the **ribs** with **1 teaspoon salt** and **½ teaspoon pepper**. Add them to the slow cooker and stir to combine. Cover and cook on low heat until they are tender and a fork can easily pierce the meat, 6 to 7 hours.

3. Line a sheet pan with aluminum foil. Transfer the ribs to the sheet pan and season all over with 1 teaspoon salt and ½ teaspoon pepper. Arrange the ribs in a single layer with the meaty side up.

4. Carefully spoon off and discard as much fat as possible from the top of the cooking liquid in the slow cooker. Transfer the cooking liquid to a saucepan and simmer uncovered over high heat until syrupy and reduced by half (to about 1 cup), 10 to 15 minutes.

5. Arrange a rack in the upper third of the oven and switch the oven to broil. Brush the ribs with half the sauce and broil on the top rack until charred in spots, 4 to 5 minutes. Top with the **cilantro**, **scallions**, and **sesame seeds** as you like, then serve with **rice**.

MAKE IT IN THE OVEN

Arrange a rack in the upper third of the oven and preheat the oven to 175°F. Line a sheet pan with aluminum foil (preferably heavy-duty if you have it). In a large pot, stir together the sauce ingredients, then add the ribs and toss to coat. Transfer the ribs and half the sauce to the sheet pan, with ribs meaty side up, and season with another 1 teaspoon salt and ½ teaspoon pepper. Cover tightly with foil. Bake until the ribs are tender and a fork can easily pierce the meat, 6 to 7 hours. Pour the cooking juices from the sheet pan into the remaining sauce in the pot, then simmer over medium-high heat until syrupy and reduced by half (to about 1 cup), 10 to 15 minutes. Continue with step 5 to get a char on the ribs, then serve.

SLOW COOKER CHICKEN ENCHILADA CASSEROLE

Serves 4 to 6

PREP
20 minutes

COOK
6 to 7 hours

I was a mom in the 1980s, so casseroles were a large part of my weeknight repertoire. They are versatile, easy, and delicious—the perfect way to serve a yummy weeknight meal to the family. I'm here to say: Casseroles are back! Though my classics include baked ziti, breakfast casseroles, chicken divan (and I could go on), I love playing with new flavors, too, like this chicken enchilada casserole.

This is one of my favorite Tex-Mex-inspired dishes. It's really a cross between enchiladas and white chicken chili. It has all the flavor of green enchiladas with the crispy-gone-soft appeal of chilaquiles and the creaminess of white chicken chili. Serve it up with avocado, sour cream, and pickled jalapeños.

4	boneless, skinless chicken breasts (2 to 3 pounds total)
2	teaspoons ground cumin
1	teaspoon chili powder, plus more for garnish
	Kosher salt and freshly ground black pepper
1	large red onion, coarsely chopped
1	(10-ounce) package frozen corn (about 2 cups; no need to thaw)
1	(15-ounce) can black beans, drained but not rinsed
1	(4-ounce) can diced green chiles
3	chicken bouillon cubes, or 1 tablespoon bouillon powder or paste
1	(16-ounce) jar salsa verde
½	(8- to 10-ounce) bag sturdy tortilla chips
2	cups (8 ounces) shredded pepper Jack or Monterey Jack cheese
1	cup fresh cilantro leaves and tender stems
	For serving: crumbled Cotija or feta cheese and/or sour cream (optional)

1. In a 5- to 8-quart slow cooker, add the **chicken breasts** and toss with the **cumin**, **chili powder**, ½ **teaspoon salt**, and ½ **teaspoon pepper**. Reserve a handful of the chopped **onion** for serving, then top the chicken with the remaining onion, **corn**, **beans**, **green chiles**, and **bouillon**. Pour in all but ½ cup of the **salsa verde**. Cover and cook on low until the chicken is cooked through, 6 to 6½ hours.

2. Use 2 forks to *coarsely* shred the chicken in the slow cooker. Stir to combine, adding half the **tortilla chips**, **half the pepper jack cheese**, and **half the cilantro** and season to taste with salt and pepper. Top with the remaining chips, cheese, and salsa. Cover the slow cooker, switch the heat to high, and cook until the cheese has melted, 10 to 15 minutes.

3. To serve, spoon the chicken mixture into bowls or onto plates, sprinkle with the remaining onion and cilantro, a sprinkle of chili powder, and the Cotija cheese and/or **sour cream** (if using).

MAKE IT IN THE OVEN

Preheat the oven to 375°F. Lightly grease a 9 × 13-inch baking dish. Season the chicken with the spices and salt, transfer to the baking dish, and bake until cooked through, about 20 minutes. Once cooled, shred the chicken. In a large bowl, combine the onion (reserve a little for topping), corn, beans, green chiles, bouillon, and all but ½ cup of the salsa. Stir in half the tortilla chips, then fold in the shredded chicken and half the cheese. Transfer to the baking dish and top with the remaining ½ cup salsa, cheese, and tortilla chips. Bake for 20 to 30 minutes and serve with your desired toppings.

FRENCH ONION SOUP POT ROAST

Serves 6 to 8

PREP
10 minutes

COOK
6 to 8 hours

Do you love French onion soup?! So do I! I even have a fabulous slow cooker recipe for it in *Celebrate with Babs*. If you love all the delicious flavors of French onion soup, then you're going to be head over heels for this pot roast.

The key to this recipe is the sweet caramelized onions that add just the right amount of flavor to this fork-tender, melt-in-your-mouth pot roast. They help create the most delicious belly-warming gravy. The dish pairs well with mashed potatoes (add a little grated Gruyère) or some bread broiled with Gruyère on top—like a French onion soup. All the components pull together for a truly great roast dinner, ready to go with very little effort on your part!

2 cups low-sodium beef broth

2 tablespoons unsalted butter

1 tablespoon soy sauce

1½ teaspoons dried thyme

1 (4-pound) boneless beef chuck roast

Kosher salt and freshly ground black pepper

6 tablespoons neutral oil, such as avocado

4 large yellow onions, sliced (about 9 cups)

3 tablespoons all-purpose flour

½ cup dry white wine

BABS SAYS

Caramelizing onions isn't difficult, but it does take a little time. The onions are the star of this roast, so be patient! The 15 to 20 minutes out of your day you take to make these babies right, I promise, will be rewarded!

♥

If you don't have (or want to cook with) white wine, you can substitute chicken broth, apple cider vinegar, or lemon juice.

1. In a 5- to 8-quart slow cooker, stir together the **broth**, **butter**, **soy sauce**, and **thyme**. Pat the **meat** dry and season all over with **2 teaspoons salt** and **½ teaspoon pepper**.

2. In a Dutch oven, heat 3 tablespoons of the **oil** over medium-high heat. Sear the meat until a deeply golden crust has formed on all sides, 8 to 10 minutes, then transfer to the slow cooker.

3. Add the remaining 3 tablespoons oil to the Dutch oven. Stir in the **onions**, adding a few cups at a time. Season with 2 teaspoons salt. Cover and let steam, stirring once or twice, until softened and just beginning to brown, 3 to 6 minutes. Reduce the heat to medium and partially cover. Stir frequently until the onions are a deep brown, 15 to 20 minutes. Every time you see browned bits on the bottom, add a couple of tablespoons of water and scrape up the bits.

4. Sprinkle in the **flour** and stir until combined, about 1 minute. Turn off the heat, add the **wine**, and scrape up the browned bits from the bottom. Scrape the onions into the slow cooker. Cover and cook on low until the meat is fork-tender, 6 to 8 hours.

5. Skim the fat from the top of the sauce. Transfer the meat to a platter, then slice or shred the meat and serve with the onion sauce.

MAKE IT IN A DUTCH OVEN

Sear the meat as instructed, then set it aside and continue as instructed. Return the meat to the pot along with the broth, butter, soy sauce, and thyme. Cover and cook in a preheated 300°F oven for 3 to 5 hours.

MRS. MURPHY'S ITALIAN COUSINS CHICAGO BEEF SANDWICHES

Serves 8 to 10

PREP
10 minutes

COOK
6 to 8 hours

My uncle Al made the Italian beef sandwiches at Mrs. Murphy's Italian Cousins, our family's restaurant in Chicago. The beef was cooked in large roasters and sliced super thin on our professional meat slicer. The drippings made a fabulous au jus for this iconic Chicago sandwich. Uncle Al was the King of Italian Beef.

The keys to a good Italian beef sandwich are how thinly you can slice that beef and the delicious juice. If you don't have a meat slicer at home, I recommend that you shred it instead. You'll get the same amazing au jus that makes this sandwich and succulent beef so delectable. Your slow cooker (or Dutch oven) simmers the broth into a concentrated flavor bomb. Pile the beef on crusty bread, add some of its juices, then top with some sweet peppers and giardiniera.

---

1   tablespoon Italian seasoning

1   tablespoon garlic powder

1   tablespoon onion powder

½   teaspoon red pepper flakes

      Kosher salt and freshly ground black pepper

1   (3- to 4-pound) boneless beef rump roast, patted dry, at room temperature

4   cups beef broth

2   tablespoons unsalted butter

5   garlic cloves, smashed

3   green bell peppers, sliced ½ inch thick

2   dried bay leaves

2 or 3 loaves of French bread, cut into 6-inch lengths (or 8–10 ciabatta rolls) and split horizontally but still attached on one side

      For serving: mild or hot giardiniera, preferably Chicago-style, roughly chopped into ½-inch pieces if larger than that

1. In a small bowl, stir together the **Italian seasoning, garlic powder, onion powder, pepper flakes,** and **1 teaspoon each salt and pepper.** Rub half the spice mixture all over the **meat,** then place the beef in a 5- to 8-quart slow cooker.

2. Add the **broth, butter, garlic, bell peppers,** and **bay leaves** and the remaining seasonings to the slow cooker. Make sure the beef and peppers are submerged. Cover and cook on low until the meat is fork-tender, 6 to 8 hours.

3. Remove and shred the meat (otherwise you won't get it thin enough). Add the beef to the gravy in the slow cooker and cook on low until warm, 3 to 5 minutes. Remove and discard the bay leaves.

4. Pile the beef shreds and peppers onto the **bread,** top with the **giardiniera,** and add *plenty* of beef juice. We like our beefs wet!

MAKE IT IN A DUTCH OVEN

Follow steps 1 and 2 using a Dutch oven. Cover and cook in a preheated 300°F oven until the meat is fork-tender, 3 to 5 hours. Shred the meat, return it to the juices in the Dutch oven, and rewarm gently. Assemble the sandwiches as directed.

Chicago giardiniera is different from the types you typically find at the grocery store; it's spicier and has more oil, so if you're interested in the real deal, you can find something like Marconi brand on Amazon. But your sandwich will be *just* as tasty, regardless!

♥

Alternatively, use thin-sliced roast beef from the deli! Make the broth in the slow cooker, but add all the spices at once. Cook on low for 3 hours, until flavorful. Add 3 pounds (or ¼ pound per person) of your deli-sliced roast beef to the sauce, turn off the slow cooker, and let sit until warmed through, about 20 minutes. (It's even better the next day!)

LAMB LOVERS' RAGU

Serves 4 to 6

PREP
15 minutes

COOK
6 hours 30 minutes to
7 hours 30 minutes

I was born a lamb lover. I love lamb chops, kebabs, rack of lamb, and lamb stew. This lamb ragu is a nod to both my heritages. Tender, hearty, and so flavorful, it will fill your house with the most amazing aroma as it simmers away, marrying Lebanese and Italian traditions. Serve this over polenta, risotto, or mashed potatoes, or toss it with wide noodles, like pappardelle.

LAMB RAGU

1   (28-ounce) can whole tomatoes, undrained

1   sprig fresh rosemary

Pinch of red pepper flakes

Kosher salt and freshly ground black pepper

2½ to 3 pounds boneless lamb shoulder

2   tablespoons neutral oil, such as avocado

2   carrots, peeled and coarsely chopped

6   garlic cloves, thinly sliced

2   tablespoons tomato paste

1½   teaspoons fennel seeds

½   cup dry red wine

HERB RICOTTA (OPTIONAL)

1   cup whole-milk ricotta

½   cup finely chopped fresh parsley

Grated zest of 1 lemon

1   garlic clove, finely grated

Kosher salt

BABS SAYS

If you're serving this with pasta, loosen the sauce with a little pasta cooking water to help coat the pasta, and be sure to top it all off with some Parmesan or pecorino.

♥

If lamb isn't your thing, substitute pork shoulder.

1. **Prepare the lamb ragu:** Pour the **tomatoes** and their juices into a 5- to 8-quart slow cooker. Use your hands to squeeze the tomatoes into chunks. Add the **rosemary**, **pepper flakes**, **½ teaspoon salt**, and **¼ teaspoon pepper**.

2. Pat the **lamb** dry and season all over with 1 teaspoon salt and ½ teaspoon pepper. In a Dutch oven or large skillet, heat the **oil** over medium-high heat. Add the lamb and brown on all sides, 10 to 12 minutes. Transfer the lamb to the slow cooker.

3. Drain off all but 2 tablespoons of the fat in the pan. Reduce the heat to medium, add the **carrots** and **garlic**, and cook until the garlic is softened, 2 to 4 minutes. Add the **tomato paste** and **fennel seeds** and stir until the tomato paste is a shade darker, 3 to 5 minutes. Turn off the heat, add the **wine**, and scrape up the browned bits on the bottom. Scrape this mixture into the slow cooker.

4. Cover the cooker and cook on low until the lamb is fork-tender, 6 to 7 hours. Remove and discard the rosemary sprig. Skim the top layer of fat from the sauce. Use 2 forks to shred the lamb directly in the cooker, discarding any large pieces of fat. Stir the lamb into the sauce. Season to taste with salt and pepper.

5. **If making the herb ricotta:** When the lamb is just about done, in a small bowl, stir together the **ricotta**, **parsley**, **lemon zest**, garlic, and a pinch of salt. Serve the ragu topped with the ricotta.

MAKE IT IN A DUTCH OVEN

Sear the meat as instructed in step 2, set it aside, then continue with step 3. Return the lamb to the pot, along with the tomatoes, rosemary, and pepper flakes. Cover and cook in a preheated 325°F oven until fork-tender, 2 to 3 hours.

CHICKEN TIKKA MASALA

Serves 4

PREP
10 minutes

COOK
6 to 9 hours

My daughter Erin worked in London for four years after college. While she was there, she developed a deep love for Indian foods and flavors. I'd go and visit her once a year, and she always brought me to the most wonderful Indian restaurants. That's where I had my first taste of chicken tikka masala—chicken charred in a tandoor oven and stewed in a creamy, tomatoey sauce, popularized by Indians living in Britain.

I was able to bring a little bit of those visits back with me to the States, where I tinkered until I got this recipe, which I still enjoy to this day. This makes a wonderful dish, one of my grandson Charlie's favorites!

½ cup plain whole-milk yogurt (not Greek)

2 teaspoons garam masala

2 teaspoons ground cumin

1 teaspoon ground turmeric

1 teaspoon smoked paprika

½ to 2 teaspoons cayenne

Kosher salt

2 pounds boneless, skinless chicken thighs, cut into roughly 1-inch pieces

1 yellow onion, finely chopped

5 garlic cloves, finely chopped or grated

1 (1-inch) piece fresh ginger, finely chopped or grated (no need to peel)

1 (15-ounce) can tomato sauce

½ cup heavy cream, or more as needed

For serving: rice, finely chopped fresh cilantro, and naan

1. In a 5- to 8-quart slow cooker, stir together the **yogurt**, **garam masala**, **cumin**, **turmeric**, **paprika**, **cayenne** to taste, and **1 teaspoon salt**. Add the **chicken** and stir to coat. Scatter with the **onion**, **garlic**, **ginger**, and ½ teaspoon salt, then pour in the **tomato sauce** and stir. Cover and cook on low until the chicken is cooked through, 6 to 8 hours.

2. Stir in the **cream** and taste the sauce: if it's too spicy, add a bit more cream. If you like a thicker sauce, cook over high heat, uncovered, until reduced, 30 minutes to 1 hour.

3. Serve over **rice**, topped with **cilantro**, and have **naan** alongside, as you like.

MAKE IT IN A DUTCH OVEN

Place all the ingredients in a Dutch oven, cover, and cook in a preheated 400°F oven until the chicken is cooked through, 30 to 40 minutes.

BABS SAYS

You can use garlic-ginger paste, which you can find in Asian specialty stores or in the international foods aisle at the grocery store.

FUN with **FONDUE BAKED POTATO BAR**
(page 190)

FUN with FONDUE
BAKED POTATO BAR

Serves 6 to 8

PREP
20 minutes

COOK
6 to 7 hours

Near the top of my comfort food list is fondue; and what's at the very top? Baked potatoes. Here, I've combined my love for baked potatoes with the joy of fondue and turned it into a super-simple slow cooker meal. Vegetables like broccoli, Brussels sprouts, and cauliflower, along with salami and roasted potatoes, are classic ingredients to dip into fondue, but this recipe flips it and loads the baked potatoes with fondue sauce and salami-roasted Brussels sprouts. The salami becomes crisp like chips. Divine! Other things you could add to the baked potato bar (or dip right into the fondue sauce) are cornichons, pickled onions, and thinly sliced apples.

BAKED POTATOES

6 to 8 russet potatoes
(about 8 ounces each),
scrubbed and patted dry

3 tablespoons extra-virgin
olive oil

Kosher salt and freshly ground
black pepper

BRUSSELS SPROUTS

1 pound Brussels sprouts,
trimmed and halved

2 tablespoons extra-virgin olive oil

Kosher salt and freshly ground
black pepper

4 ounces salami slices, cut into
1-inch pieces

> BABS SAYS
>
> This slow cooker method for baked potatoes is also perfect for families with staggered eating times: people can reach into the slow cooker and grab a potato to eat with dinner. Plus, it's a great way to have a baked potato for dinner in the summer, when you don't want to run the oven for an hour.

1. **Make the baked potatoes:** Prick the **potatoes** all over with a fork and transfer to a 5- to 8-quart slow cooker. Sprinkle with the **olive oil**, **1 teaspoon salt**, and a few grinds of **pepper** and toss to coat. Add ½ **cup water**, cover, and cook on low until the potatoes are easily pricked with a fork, 5 to 7 hours. Keep the potatoes in the slow cooker on warm until ready to eat.

2. **Roast the Brussels sprouts:** An hour before you're ready to eat, preheat the oven to 425°F. Line a sheet pan with parchment paper.

3. Toss the **Brussels sprouts** on the sheet pan, add the olive oil, and ½ teaspoon each salt and pepper and toss to coat. Spread into an even layer, then top with the **salami**. Roast, stirring halfway through, until the sprouts are tender and the salami is golden, 15 to 20 minutes.

4. Transfer the baked potatoes to a cutting board and keep the slow cooker on the warm setting (you'll use it for the fondue in a few minutes).

FONDUE

¼ cup kirsch or other brandy

1 tablespoon all-purpose flour

1 large garlic clove, halved

1 cup dry white wine

Juice of ½ lemon
(about 1½ tablespoons)

8 ounces Emmental cheese,
cut into small cubes or
shredded

8 ounces Gruyère cheese,
cut into small cubes or
shredded

Pinch of freshly grated nutmeg

Pinch of black pepper (optional)

For serving: butter, sour cream,
sliced scallions or chives, crispy
bacon, grated Cheddar, roasted
broccoli or cauliflower, salsa,
barbecue sauce

5. **Make the fondue:** In a small bowl, whisk together the **kirsch** and **flour** until the flour is dissolved.

6. Rub the **garlic** vigorously on the inside of a large saucepan, then discard the garlic. Add the **wine** and bring to a boil over medium-high heat. Reduce the heat to medium-low and stir in the **lemon juice**. Add the **cheese** in handfuls, stirring slowly and continuously between each addition to prevent lumps. Add the kirsch mixture and stir to combine. Season with the **nutmeg** and pepper (if using). Continue to stir until the fondue is smooth and just bubbling, 2 to 3 minutes. Pour into the slow cooker, cover, and keep on the warm setting.

7. Working one at a time, hold a hot potato with a kitchen towel and slit it open lengthwise. Push the 2 ends toward each other to fluff up the middle. Season the potato insides with a little salt.

8. To serve, let people build their own baked potatoes by layering with some of the Brussels sprouts and salami, then the fondue. Sprinkle with toppings of your choosing.

MAKE IT IN THE OVEN

To bake the potatoes in the oven, preheat the oven to 400°F. Prep the potatoes the same way (pricking with a fork and seasoning with oil, salt, and pepper) and place directly on the middle oven rack. Place a sheet pan or piece of aluminum foil on the rack beneath the potatoes. Roast until easily pricked with a fork, 1 hour to 1 hour 15 minutes.

STOUT BRISKET CHILI

Serves 6 to 8

PREP
45 minutes

COOK
7 to 8 hours

Several years ago, Bill, our daughters, and I traveled to Ireland. While there, we visited the Guinness Storehouse. Guinness is probably the most famous stout: that dark beer that *must* have the frothy head on top of the pint. You don't have to use Guinness for this stick-to-your-ribs chili, but I would recommend you do!

Chili gets better with time, so it will be even tastier the next day. And don't worry about the kiddos—the alcohol cooks off. This is one of my one-year-old grandchild Willa's favorite meals. She loves it!

2   tablespoons all-purpose flour

1   tablespoon ground cumin

1   tablespoon chili powder

     Kosher salt and freshly ground black pepper

1   (2½- to 3-pound) boneless brisket, fat trimmed and meat cut into ½-inch cubes

3   slices thick-cut bacon, chopped into small pieces

2   yellow onions, cut into ½-inch pieces

1   jalapeño, thinly sliced

¾   cup stout beer (half a 12-ounce bottle)

2   (15-ounce) cans black or kidney beans, drained but not rinsed

1   (15.5- to 16-ounce) jar mild salsa

2   tablespoons soy sauce

1   teaspoon apple cider vinegar

     Toppings: shredded Cheddar, sour cream, hot sauce, sliced scallions, chopped white onion, cilantro, Fritos, and/or crushed tortilla chips

BABS SAYS

You can use stew meat here instead of brisket to cut down on the prep time.

1. In a large bowl, stir together the **flour**, **cumin**, **chili powder**, **½ teaspoon salt**, and **½ teaspoon pepper**. Add the **beef** and toss to coat.

2. Add the **bacon** to a large skillet or Dutch oven and set over medium-high heat. Cook, stirring often, until golden and crisp, 5 to 7 minutes. Turn off the heat, then use a slotted spoon to transfer the bacon to a 5- to 8-quart slow cooker.

3. Return the skillet with the bacon drippings to medium-high heat and add half the beef. Sear, stirring occasionally, until browned, 2 to 4 minutes. Transfer to the slow cooker and repeat with the remaining beef. Add any remaining spice mix from the bowl to the slow cooker.

4. Add the **onions** and **jalapeño** to the skillet and cook, until browned in spots, 3 to 5 minutes. Add the **beer** and scrape up the browned bits on the bottom of the skillet. Add everything to the slow cooker.

5. Add the **beans**, **salsa**, and **soy sauce** to the slow cooker. Stir to combine (the meat will not be completely submerged). Cover with the lid and cook on low until the beef is tender, 6 to 7 hours.

6. Stir the **vinegar** into the cooker and season to taste with salt and pepper. Serve portions of the stew with **toppings** as desired. (Leftovers will keep for 3 days in the refridge and 4 months in the freezer.)

MAKE IT IN A DUTCH OVEN

Follow the instructions but set aside the seared ingredients in a large bowl as you brown everything. Return all the ingredients to the Dutch oven. Cover and cook in a preheated 325°F oven until the beef is tender, 1½ to 3 hours. Uncover and continue to cook until the stew has thickened, 30 minutes to 1 hour. Add beer as needed to loosen.

LOVE BY THE SPOONFUL CHICKEN NOODLE SOUP

Serves 4 to 6

PREP
10 minutes

COOK
6 hours 30 minutes to
8 hours 30 minutes

Whatever happens to be ailing you, this chicken noodle soup will fix it! To make chicken soup the way *my* mother did, you simmer a stock of chicken and aromatics (including vegetables), strain the stock, then add new vegetables and simmer until they're tender. I appreciate that effort, but if you don't have that kind of time, this is your recipe!

In the slow cooker, we start with chicken stock for extra flavor, and the vegetables don't get mushy, so you can still eat them. It makes cooking homemade chicken soup so much easier. Bone-in chicken thighs provide the fat, bone, and cartilage—aka flavor—of a whole chicken without as much effort. If you prefer white meat, though, you could substitute with four bone-in, skin-on breasts.

---

2   pounds bone-in, skin-on chicken thighs (4 to 6 thighs)

6   cups chicken broth

4   carrots, peeled and sliced into ¼-inch-thick rounds (about 8 ounces)

4   garlic cloves, finely chopped

3   celery stalks, sliced

2   tablespoons unsalted butter

8   sprigs fresh parsley and ¼ cup finely chopped leaves

6   sprigs fresh thyme

2   dried bay leaves

1½   teaspoons onion powder

     Kosher salt and freshly ground black pepper

3   cups wide egg noodles (about 6 ounces)

     For serving: lemon wedges

BABS SAYS

If you're making the soup ahead, boil the noodles separately. If they sit in the soup, they will continue to drink up the liquid, turning mushy and leaving you with not as much broth.

1. In a 5- to 8-quart slow cooker, combine the **chicken**, **broth**, **carrots**, **garlic**, **celery**, **butter**, **parsley sprigs**, **thyme sprigs**, **bay leaves**, **onion powder**, **2½ teaspoons salt,** and **1 teaspoon pepper**. Cover and cook on low until the chicken easily shreds with a fork, 6 to 8 hours.

2. Transfer the chicken to a bowl and set aside to cool slightly. Remove and discard the bay leaves and herbs from the slow cooker. Stir the egg **noodles** and ½ teaspoon salt into the slow cooker, cover, and cook on low until the noodles are al dente, 15 to 20 minutes.

3. While the noodles are cooking, remove and discard the chicken skin and bones. Using 2 forks, shred the chicken meat. Once the noodles are cooked, return the shredded chicken to the slow cooker along with half the chopped parsley. Season to taste with salt and pepper.

4. Serve the chicken soup topped with the remaining chopped parsley and a squeeze of **lemon**.

MAKE IT IN A DUTCH OVEN

For step 1, use a Dutch oven for the ingredients and simmer on the stove until the chicken is tender and the broth is flavorful, 1½ to 2 hours. Cook the noodles for just 7 or 8 minutes.

DR PEPPER PULLED PORK

Serves 4 to 6

PREP
10 minutes

COOK
6 hours 30 minutes to
8 hours 30 minutes

You know those Saturdays you wish you could be in four places at once? And on top of that, when those "four places" converge into one for dinnertime, and they're famished, you have to think about what to feed them. Well, I can't help you be in four places at one time, but I *can* help you get a delicious meal ready for when everyone gets home—with very little thought or effort on your part.

This one involves soda! All you need to do ahead is sauté a pork shoulder and some onions. After adding a can of Dr Pepper and some spices to your slow cooker, throw in your pork and onions, and voilà! When you return from here, there, and everywhere, the most delicious pulled-pork sandwiches with pickles and potato chips will be awaiting you. A perfect way to end an activity-filled day!

---

1 (12-ounce) can Dr Pepper

¾ cup ketchup

¼ cup apple cider vinegar

2 tablespoons brown sugar

1 tablespoon Dijon mustard

3 teaspoons chili powder

Kosher salt and freshly ground black pepper

1 (3- to 4-pound) boneless pork shoulder, patted dry

2 tablespoons neutral oil, such as avocado

1 large yellow onion, sliced ½ inch thick

BABS SAYS

Cola is actually a great tenderizer for tough cuts of meat! It has higher acidity than lemon juice, so it breaks down the proteins without ruining the meat.

1. In a 5- to 8-quart slow cooker, stir together the **Dr Pepper**, **ketchup**, **vinegar**, **brown sugar**, **mustard**, **1 teaspoon of the chili powder**, **½ teaspoon salt**, and **¼ teaspoon pepper**. Rub the **pork shoulder** all over with the remaining 2 teaspoons chili powder, 1½ teaspoons salt, and ½ teaspoon pepper.

2. In a large skillet, heat the **oil** over medium-high heat. Add the pork and brown on all sides, 8 to 10 minutes. Transfer the pork to the slow cooker.

3. With the skillet still over medium-high heat, add the **onion** and ¼ teaspoon salt and cook, scraping up the browned bits, until the onion is just starting to brown, 2 to 3 minutes. Scrape the onion and any drippings into the slow cooker. Cover the slow cooker and cook on low until the pork easily shreds with a fork, 6 to 8 hours.

4. Transfer the pork to a bowl and shred using 2 forks. If you want to make your own barbecue sauce, transfer the cooking liquid to a large skillet and simmer over medium-high heat until reduced by half, 15 to 20 minutes. Toss the pork with ½ cup of the sauce and serve the rest alongside.

MAKE IT IN A DUTCH OVEN

Season and brown the pork shoulder and onions in the pot, as instructed, then add the sauce ingredients. Cover and cook in a preheated 300°F oven until the pork easily shreds with a fork, 3 to 4 hours. Finish the sauce as directed.

BREAD BOWL
BROCCOLI-CHEDDAR SOUP

Serves 4

PREP
30 minutes

COOK
6 hours 30 minutes to
7 hours

My grandchildren, all nine of them, are so wonderful. They keep me young and they keep me current. I didn't need their help, however, to discover Panera's amazing broccoli Cheddar soup; it is my granddaughter Mary's absolute favorite. So, this one's for her! This soup is a copycat of that heavenly soup but very hands-off—it's a total dump dinner. You could skip the bread bowls because the soup is amazing all on its own, but come on—a bread bowl is fun!

1   (12-ounce) package broccoli florets (about 5 cups)

2   large carrots, peeled and coarsely grated

4   cups vegetable or chicken broth

4   tablespoons (½ stick) unsalted butter

1   tablespoon Dijon mustard

½   teaspoon onion powder

½   teaspoon garlic powder

¼   teaspoon freshly grated nutmeg

     Kosher salt and freshly ground black pepper

¼   cup all-purpose flour

¾   cup heavy cream

4   cups (1 pound) shredded sharp yellow Cheddar cheese

1   cup (4 ounces) grated Parmesan cheese

     Hot sauce

4   small crusty round bread loaves (6 to 8 ounces each)

BABS SAYS

To keep condensation on the lid of your slow cooker from dripping into your yummy soup, or whatever you're making, just tuck a kitchen towel under the lid before placing it on top of the slow cooker.

1. In a 5- to 8-quart slow cooker, combine the **broccoli**, **carrots**, **broth**, **butter**, **mustard**, **onion powder**, **garlic powder**, **nutmeg**, **½ teaspoon salt**, and **¼ teaspoon pepper**. Cover and cook on low until the broccoli is tender and falling apart, 6 to 6½ hours.

2. Sprinkle the **flour** over the soup in the cooker and whisk vigorously to combine and break up the broccoli. Cover again and cook until the soup has thickened slightly, 20 to 30 minutes.

3. Turn off the slow cooker. Blend the contents with an immersion blender or in batches in a stand blender until mostly smooth but with some broccoli pieces visible. Stir in the **cream**, **2 cups of the Cheddar**, and **½ cup of the Parmesan** until melted. Season to taste with **hot sauce**, salt, and pepper. Keep warm.

4. While the soup is cooking, prepare the **bread** bowls. Cut a ¼- to ½-inch-thick slice off the top of each loaf and reserve the tops. Hollow out the inside of each loaf, leaving about ½ inch of bread along the sides and bottom. (Save the interior of the bread for another use, like for croutons or bread crumbs.)

5. Right before serving, arrange a rack in the upper third of the oven and set the broiler to high. Line a sheet pan with aluminum foil.

6. Place the loaf tops cut side up on the sheet pan. Sprinkle with ½ cup of the Cheddar and the remaining Parmesan. Broil until the cheese is melted and starting to brown in spots, 1 to 3 minutes. (Simultaneously, you can warm the bread bowls on the bottom rack, if you'd like.) Cut the bread tops into 1-inch sticks.

7. Ladle the soup into the bread bowls and top with the remaining 1½ cups Cheddar. Serve immediately with hot sauce and the cheesy breadsticks for dipping.

MAKE IT IN A DUTCH OVEN

In a large Dutch oven, melt the butter over medium heat, whisk in the flour, and cook, stirring, for 2 minutes. Add the broth to the pot and bring to a boil. Add the broccoli, carrots, mustard, and spices, reduce the heat to a simmer, then cover and cook until the broccoli is tender, 20 to 30 minutes. Continue with the instructions.

Sunday Suppers

Let me tell you a little about Vincenza and Luigi. They were my grandparents. When I was growing up, Sunday started with Mass and then it was off to my grandparents' for supper. Our entire family gathered in the basement for a big meal with my sixteen aunts and uncles and twenty cousins!

Sure enough, the tradition continued. When I was newly married and my husband, Bill, was away on active duty for the National Guard, I went to live with Vincenza and Luigi. Every night, Vincenza would have a beautifully set table and a warm inviting meal waiting for me when I got home. But Sundays? Forget about it. Italian families know how to do Sunday supper. Luigi would draw a carafe of wine from the oak casks he had in the basement, and we would sit down to some of the most memorable meals of my life. I can still smell my grandmother's chicken roasting in the oven, while her fragrant gravy packed with sausage, meatballs, and braciola simmered on the stove. I can still hear the delightful sound of wineglasses clinking away with lots of joy and happiness. I can still see a kitchen filled with a family's love and laughter.

Sundays are a perfect day for slowing down. I know it's hard to gather the family around the dinner table. It can even feel impossible. But once a week, at least, it's so important to *try*.

The recipes in this chapter are near and dear to my heart. I've been making them for *my* family for nearly fifty years. They take a little more time and call for a few more ingredients. But how worth it they are when you sit down to eat with *your* loved ones and share a meal, some stories, and laughter.

EASY ROAST CHICKEN

Serves 4

PREP
20 minutes

COOK
1 hour

I tried to use Sunday dinner as an opportunity for my kids to participate in the mealtime routine. Shawn would set the table, Erin would fill the water glasses, Bill would help me bring food out to the table, and Liz would sometimes use her creativity to make place cards, even though we always sat in the same place! The point was: Sunday dinner was special. So, recipes like my classic but *easy* roasted chicken fit the bill.

The prep is done in under 20 minutes, with most of the dish's delicious succulence coming from the time it spends roasting away in the oven. You can use whatever fresh herbs you like to flavor the chicken and use the dried version of those same herbs to season a nice pile of crisp roasted potatoes. Perfection.

1   whole chicken (4 to 4½ pounds)
    Kosher salt and freshly ground black pepper

¼   yellow onion

½   small lemon

1   garlic head, halved horizontally through the middle, left unpeeled
    A few sprigs fresh herbs, such as rosemary, thyme, and sage

2   tablespoons extra-virgin olive oil

> **BABS SAYS**
>
> If you have room in your oven, roast some potatoes, too. Cut them into 1-inch chunks, toss them generously with olive oil, salt, and pepper on a sheet pan, and roast on the lower rack during the last 35 to 40 minutes of the chicken's cook time.

1. Place a large cast-iron skillet in the cold oven and preheat the oven to 450°F.

2. Remove any giblets from the inside of the **chicken** and discard. Dry the chicken inside and out. Sprinkle the inside of the chicken with **½ teaspoon salt** and **¼ teaspoon pepper**. Stuff the cavity of the chicken with the **onion quarter**, **lemon half**, one half of the **garlic** (save the rest for another use), and **herb sprigs**.

3. Take the fatty piece of flap skin on one side of the cavity (behind the leg) and cut a ½- to 1-inch slit in the skin. Repeat on the other side. Carefully thread the chicken legs, crisscrossed, through the holes to close the chicken cavity. Brush the outside of the chicken with the **olive oil** and sprinkle liberally with additional salt and pepper.

4. Carefully remove the skillet from the oven and place the chicken breast side up in the skillet. Return the skillet to the oven and bake until a thermometer registers 165°F in the thickest parts, 50 minutes to 1 hour.

5. Let the chicken rest for 10 minutes, then discard the items in the cavity and carve the chicken. Enjoy and keep any extras for yummy leftovers.

ROAST BEEF with
ROASTED GARLIC RED WINE SAUCE

Serves 6 to 8

PREP
20 minutes

COOK
1 hour 30 minutes

Beth O'Brien and I met in the third grade. We became fast friends and remained very close throughout our high school years. Sunday dinner at the O'Briens' was slightly different from how it was at my house; their menu *always* included roast beef. Walking into Beth's house and getting to smell that roast cooking away in the oven was absolute heaven.

Roast beef definitely goes hand in hand with Sunday dinner for me because of Mrs. O'Brien's delicious Sunday roasts. I've made plenty on my own since those days, and this one, I have to say, is exceptional. You roast whole heads of garlic alongside the beef, then add the roasted cloves to the red wine sauce for a boost of caramelized flavor. You can serve this with green beans, like my friend Beth's family did, and roasted or mashed potatoes. So good!

---

2   garlic heads

1   (3- to 4-pound) boneless beef round roast (top, eye, or bottom)

3   tablespoons extra-virgin olive oil

2   tablespoons finely chopped fresh rosemary

    Kosher salt and freshly ground black pepper

4   tablespoons (½ stick) unsalted butter, at room temperature

1   tablespoon tomato paste

2   cups beef broth

1½ cups dry red wine

1   tablespoon sugar

1   tablespoon all-purpose flour

1. Preheat the oven to 450°F.

2. Pick off 4 cloves from one **garlic** head. Thinly slice each clove into 3 pieces. Pat the **roast** dry and place in a large ovenproof skillet (preferably cast iron). Make 12 small slits all over the beef and stick 1 piece of garlic in each slit. Sprinkle the beef with **2 tablespoons of the olive oil**, the **rosemary**, **1 tablespoon salt**, and **1 teaspoon pepper** and rub to coat. (You can cover and refrigerate the beef up to overnight.)

3. Using a sharp knife, slice about ¼ inch off the tops of the garlic heads so the cloves are exposed. Place the garlic heads on a piece of aluminum foil, then drizzle with the remaining olive oil and sprinkle with a pinch of salt and pepper. Wrap the cloves in the foil and place in the skillet alongside the beef.

4. Roast the meat for 15 minutes, then reduce the oven temperature to 325°F. Continue to cook until the beef registers between 120°F and 125°F internally for medium-rare, 40 minutes to 1 hour. Transfer the beef and garlic to a cutting board to rest while you make the sauce (or at least 30 minutes).

5. Pour off any fat from the skillet. Add **3 tablespoons of the butter** and melt over medium heat. Squeeze the garlic cloves from one of the heads directly into the skillet (save the other for another use). Add the **tomato paste** and stir, breaking up the garlic, until the

(recipe continues)

The leftover roast beef is great
for sandwiches and is best sliced
cold right before serving. Use the
leftover roasted garlic to stir into
mayo for the sandwiches, too.

♥

Freeze your tomato paste in ice cube
trays! Measure out 1 tablespoon
portions into the individual cube
sections. Once frozen, pop the
cubes into a freezer bag.

tomato paste is caramelized and brick red, 2 to 4 minutes. Add the **broth**, **wine**, and **sugar** and scrape up any browned bits on the skillet bottom. Bring to a simmer over medium-high heat, then reduce the heat to medium and simmer until reduced by half, 15 to 20 minutes.

6. In a small bowl, using a fork, mash the **flour** and remaining tablespoon butter into a paste. Add the butter-flour paste to the sauce in the skillet and whisk to combine. Simmer over medium-high heat until thickened, 1 to 3 minutes. Season to taste with salt and pepper. Pour the sauce through a fine-mesh strainer, if desired.

7. Pour any juices that have collected on the cutting board into the sauce. Very thinly slice the beef across the grain. Serve with the red wine sauce. Slice only what you'll eat that day.

HOMEMADE RICOTTA GNOCCHI
with SAGE BUTTER AND MUSHROOMS

Serves 6

PREP
30 minutes,
plus 15 minutes
freezing time

COOK
30 minutes

I'm going to be honest with you; this recipe will require a little time, but *not* a lot of effort. Gnocchi is the easiest homemade pasta to make. No special equipment is required, and it's a fun cooking project. You can also make a double batch and freeze it. Your future self will thank you for having such an elegant meal ready to go.

Butter and sage sauce is a classic to serve with gnocchi, but you can also serve them with fresh tomato sauce, marinara, pesto, or any other sauce you like; it's a versatile pasta. The sauce here—a combination of mushrooms and sage butter—would also work well with ravioli or tortellini.

GNOCCHI

1½ cups (12 ounces) high-quality whole-milk ricotta (such as Calabro)

Heaping ¼ cup (1 ounce) grated Parmesan cheese

1 large egg

1 large egg yolk

Kosher salt and freshly ground black pepper

½ teaspoon freshly grated nutmeg

Heaping ¾ cup (about 100g) all-purpose flour, or more as needed

SAUCE

3 tablespoons extra-virgin olive oil

1 pound fresh mushrooms (such as maitake, oyster, or cremini, or a mix), stems trimmed, caps torn or chopped into bite-size pieces

Kosher salt and freshly ground black pepper

6 tablespoons unsalted butter

20 fresh sage leaves

For serving: grated Parmesan cheese

1. **Make the gnocchi:** Line a sheet pan with a double layer of paper towels or kitchen towels. Use the back of a spoon or spatula to spread the **ricotta** onto the towels in an even layer. Top the ricotta with another double layer of paper towels, pressing down to help absorb the moisture. Let sit for 5 minutes.

2. Scrape the drained ricotta into a large bowl. Add the **Parmesan, egg** and **egg yolk**, **1 teaspoon salt**, **¼ teaspoon pepper**, and the **nutmeg**. Whisk to combine thoroughly, then switch to the spatula and fold in the **flour**. Knead with the spatula until the dough comes together in a ball. It will be sticky but shouldn't be loose; if it's loose after a minute of kneading, add another tablespoon or two of flour.

3. Transfer the dough to a well-floured surface. Coat the dough with flour and pat into a 6-inch square. Use a sharp knife or bench scraper to cut the dough into 9 equal pieces (2 cuts in both directions). Cover with a kitchen towel.

4. Line a sheet pan with parchment paper. Working with one piece of dough at a time, roll the dough into ½-inch-wide logs. Use your knife or bench scraper to cut the logs into 1-inch pieces. Place the gnocchi on the sheet pan. Place in the freezer for at least 15 minutes. (To make ahead, freeze the gnocchi until solid, about 1 hour, then transfer to a zip-top bag and freeze for up to 1 month.)

(recipe continues)

5. **Make the sauce:** In a large nonstick skillet, heat the **oil** over medium-high heat. Add the **mushrooms** and ½ teaspoon salt and cook, stirring occasionally, until golden brown, 10 to 15 minutes. Push the mushrooms to one side of the skillet. Into the empty side, add the **butter** and **sage**. Stir until the sage is crisp and dark green, and the butter smells toasted and golden, 3 to 5 minutes.

6. Meanwhile, bring a large pot of salted water to a boil over high heat. Add the gnocchi and gently stir once to prevent sticking. Cook until completely tender and squishy but not gooey, 3 to 4 minutes (or 5 to 7 minutes if gnocchi were totally frozen). Reserve 1 cup of the pasta cooking water, then drain the gnocchi.

7. Add the gnocchi and ¼ cup pasta water to the mushrooms in the skillet. Set over high heat and stir gently until glossed with butter. Add more pasta water as needed, until the gnocchi are coated. Divide the gnocchi among plates. Top with the **Parmesan** and pepper and serve immediately.

MY SUPER CHEESY LASAGNA

Serves 6 to 8

PREP
25 minutes

COOK
1 hour 30 minutes

I've mentioned my friend and mentor Ida. It's impossible to forget a cook like Ida Sylvestri. An absolute legend; her lasagna recipe is one of the reasons. She made it only once a year. It was a *seven*-layer masterpiece. Noodles by hand, ricotta from scratch, layers of cheese, meatballs, salami, her secret marinara, a layer of hard-boiled eggs! It took days to make, and it was out of this world. But this labor of love is not something I've ever tried myself. I've never had that kind of time . . . or patience!

If you, like me, don't have three days to make one recipe, I've created a lasagna inspired by the care and attention Ida put into hers. It doesn't have as many layers as hers, but it does have just as much love. Mixing heavy cream into the ricotta makes a luscious cheese sauce. Using marinara instead of canned tomatoes means a much shorter simmer time for the sauce. Instead of no-boil noodles, which are a common shortcut, here you'll soak the traditional noodles in cold water before using them. That gives you the crispy edges that are so classic but saves you the time of boiling them separately—they cook right in the sauce. I use two different mozzarellas here, fresh for milky creaminess and low moisture for that iconic cheese pull. I have to say, this one would definitely be Ida approved!

1	pound dried lasagna noodles (not no-boil)
1	pound sweet Italian sausage, casings removed
1	yellow onion, finely chopped
1	pound ground beef (80% lean)
4	garlic cloves, thinly sliced
	Kosher salt and freshly ground black pepper
2	(24-ounce) jars marinara sauce (6 cups)
1	(16-ounce) container whole-milk ricotta (2 cups)
¼	cup heavy cream
16	ounces fresh mozzarella cheese, grated or torn

1. Spread the dried **lasagna noodles** on a sheet pan and cover with cold water. Let soak while you prepare the other components.

2. Combine the **sausage** and **onion** in a Dutch oven or large heavy-bottomed pot over medium-high heat. Cook, stirring to break up large pieces, until the onion is tender and the sausage is lightly browned, 10 to 12 minutes. Add the **beef**, **garlic**, **1 teaspoon salt**, and a few grindings of **pepper** and cook, breaking up large pieces, until the beef is no longer pink, 5 to 7 minutes. Drain off all but a few tablespoons of the liquid. Add the **marinara**, scrape up any browned bits, reduce the heat to low, cover, and simmer until flavorful, about 10 minutes.

3. While the sauce is simmering, preheat the oven to 350°F.

(recipe continues)

2 cups (8 ounces) grated low-moisture mozzarella cheese

2 cups (8 ounces) grated Parmigiano-Reggiano cheese

½ cup chopped fresh basil

½ cup chopped fresh parsley leaves and tender stems

A few gratings of nutmeg

Nonstick cooking spray or olive oil

BABS SAYS

Here's a simple way to freeze any leftovers. Line an 8-inch square baking pan with enough aluminum foil so it hangs over the sides. Layer plastic wrap onto it the same way. Place the cooled leftovers onto the plastic wrap and fold it over your lasagna, then fold over the foil. Place that, along with the pan, in your freezer. Once frozen, take the foil packet out of the pan and place into a freezer bag. Label with the contents and date. Extra freezer room!

♥

If you're hand-grating your cheese, place an open storage bag under the grater so it catches all the cheese.

4. In a large bowl, stir together the **ricotta**, **cream**, **1½ cups of the fresh mozzarella**, **three-quarters of the low-moisture mozzarella**, **1 cup of the Parmigiano-Reggiano**, the **basil**, **parsley**, **nutmeg**, 1 teaspoon salt, and a few grindings of pepper.

5. Spread 1 cup of the meat sauce on the bottom of a 9 × 13-inch baking dish. Place the dish on a sheet pan. Top with one layer of noodles and press down. Break the noodles to fill in any gaps. Top the noodles with 2 cups of the meat sauce, then dollop with one-third of the ricotta mixture (a heaping 1½ cups; no need to spread into an even layer). Repeat twice with more noodles, sauce, and ricotta, pressing down each layer. Finish with the last of the noodles and sauce. Top with the remaining mozzarellas and the Parmigiano-Reggiano.

6. Grease a piece of aluminum foil with **cooking spray** or a little olive oil, then use it to cover the baking dish tightly, greased side down. Bake until the noodles are tender, 30 to 35 minutes. Remove the foil, increase the heat to 425°F, and continue to bake until the lasagna is golden brown, the edges are crisp, and the sauce is bubbling, 25 to 30 minutes more. Let rest for 15 minutes before serving.

COUSIN JIM'S CHICKEN CACCIATORE

Serves 6

PREP
30 minutes

COOK
45 minutes

My cousin Jim was a true Renaissance man. He played hockey; he was a golf pro; he was funny, kind, and handsome. Among his many passions was food. He loved good food, good wine, and the art of entertaining. One day, he found out the famous Gene & Georgetti Steakhouse in Chicago was looking for a lunch chef. He was an excellent—and I mean *excellent*—cook, but he wasn't a trained chef and had never worked in a restaurant kitchen. Nevertheless, he walked in, impressed the manager, and was hired. He learned so much in that kitchen and he worked there for over a decade.

When Jim passed, his wife gave me his most prized possession, knowing how much I would appreciate it. It was his handwritten recipe book with all his favorite dishes. I was grateful and so eager to start cooking from it! I opened it up to this cacciatore recipe, and as with all really talented cooks, he had included no measurements. Just a list of ingredients and rough instructions. Food was art and art was food, so basically, he winged it. So, I went to work and tweaked this recipe so anyone can make and enjoy it. It's a rustic, juicy, one-pan comfort dinner. This one's for Jim.

6	boneless, skinless chicken breasts (8 ounces each)
½	cup all-purpose flour
	Kosher salt and freshly ground black pepper
¼	cup extra-virgin olive oil, or more as needed
5	tablespoons unsalted butter
1	green bell pepper, coarsely chopped
1	red bell pepper, coarsely chopped
12	ounces cremini mushrooms, halved or sliced if large
1	large yellow onion, chopped
3	garlic cloves, finely chopped
2	shallots, chopped
2	teaspoons Italian seasoning

1. Set one hand on top of one **chicken breast** to hold it in place, then cut through the middle so you have 2 thinner cutlets. Repeat with the 5 remaining breasts. Pat the chicken dry with paper towels. Cover the chicken cutlets with plastic wrap or wax paper and pound to an even thickness of about ½ inch. On a large plate, mix the **flour** with **¾ teaspoon salt** and **½ teaspoon pepper**. Dip the chicken cutlets in the flour and coat all sides, tapping off the excess.

2. In a large skillet, heat the **olive oil** and **2 tablespoons of the butter** over medium-high heat until the butter is foamy. Working in batches (do not overcrowd), add the chicken cutlets and cook until golden on both sides, 2 to 4 minutes per side. (It might not be cooked through yet.) Reduce the heat if the flour is burning and add more oil as needed. Set the cutlets aside.

3. In the same skillet, add the **bell peppers**, **mushrooms**, **onion**, **garlic**, and **shallots** and stir. Cook until juicy, 2 to 4 minutes. If the skillet is dry, add another tablespoon or two of olive oil. Add the **Italian seasoning** and ½ teaspoon salt. Reduce the heat to medium and cook for about 10 minutes, stirring frequently, until softened.

(recipe continues)

1⅓ cups marinara sauce

⅔ cup dry red wine

⅔ cup chicken broth

1 cup pitted Kalamata olives

For serving: rice pilaf, linguine, or polenta

BABS SAYS

You could also make this in a slow cooker. After the chicken is browned, add it with the remaining ingredients to a slow cooker and cook on low for 7 to 8 hours.

♥

Make sure to use both oil and butter. Butter adds that creamy flavor, but if you were to use all butter, it would burn. You could use all oil, but you'd miss that layer of sweet butter flavor.

4. Add the **marinara**, **wine**, **broth**, and remaining 3 tablespoons butter. Stir until the butter is melted. Once simmering, add the chicken cutlets and turn to coat in the sauce. Add the **olives**. Reduce the heat to medium-low, cover the skillet, and cook until the chicken registers 165°F, 5 to 10 minutes.

5. Transfer the chicken to a serving platter. Boil the sauce in the skillet for about 5 minutes to thicken slightly. Spoon the sauce over the chicken and serve with **rice pilaf**, **linguine**, or **polenta**. (Leftovers can be stored in an airtight container, refrigerated, for 4 to 5 days or frozen for up to 3 months. Let thaw overnight in the refridge.)

LOBSTER ROLL COBB SALAD

4 servings

PREP
20 minutes

COOK
20 minutes

Bill and I took the kids for a family vacation to Acadia National Park, in Maine, many years ago. That trip was when I had my first classic Maine lobster roll. Sweet, succulent lobster is mixed with a light tarragon mayo and some celery for crunch—such a delight!

Here, I've taken my love for lobster rolls and reimagined them into this Cobb salad. It's all the best things about lobster rolls and Cobb salads into one—plus, it's hearty and special enough for a Sunday supper. You'll use half the lobster you would for lobster rolls (better on the budget!), and you're still feeding the whole family. It's an ideal make-ahead summer meal. Swap the lobster for crab, shrimp, grilled salmon, or even canned fish, if you like!

BUTTERMILK DRESSING

- ½ cup well-shaken buttermilk
- ½ cup mayonnaise
- 3 tablespoons thinly sliced fresh chives
- 1 tablespoon fresh lemon juice (from 1 lemon)
- 2 teaspoons thinly sliced fresh tarragon

  Kosher salt and freshly ground black pepper

SALAD

- 8 ounces lobster meat, coarsely chopped
- 1 celery stalk, finely chopped

  Kosher salt and freshly ground black pepper

- 4 large eggs
- 8 slices thick-cut bacon
- 2 hot dog buns, preferably brioche
- 1 avocado
- 2 large heads romaine lettuce, or 4 heads Little Gem lettuce, thickly sliced
- 1 pint cherry tomatoes, halved, or 1 cup chopped ripe tomatoes
- 1 tablespoon of herbs combined, any breakdown you would want

1. **Make the dressing:** In a jar, shake together the **buttermilk**, **mayonnaise**, **chives**, **lemon juice**, **tarragon**, and **½ teaspoon each salt and pepper.**

2. **Make the salad:** In a medium bowl, stir together the **lobster meat**, **celery**, and 2 tablespoons of the dressing. Season the lobster to taste with salt and pepper. Cover the bowl and refrigerate both the lobster and the remaining dressing until ready to serve.

3. Bring a medium saucepan of water to a boil over high heat. Gently lower in the **eggs**, reduce the heat to low, and simmer for 8½ minutes. Transfer the eggs to an ice bath to cool.

4. Add the **bacon** to a large skillet over medium heat. Cook until crisp, 2 to 4 minutes per side. Transfer to a paper towel–lined plate and set aside.

5. Pour off all but 2 tablespoons of the bacon fat from the skillet. Add the **buns** cut sides down and cook over medium heat until toasted, 2 to 4 minutes. Cut the buns into 1-inch pieces.

6. Peel and quarter the eggs. Coarsely chop the bacon. Pit and thinly slice the **avocado**. Arrange the **lettuce** on a large platter or individual serving plates. Drizzle with a little of the dressing, season with salt and pepper, and toss to combine. On the lettuce, arrange the dressed lobster, egg quarters, and bacon bits, then add the croutons, the **tomatoes**, and avocado. Sprinkle with salt, pepper, and the herbs. Eat right away, with more dressing alongside for drizzling over.

MY GRANDMA'S GREEK CHICKEN & POTATOES

Serves 4 to 6

PREP
30 minutes,
plus 1 to 3 hours
marinating time

COOK
1 hour

You would not be reading this right now if not for *this* recipe. It literally started it all. It's the very first recipe I posted to social media. How could I not include it? My grandmother, as I've mentioned, was a talented cook. She was an Italian immigrant and raised nine children. She was constantly in the kitchen (or the garden). I don't know what it is about a grandmother's cooking; there is always something she can put in the oven or on the stove that brings that extra bit of comfort. Like a warm hug from the inside out. When they're gone, whatever that special something is, remains with you. A reminder of her love.

This is that dish for me. It's deceptively simple; the prep is very minimal. But in the end, you get succulent chicken and potatoes that are crisp on the outside but very tender inside, all of it complemented by the classic Mediterranean flavor combination of lemon, garlic, and oregano. From my grandma's kitchen to yours!

---

6 tablespoons extra-virgin olive oil

6 garlic cloves (or more if you like garlic), finely chopped

Juice of 3 lemons (about ½ cup)

2 tablespoons dried oregano

Kosher salt and freshly ground black pepper

3 to 3½ pounds bone-in, skin-on chicken pieces, such as breasts, thighs, and legs

4 Yukon Gold potatoes (2 pounds total), peeled and quartered lengthwise

½ teaspoon garlic powder

> **BABS SAYS**
>
> Oregano is one of those rare herbs I prefer dried to fresh. Dried has a milder flavor, is less peppery, and is so much easier to find!
>
> ♥
>
> You could sprinkle fresh herbs and some lemon zest on the completed dish for an extra little kick and a pop of color.

1. In a large bowl, stir together **3 tablespoons of the olive oil**, the **garlic**, one-third of the **lemon juice** (about 3 tablespoons), **1 tablespoon of the oregan**o, **2 teaspoons salt**, and **1 teaspoon pepper**. Add the **chicken** and toss to coat. Cover the bowl and refrigerate for 1 to 3 hours.

2. Preheat the oven to 425°F.

3. On a sheet pan, toss the **potatoes** with the remaining 3 tablespoons olive oil, the remaining lemon juice (about 5 tablespoons), remaining 1 tablespoon oregano, the **garlic powder**, 1 teaspoon salt, and a few grindings of pepper. Place the chicken on the sheet pan and pour on the remaining marinade. Bake until the potatoes are tender, the breast meat is at least 155°F, and the dark meat registers at 165°F in the thickest parts, 45 minutes to 1 hour. Serve immediately.

CHICKEN CORDON BLEU PASTA

Serves 4 to 6

PREP
10 minutes

COOK
40 minutes

There were lots of things my kids got excited about during our trips to Costco, but the *main* attraction was always the free samples! (I would like to thank all the Costco employees who were patient with my children while they acted like I never fed them.) Of all Costco's samples, my daughter Elizabeth's favorite was the chicken cordon bleu. Crispy-crusted chicken with a surprise inside of melted cheese and ham, this classic dish deserves its cordon bleu— its blue ribbon!

I wanted to bring this winning combination to a baked pasta for the whole family to dig into. The pasta is crispy and melty, all the things you love about the traditional, in a much more convenient delivery system. It's a rich cheese sauce studded with pasta, chicken, ham, and peas, all blanketed in a delightful breadcrumb topping. I'd never make Elizabeth choose between my pasta and Costco's dish, but knowing my daughter, she'd choose her mom's!

Kosher salt

1 pound medium shells

1 cup frozen peas (no need to thaw)

5 tablespoons unsalted butter

½ cup panko bread crumbs

¼ teaspoon garlic powder

Freshly ground black pepper

3 tablespoons all-purpose flour

3 cups chicken stock

1 cup heavy cream

2 cups (8 ounces) grated or chopped Gruyère or Swiss cheese

½ cup (2 ounces) grated Parmesan cheese

1½ teaspoons Dijon mustard

1 cup diced cooked chicken (about 1 rotisserie breast)

6 to 8 ounces boneless thick-cut ham, diced

1. Preheat the oven to 400°F.

2. Bring a medium pot of **salted water** to a boil over high heat. Add the **pasta** and cook until 1 minute shy of al dente according to the package directions. Place the **peas** in a colander and drain the pasta over them.

3. In a 12-inch ovenproof skillet, melt **2 tablespoons of the butter** over medium-high heat. Add the **panko** and cook, stirring, until golden brown, 3 to 5 minutes. Turn off the heat, transfer the panko to a small bowl, then stir in the **garlic powder** and ¼ teaspoon salt and **¼ teaspoon pepper**. Wipe out the skillet.

4. In the same skillet, melt the remaining 3 tablespoons butter over medium heat. Whisk in the **flour** and cook until golden in color, 1 to 2 minutes. Gradually whisk in the **stock** and **cream**. Simmer, whisking occasionally, until slightly thickened and the sauce coats the back of a spoon, about 10 minutes. Turn off the heat and whisk in the **cheeses** and **mustard** until smooth.

5. Stir the pasta and peas and then the **chicken** and **ham** into the skillet. Season to taste with salt and pepper. Sprinkle with toasted panko and bake until the sauce is bubbling, about 15 minutes. Wait 10 minutes before serving.

PESTO RACK OF LAMB
with TOMATO-MOZZARELLA SALAD

Serves 4 to 6

PREP
30 minutes,
plus 2 or more hours
marinating time

COOK
40 minutes

This recipe screams summer to me, and the star here is the pesto. It does triple duty as an herb marinade for the lamb, a dressing for the salad, and a sauce for serving. And let me tell you, I have eaten it by the spoonful; it's that good.

The salad, inspired by the classic caprese, leans in to the freshness of summer tomatoes and basil and the creaminess of mozzarella, with some cucumbers and nuts for a little crunch. And there is nothing better than grilled lamb.

This is a must for a Sunday supper on the patio, a little more relaxed with the music of ice clinking in your glass under the summer sun!

PESTO

2 cups packed fresh basil leaves

Heaping ½ cup (about 2 ounces) grated Parmesan cheese

½ cup extra-virgin olive oil, or more as needed

½ cup toasted pine nuts or walnuts

2 garlic cloves, peeled but whole

Kosher salt and freshly ground black pepper

LAMB

2 racks of lamb (about 3 pounds total), rib bones frenched

Kosher salt

SALAD

2 tablespoons extra-virgin olive oil

2 tablespoons red wine vinegar

Kosher salt and freshly ground black pepper

2 pints cherry tomatoes, halved, or 3 to 4 large ripe tomatoes (about 20 ounces), cut into bite-size pieces

4 mini cucumbers, chopped into bite-size pieces

8 ounces mini mozzarella balls, such as bocconcini or ciliegine, halved

¼ cup toasted pine nuts or walnuts

1. **Make the pesto:** In a food processor, combine the **basil, Parmesan, olive oil, pine nuts, garlic,** and **½ teaspoon each salt and pepper**. Pulse until a paste forms. Season to taste with salt and pepper. Keep in the refridge until ready to use.

2. **Marinate the lamb:** Pat the **lamb** dry, season the meat with 1 teaspoon salt, then coat with ¼ cup of the pesto. Refrigerate for 2 to 8 hours to marinate. Place the remaining pesto in an airtight container, drizzle with a couple of tablespoons of olive oil to cover, and refrigerate (the oil keeps it from oxidizing).

3. When you're ready to eat, heat the grill to medium hot and set the coals for two-zone grilling, leaving half the grill with coals not turned on. Clean and grease the grill grates.

4. Take the lamb and pesto out of the refridge.

5. Grill the lamb until browned all over, 6 to 8 minutes, moving the meat away from the heat as needed if flare-ups occur. Move the lamb to the cooler part of the grill, cover, and cook until it reaches 125°F for medium-rare, 8 to 12 minutes longer. Let rest for at least 5 minutes.

6. **Make the salad:** In a large bowl, combine the olive oil, **vinegar**, ¼ cup of the pesto, 1 teaspoon salt, and ½ teaspoon pepper. Stir in the **tomatoes, cucumbers, mozzarella,** and **pine nuts.** Season to taste with salt and pepper.

7. Slice the racks of lamb into individual chops. Serve the lamb and salad with the remaining pesto alongside for drizzling.

KISS OF SUMMER SHRIMP & GRITS

Serves 4

PREP
15 minutes

COOK
35 minutes

Grits are such a southern staple that there are entire grocery aisles dedicated to all the varieties. I learned that from my time living in Virginia, where I had more than my fair share of cheese grits. So, I need to include my spin on this comforting dish for you. This shrimp and grits recipe is a light, summery, veggie-heavy take on the classic. There are corn kernels in the grits, and the shrimp is cooked quickly with squash and fresh tomatoes. White and rosé wine both work in this recipe and equally well chilled in a glass while you enjoy it!

4	ripe plum tomatoes, halved lengthwise and sliced ½ inch thick
	Kosher salt
1	cup old-fashioned grits (not instant)
1	cup (4 ounces) grated sharp Cheddar cheese
1	cup fresh or frozen corn (no need to thaw)
3	tablespoons unsalted butter
	Freshly ground black pepper
3	slices thick-cut bacon, coarsely chopped with scissors
2	summer squash or zucchini, halved lengthwise and sliced into ¼-inch-thick half-moons
4	scallions, thinly sliced, white and green parts separated
2½	teaspoons Old Bay seasoning
1	pound extra-large shrimp (10–12 count), peeled and deveined
½	cup dry white wine or rosé

> **BABS SAYS**
>
> I am the last person to judge a cooking shortcut. But here, I must discourage you from using quick-cooking grits. They have a soft, almost Cream of Wheat texture, which is lovely for some things but maybe not for this.

1. In a colander, toss the **tomatoes** with **½ teaspoon salt**. Set in the sink to drain.

2. In a medium saucepan, bring **5½ cups water** and 1 teaspoon salt to a boil over medium-high heat. Gradually whisk in the **grits**, then reduce the heat to low. Very gently simmer, stirring often and scraping the bottom and sides of the pot, until the grits are tender, thick, and creamy, 25 to 30 minutes. (If the grits get too thick, add a tablespoon of water.) Stir in the **Cheddar**, **corn**, **2 tablespoons of the butter**, and **½ teaspoon pepper**. Cook, stirring, until the cheese is melted and the corn is heated through, about 2 minutes more. Cover and remove from the heat, stirring occasionally.

3. Meanwhile, add the **bacon** to a large nonstick skillet and heat over medium heat. Once sizzling, cook, stirring often, until the bacon is golden brown, 4 to 6 minutes. Use a slotted spoon to transfer the bacon pieces to a paper towel–lined plate.

4. Remove all but 2 tablespoons of bacon fat from the skillet. Add the **squash** in a single layer, set the skillet over medium-high heat, and cook, stirring halfway through, until golden all over, 3 to 5 minutes. Sprinkle with the **scallion whites** and **Old Bay seasoning** and stir until fragrant, just a minute. Add the **shrimp**, tomatoes from the colander, and the **wine** and stir until the shrimp are just pink and the tomatoes are just softened, 2 to 4 minutes. Stir in the remaining tablespoon butter until melted.

5. Thin the grits with hot water, as needed, then spoon onto plates. Serve the shrimp and sauce over the grits. Top with the scallion greens, the bacon, and more pepper.

MAMA'S STUFFED PEPPERS

Serves 4

PREP
25 minutes

COOK
1 hour 10 minutes

My mother was a master of simplicity and comfort, and this stuffed pepper recipe is straight from her kitchen. The meat and rice combination makes such a satisfying stuffing; it's already full of flavor and then you add the sweet bite of red or yellow bell peppers in a warm blanket of savory tomato sauce. Heavenly. It's a family meal that can be assembled early in the day and refrigerated until you're ready to serve dinner. Just make sure you allow the stuffed peppers to come to room temperature before baking.

4   large red or yellow bell peppers

3   tablespoons extra-virgin olive oil

    Kosher salt and freshly ground black pepper

1   yellow onion, chopped

2   large garlic cloves, finely chopped

8   ounces sweet Italian sausage, casings removed

8   ounces ground beef (80% lean)

2   cups cooked white rice

¼   cup chopped fresh parsley, plus more for garnish

1   large egg, beaten

½   cup (2 ounces) grated Pecorino Romano cheese

1   (15-ounce) can tomato sauce

    Nonstick cooking spray

> **BABS SAYS**
>
> Cooked rice is one of those staples you want to have around, preferably ready to go. You don't want to keep it in the refridge for more than a day, *but* you can freeze it. Don't be afraid to make some extra; after cooking, cool it down quickly in a shallow dish or pan in the refridge. Scoop it into zip-top bags for individual servings and load up your freezer.

1. Preheat the oven to 400°F.

2. Cut the tops off the **peppers**, pull out the cores, and discard the seeds, membranes, and tops, keeping the peppers intact. Brush the skins of the peppers with **1 tablespoon of the olive oil**. Sprinkle the insides of the peppers with **salt** and **pepper**. Heat a large skillet over medium-high heat and very lightly brown the outsides of the peppers, 1 to 2 minutes. Transfer the peppers to a baking dish in which they can fit snugly upright, like an 8-inch square pan or cast-iron skillet, or a 9-inch square or other 2½-quart baking dish. Slice off a bit of the bottom to keep them from falling over.

3. In the same skillet, over medium-high heat, heat the remaining 2 tablespoons olive oil. Add the **onion** and cook until softened, 2 to 4 minutes. Add the **garlic** and cook until fragrant, 30 seconds. Next add the **sausage** and **beef** and season with 1 teaspoon salt and ½ teaspoon pepper. Break up any clumps of meat with a wooden spoon and cook until no longer pink, 3 to 5 minutes.

4. Using a slotted spoon, transfer the meat mixture to a large bowl. Add the **rice, parsley, egg, ⅓ cup of the cheese**, and **½ cup of the tomato sauce**. Use your hands to thoroughly combine.

5. Generously stuff the peppers with the meat mixture, mounding the tops slightly. Sprinkle the tops of the peppers with the remaining cheese. Mix the remaining tomato sauce with ½ cup water and pour around the peppers in the baking dish.

6. Spray a piece of aluminum foil with **cooking spray**, then use it to cover the baking pan tightly, coated side down. Bake until a knife easily pierces the peppers, 45 to 55 minutes. Remove and let rest for 5 minutes and garnish with parsley before serving.

PORK TENDERLOIN MARBELLA

Serves 4

PREP
20 minutes

COOK
40 minutes

When my husband, Bill, and I were newly married and wanted to entertain friends, we turned to the 1980s classic, chicken Marbella. It was a signature recipe from *The Silver Palate Cookbook*. Fancy enough for company, but easy enough to make anytime. It's beloved for the sweet and briny combination of flavors from ingredients like prunes, brown sugar, capers, olives, and wine. I eventually decided to take this idea in a different direction with pork tenderloin, which is just as entertaining-worthy. It's so good, and chicken shouldn't have all the fun!

As the pork braises, its juices fortify the liquid into a luscious sauce. This recipe is elegant enough for a Sunday meal or to serve to company, but don't be afraid to make it on a weeknight—because it's that super simple and easy!

---

2   (1-pound) pork tenderloins, silver skin removed, meat patted dry

Kosher salt and freshly ground black pepper

2   tablespoons neutral oil, such as avocado

1   yellow onion, thinly sliced

4   garlic cloves, thinly sliced

1   cup dried pitted fruit (apricots and prunes are both great), halved if large

1   cup mixed pitted olives (if you can't find mixed, just use green)

1   cup dry white wine

¼   cup drained capers

2   tablespoons brown sugar

1   tablespoon dried oregano

For serving: chopped fresh parsley

1. Preheat the oven to 350°F.

2. Season the **pork** all over with **2 teaspoons salt** and a few grindings of **pepper**. In a 12-inch ovenproof skillet, heat the **oil** over medium-high heat until shimmering. Add the pork and sear until golden underneath, 2 to 4 minutes. Flip the pork over and add the **onion** and **garlic**. Stir the vegetables around and cook until the pork is browned on the second side, another 2 to 4 minutes.

3. Add the **fruit**, **olives**, **wine**, **capers**, **brown sugar**, and **oregano** and stir to combine. Place the skillet in the oven and roast, uncovered, until the thickest part of the tenderloin registers between 140° and 145°F, 17 to 23 minutes. Transfer the pork to a cutting board and rest for 10 minutes.

4. Return the skillet to medium-high heat on the stove and simmer the sauce until thickened slightly, 3 to 5 minutes. Slice the meat, spoon on the pan juices, and sprinkle **parsley** over the top.

BABS SAYS

The pork and its sauce would be delicious with crusty bread, polenta, pasta, or mashed potatoes, and/or roasted broccoli.

♥

You don't want the meat's silver skin because it's tough and will cause the tenderloin to curl when cooking. To remove it, wiggle a sharp, narrow knife underneath the start of the silver skin and peel. Don't go too deep into the meat. You can also ask your butcher to do it for you!

AUNT LOUISE'S EGGPLANT PARMESAN

Serves 6 to 8

PREP
30 minutes

COOK
1 hour 30 minutes

My older sister, Louise, is my only sibling. Louise has a heart of gold and is one of the most generous people I know. She also makes the *most* amazing eggplant Parmesan I've ever tasted. It does take a lot of time and involves quite a bit of frying, so this recipe is my simpler twist on her classic.

I've traded frying for roasting, but the only thing sacrificed here is the half day you'd spend in front of a pot of hot oil. All the wonderful flavors you love in an eggplant Parmesan come through. The perfectly cooked eggplant is nestled in a rich, well-balanced bubbling tomato sauce that's interrupted only by heaps of cheese. I can't think of anything better than that!

EGGPLANT

3   large eggplants
    (about 2½ pounds total)

6   tablespoons extra-virgin olive oil

2   teaspoons kosher salt

2   teaspoons dried oregano

SAUCE

2   tablespoons extra-virgin olive oil

4   garlic cloves, finely chopped or
    grated

½   teaspoon dried oregano

    Pinch of red pepper flakes

    Kosher salt

1   (28-ounce) can crushed tomatoes

2   teaspoons sugar

ASSEMBLY AND SERVING

4   cups (16 ounces) shredded low-
    moisture mozzarella cheese

    Heaping ½ cup (2 ounces) grated
    Parmesan or Pecorino cheese

20 fresh basil leaves, torn if large,
    plus more for serving

    Nonstick cooking spray

1. Preheat the oven to 425°F.

2. Slice off the bottom and top of the **eggplant**, then stand it on the wide end and slice lengthwise into ¼-inch-thick planks. Divide the eggplant between 2 sheet pans and drizzle each pan with half the **olive oil**, **salt**, and **oregano**, then flip over and drizzle with the remaining oil, salt, and oregano (the eggplant won't be fully coated). Spread the eggplant into an even layer; it's okay if slices overlap. Roast until tender and golden, 15 to 20 minutes per side. Reduce the temperature to 350°F.

3. **Make the sauce:** In a medium saucepan, heat the olive oil, **garlic**, oregano, **pepper flakes**, and 1¼ teaspoons salt over medium heat. Cook until sizzling and fragrant but not browned, 1 to 3 minutes. Add the **tomatoes**, then rinse the can with ½ cup water and add that to the pan. Increase the heat to medium-high and bring to a boil. Stir in the **sugar**, cover the pan, and remove from the heat.

4. **Assemble the dish:** Spread 1 cup of the tomato sauce on the bottom of a 9 × 13-inch or other 3-quart baking dish. Top with a single layer of the roasted eggplant, then follow with 1 cup of the sauce and one-third of the **mozzarella** and **Parmesan** (you can eyeball it). Sprinkle with **half the basil leaves**. Repeat with another layer of eggplant, 1 cup of sauce, one-third of the cheeses, and the remaining basil. Finish with the remaining eggplant, remaining sauce, and remaining cheeses. Lightly grease a piece of aluminum foil, then use it to cover the dish tightly.

5. Place the baking dish in the oven and bake until the sauce is bubbling and the cheese has melted, about 40 minutes. Remove the foil and bake until the cheese on top is golden, another 15 to 20 minutes. Let sit at least 10 minutes, then sprinkle with more basil before serving.

Sweet Tooth

The Costello family was always in charge of the cotton candy and snow cone booth at Saint Mary's Fall Festival. Pouring that pure crystalline sugar into the cotton candy maker was, by far, my children's favorite job. Plus, they got unlimited cotton candy! By the time we all got home from a "hard" day's work, we looked like glazed donuts, covered in sugar from head to toe. Needless to say, my children all inherited my sweet tooth!

Sometimes you just need a little something to end a meal. Even a weekday meal. Something sweet to look forward to and satisfy any lingering cravings.

We always had a jar of cookies on hand at the house. I'm so famous for my love of cookies that my son Bill got me a cookie jar when he was twelve, which I still use to this day—that, and a jar from my grandchildren, which has their handprints on it. They're truly treasures and they're even better when I get to fill them!

Not everyone has dessert every day, of course, but the recipes in this chapter, made one time, will provide you with several days' worth of delectable treats—*if* they're not gobbled up all at once. I'm a mom and a grandma; I know how that goes!

Whether you have dessert every day or just occasionally, like everything in this book, these recipes are simple to assemble and require minimal effort and clean-up. Whether you like chocolate, vanilla, or fruit, I have something for you in this chapter. Here's your permission to be a little indulgent!

FAMOUS CHOCOLATE CHIP COOKIES

Makes about
10 cookies

PREP
15 minutes,
plus 8 hours
refrigeration time

COOK
25 minutes

You can't have an everyday book without including your best chocolate chip cookie recipe. This is mine. So, for the first time in these pages, you will get to know my unintentionally super-secret recipe for my famous (to anyone that's tried them) chocolate chip cookies.

The recipe took some tinkering and some trial and error based on the best chocolate chip cookies I've had—and let me tell you, that's a lifetime of testing! These are the ultimate grandma cookies. Crispy on the outside and gooey, almost doughy on the inside. They are big cookies, too. I'd recommend you put them into your favorite cookie jar when you're done, but I don't think they'll last (or fit)!

2   sticks (8 ounces/225g) unsalted butter, cold

1   cup (200g) granulated sugar

¼   cup (50g) packed dark brown sugar

1   large egg, cold

2   teaspoons vanilla extract

1½   teaspoons kosher salt

1   teaspoon instant espresso powder

¾   teaspoon baking soda

1¾   cups (224g) all-purpose flour

¾   cup (130g) chopped bittersweet chocolate

½   cup (85g) chopped milk or semisweet chocolate

Flaky sea salt (optional)

BABS SAYS

The beauty of these is that you can freeze the dough balls ahead of time and bake from frozen; they'll just need a little more time in the oven.

1. Cut 4 tablespoons (2 ounces/55g) of the **butter** into 4 pieces and add it to a large bowl.

2. Set a medium saucepan with a light-colored interior over medium heat and add the remaining 1½ sticks (6 ounces/170g) butter. Melt the butter, whisking occasionally and scraping the sides and bottom of the pot with a flexible spatula, until it foams and the milk solids turn a deep golden brown, 5 to 7 minutes.

3. Pour the hot brown butter over the cold butter in the bowl, making sure to scrape all the brown bits from the pan. Add the **granulated and brown sugar** and vigorously whisk for 90 seconds. (It's okay if the mixture looks separated and oily.) Let the mixture sit for 5 minutes, stirring once or twice to help cool it.

4. Add the **egg**, **vanilla**, **kosher salt**, and **espresso powder** and whisk until emulsified. Whisk in the **baking soda**.

5. Add the **flour** and fold it into the mixture with a flexible spatula until only a few streaks of flour remain. Add the **bittersweet and milk chocolate** and fold again until just combined.

6. Scoop the dough into 2-inch mounds and place the mounds on a parchment-lined sheet pan that fits in your refridge. Cover the dough balls with plastic wrap and refrigerate for 8 to 36 hours.

7. When you are ready to bake, arrange a rack in the center of the oven and preheat the oven to 400°F. Line a second sheet pan with parchment paper.

8. Evenly space out the mounds of dough at least 1½ inches apart,
5 to each pan. Sprinkle with **flaky sea salt** (if using). Bake one pan
at a time until the cookies are lightly browned on the edges but still
quite soft in the center, 10 to 12 minutes. Remove the sheet pan, bang
it on the counter once, and set the pan on a rack to cool. Repeat with
the remaining pan. It'll be tough, but try to let these cool for at least
10 minutes before eating.

BABS' FAVORITE KEY LIME ICEBOX CAKE

Serves 12 to 16

PREP
20 minutes

COOK
No cooking!
Just 6 hours
refrigeration time

Key lime pie and Florida are synonymous to me. I *really* look forward to having this when Bill and I go on our annual trip to Florida. I've had it as the traditional pie (and believe it or not, Publix makes a killer version), but also as ice cream bars, cookies, and cocktails. Now, here's an even better twist: Key lime icebox cake.

Time does all the work with icebox cakes, yet this one has all the components of Key lime pie: layers of graham crackers and a whipped cream filling that's tart with lime juice and sweet with condensed milk. You end up with an airy, mousse-like dessert that makes you feel you're on vacation, too!

---

6   limes

4   cups (945g) heavy cream, cold

1   (14-ounce) can sweetened condensed milk

     Kosher salt

1   (14-ounce) box graham crackers (about 30 sheets)

½   cup (110g) sour cream

1   tablespoon granulated or powdered sugar

1   teaspoon vanilla extract

BABS SAYS

Conventional (aka Persian) limes are larger and not as sweet as Key limes. They're also much easier to find year-round and outside of Florida, so they're often used in Key lime pies anyway. I prefer them here because their tartness helps balance all the dairy—and they're larger, so you don't have to squeeze a billion to get enough juice.

♥

Make sure your heavy cream is cold—it *does* make a difference. It ensures the whipped cream will be light and airy.

1. Zest enough of the **limes** to have 3 tablespoons zest, then squeeze to have ⅔ cup juice. Reserve the remaining limes for garnish.

2. In a large bowl, use a whisk or electric hand mixer to whip **2½ cups of the cream** until slightly thickened and beginning to hold its shape. Add the lime juice and zest, then add the **condensed milk** and a pinch of **salt**. Continue whipping until the mixture forms soft peaks. Scrape any zest that has collected on the whisk and gently fold back into the beaten mixture.

3. Line a 9 × 13-inch baking dish with a single layer of **graham crackers**. You may have to break them to fill the entire space. Spoon half the lime cream over the crackers (just eyeball it) and gently spread into an even layer. Top with another single layer of graham crackers, followed by the rest of the lime cream. Add a final layer of graham crackers (reserve any extra) and press down lightly.

4. In the same bowl you used to make the filling, whip the remaining 1½ cups cream, the **sour cream**, **sugar**, **vanilla**, and a pinch of salt until you have medium peaks. Gently spoon the whipped cream over the crackers and spread into an even, swoopy layer. Loosely tent the cake with aluminum foil, then refrigerate for at least 6 hours and up to 2 days.

5. When ready to serve, crush any remaining graham crackers and sprinkle them around the top edge of the cake. Zest some of the remaining limes over the top, then slice the limes and garnish the cake with the slices.

TURTLE DATE BARK

Makes about 10 pieces

PREP
15 minutes

COOK
No cooking!
Just 30 minutes
refrigeration time

Sometimes you just want a *little* something sweet. Just a nibble, not a whole brownie, cookie, or slice of cake. The kind of treat you can grab whenever you have a bit of a craving. Believe me, this will hit the spot!

This date bark is the perfect bite to end a meal when you don't need or want much more. It all comes together on a sheet pan: sweet dates, creamy almond butter, melted chocolate, and a nice crunch from pecans. It's ready in no time, and you'll have it on hand all week for whenever your sweet tooth calls!

---

20 soft Medjool dates, pitted

⅓ cup (90g) almond butter

1 cup (115g) pecan halves, toasted

1½ cups (255g) bittersweet chocolate chips

2 teaspoons coconut oil

Flaky sea salt

> **BABS SAYS**
>
> You can easily make this into a Peanut Date Bark by swapping out the almond butter and using ⅓ cup creamy peanut butter, replacing the pecans with ⅓ cup salted roasted peanuts, reducing the chocolate chips by ½ cup, and cutting the coconut oil down to 1 teaspoon.

1. Line a sheet pan with parchment paper.

2. Slit the **dates** open and arrange open side down next to each other in a large cluster on the sheet pan. With your hands or a rolling pin, press down on the dates until they are firm and flat. Cover the dates with an even layer of the **almond butter**. Add the pecans in a single layer and press to adhere.

3. In a small bowl, microwave the **chocolate chips** and **coconut oil** together on high in 30-second increments until melted, about 1 minute 30 seconds. Pour the chocolate over the dates and nuts and spread to cover. Top with a sprinkle of **flaky sea salt**.

4. Refrigerate or freeze the bark until set, about 30 minutes in the refridge or 15 minutes in the freezer. Cut into bite-size pieces. (Store the bark pieces in an airtight container in the refridge for up to 1 week.)

THE MOST DELICIOUS POUND CAKE

Makes 2 loaves

PREP
15 minutes

COOK
1 hour 10 minutes

My mother would occasionally stop at the Sara Lee outlet in Chicago after work. I still remember the sound of her peeling back the cardboard from a tin of their pound cake. It wasn't every day, but, boy, was it a nice treat!

Pound cake brings to mind special memories for me. It's a classic for a reason. Soft, comforting, and buttery, it is also a great everyday cake that goes with everything. The best part about this recipe is that it makes *two* loaves. Batch-cooking, but for dessert! This is an easy dessert served with berries, stone fruit, lemon curd, ice cream, and/or whipped cream. You can use it to make a trifle, or simply have a slice for breakfast or with your afternoon tea or coffee (it's extra good toasted in a pan with butter).

---

3   sticks (12 ounces/340g) unsalted butter, at room temperature, plus more for greasing

2½   cups (500g) sugar

8   ounces (225g) cream cheese, at room temperature

5   large eggs, at room temperature

½   cup (110g) sour cream, at room temperature

2   tablespoons vanilla extract

2½   teaspoons kosher salt

1½   teaspoons baking powder

3   cups (385g) all-purpose flour

> **BABS SAYS**
>
> Do *not* try to tap or pound the pan on the counter. It will release too much air, and you'll lose that lovely soft texture.

1. Arrange a rack in the center of the oven and preheat the oven to 325°F. Generously **butter** two 9 × 5 × 3-inch loaf pans. Line each pan with a piece of parchment paper long enough to hang over the 2 long sides.

2. In a large, deep bowl with an electric hand mixer or in the bowl of a stand mixer fitted with the paddle attachment, cream the butter and **sugar** on medium-high speed until smooth and fluffy, 7 minutes. Scrape down the sides of the bowl once or twice with a flexible spatula. Add the **cream cheese** and mix until smooth. Add the **eggs** one at a time, incorporating each before adding the next. Mix in the **sour cream**, **vanilla**, **salt**, and **baking powder** until well combined.

3. Gently fold the **flour** into the batter with a spatula just until combined.

4. Divide the batter evenly between the loaf pans and smooth the tops. Bake the loaves until golden, puffed, and a toothpick inserted into the center comes out clean, 60 to 70 minutes.

5. Set the loaves on a wire rack so the cakes cool in the pans for 10 minutes. Then carefully remove them from the pans, using the parchment paper flaps on the sides, and set them back on the rack to cool completely. Remove the parchment once cooled.

6. Slice and serve one loaf as desired. (Store the other loaf unsliced in an airtight container for up to 5 days on the counter or in the refridge so it's handy when you crave a taste. Or, slice the loaf and freeze the slices on a parchment-lined sheet pan, then place the frozen slices in freezer bags and store for up to 3 months. When you're ready to serve, just remove them from the freezer and let come to room temperature.)

VARIATIONS

LEMON LOAF: Add 1 tablespoon grated lemon zest to the batter along with the vanilla and bake as directed. (You could also add 2 tablespoons poppy seeds for a lemon-poppyseed cake.) Then make a lemon glaze by whisking together 3 cups powdered sugar, 2 teaspoons grated lemon zest, and 2 tablespoons fresh lemon juice until smooth. (Add another tablespoon of juice if the mixture is too thick.) When the cakes are cool, pour the glaze over them and let rest until the glaze is set.

CHOCOLATE CHIP LOAF: Add 2 cups chocolate chips (any kind you like) along with the flour and sprinkle a few more chips on top of the loaves just before baking.

JAM SWIRL LOAF: Transfer 2 cups of the finished batter to another bowl and stir in ⅔ cup jam or preserves (raspberry is pretty). Pour two-thirds of the plain batter into the loaf pans, then dollop with the jam batter. Carefully top the loaves with the remaining plain batter. Drag your knife through the batter to create swirls. Bake as directed.

CARAMEL APPLE CRISP

Serves 8 to 10

PREP
20 minutes

COOK
40 minutes

When my kids' love for caramel apples and *my* love for apple crisp collide, you get my famous Caramel Apple Crisp. I love making crisps. I've made them for decades because they're so much easier than a pie (you can make them all in one pan!) and just as rewarding. Here, instead of sweetening the apples in the crisp with plain old sugar, I use caramel sauce instead, which I was inspired to do because my children always licked the caramel off their caramel apples but left the apples! Those days are gone. With this, if they want the caramel, they've gotta eat the apples! Serve the crisp topped with ice cream and another pour of caramel sauce.

CARAMEL APPLES

3	pounds firm tart apples (about 6), such as Granny Smith or Pink Lady, sliced ¼ inch thick (peeled, if desired)
½	cup high-quality caramel sauce, store-bought or homemade (recipe follows), plus more for serving
1	tablespoon cornstarch
1	tablespoon apple cider vinegar
2	teaspoons vanilla extract
1½	teaspoons ground cinnamon
½	teaspoon freshly grated nutmeg
¼	teaspoon kosher salt

PECAN TOPPING

1	cup (130g) all-purpose flour
1	cup (90g) old-fashioned rolled oats
½	cup (100g) light brown sugar
½	cup (60g) finely chopped pecans
½	teaspoon kosher salt
1	stick (4 ounces/113g) unsalted butter, cut into tablespoons, at room temperature

For serving: vanilla ice cream

1. Arrange a rack in the center of the oven and preheat the oven to 375°F.

2. **Prepare the apples:** In a large bowl, stir together the **apples**, **caramel sauce**, **cornstarch**, **vinegar**, **vanilla**, **cinnamon**, **nutmeg**, and **salt**. Pour into a 10-inch cast-iron or other ovenproof skillet. Set aside.

3. **Prepare the topping:** In the same bowl (no need to clean it), stir together the **flour**, **oats**, **brown sugar**, **pecans**, and salt. Add the **butter** by tablespoons and use your fingers to rub the butter into the flour mixture until it holds together in large clumps when squeezed.

4. Now, set the skillet over medium-high heat and cook, turning the apples occasionally, until juicy and warm, 2 to 3 minutes. Remove from the heat and sprinkle the clumps of topping over the apples.

5. Place the skillet in the oven and bake until the top is golden brown and the juices are bubbling, 30 to 35 minutes. Let cool slightly, then serve warm with **vanilla ice cream** and a drizzle of caramel sauce.

(recipe continues)

HOMEMADE CARAMEL SAUCE

This is not a lot of work to make, but it does take a watchful eye. You'll end up with extra, so it's well worth the effort.

1. In an ovenproof medium skillet, sprinkle 1½ cups (300g) **sugar** evenly over the bottom, then dot with **12 tablespoons unsalted butter** and drizzle ½ **cup water** over the top. Set the skillet over medium-high heat and use a spoon to swirl occasionally until the mixture is melted and bubbling, 5 to 7 minutes. Continue to cook, swirling (not stirring!) the pan occasionally, until the caramel is a deep amber, 2 to 3 more minutes.

2. Remove the skillet from the heat and carefully add ¾ **cup heavy cream**, **2 tablespoons vanilla**, and **1 teaspoon salt**. The mixture will bubble and steam. Whisk until smooth. Makes about ½ cup.

STRAWBERRY SHORTCAKE SHEET CAKE

Serves 12

PREP
25 minutes

COOK
15 minutes

I like to end a big meal with something a little lighter—in this case, fresh strawberries. This sheet pan dessert brings some ease to the beloved strawberry shortcake. You bake one big, brown sugary biscuit on a sheet pan, then pile it with whipped cream and strawberries. The strawberries are macerated in sugar and vanilla, so they taste like their best selves even when they're not in season.

You can swap the strawberries for other berries, peaches, or nectarines, as you wish. For even less work, use store-bought biscuit dough in place of the homemade dough.

SHORTCAKE

- 3 cups (385g) all-purpose flour, plus more for rolling
- ¼ cup (50g) light brown sugar
- 4 teaspoons baking powder
- 1 teaspoon baking soda
- 1½ teaspoons kosher salt
- 1 stick (4 ounces/113g) unsalted butter, cold, cut into ½-inch pieces
- ½ cup well-shaken buttermilk
- ½ cup plus 2 tablespoons heavy cream, plus more if needed
- 1 tablespoon granulated sugar

STRAWBERRIES AND CREAM TOPPING

- 1½ pounds fresh strawberries, hulled and sliced
- 2 tablespoons plus 1 teaspoon granulated sugar
- 2 teaspoons fresh lemon juice
- 3 teaspoons vanilla extract
- 1½ cups heavy cream

1. **Prepare the shortcake:** Arrange a rack in the center of the oven and preheat the oven to 400°F. Line a sheet pan with parchment paper.

2. In a large bowl, stir together the **flour**, **brown sugar**, **baking powder**, **baking soda**, and **salt**. Add the **butter** and use your hands to toss it in the flour to coat. Use your fingers to mash each piece of butter into a flat piece, tossing it in flour as you go. Aim for pieces around the size of a nickel.

3. Make a well in the center of the flour mixture and pour in the **buttermilk** and ½ **cup of the cream**. Stir gently until just combined, with a few dry spots remaining. Use your hands to fold the dough over itself in the bowl a few times, until the dough is evenly moistened, but be careful not to overwork it. The dough should just hold together and should not be crumbly. There should still be visible pieces of butter. This may require adding another tablespoon or two of cream.

4. Turn out the dough onto the sheet pan and sprinkle a bit of flour over the top. Use your hands or a rolling pin to press or roll the dough into a rough oval ½ inch thick. (If the dough seems at all warm or the butter is very soft, refrigerate for 10 minutes.) Brush off any excess flour, then brush with the remaining 2 tablespoons cream and sprinkle with the **granulated sugar**.

(recipe continues)

5. Bake the shortcake until golden brown and crisp at the edges, 12 to 15 minutes. Let cool completely on the pan.

6. **Prepare the strawberries:** In a large bowl, stir together the **strawberries**, 2 tablespoons of the granulated sugar, the **lemon juice**, and **1 teaspoon of the vanilla**. Cover with a clean kitchen towel and let macerate briefly, stirring the mixture occasionally until ready to serve.

7. **When ready to serve, whip the cream:** In a medium bowl, combine the cream, the remaining teaspoon granulated sugar, and remaining 2 teaspoons vanilla. Use an electric hand mixer or whisk to beat the mixture to medium peaks.

8. Transfer the shortcake to a serving platter (or leave on the sheet pan!). Top with swoops of whipped cream, then carefully spoon the strawberries and their juices over the cream. Slice with a serrated bread knife and serve immediately.

CHOCOLATE MAYONNAISE SNACK CAKE

Makes one
9 × 13-inch cake

PREP
15 minutes

COOK
45 minutes

Chocolate mayo cake is an easy way to get a deliciously moist cake without having to use a ton of ingredients. Let me assure you, you cannot taste the mayo—only the delicious results! This is a Depression-era cake born from how difficult it could be to access fresh ingredients, namely eggs, butter, and milk. This cake instead uses mayo, which, after all, is a combination of eggs and oil.

I found a recipe for chocolate mayo cake in one of my mother's old cookbooks, and it was just as good as I remember. My version adds coffee to help enhance the chocolate flavor and adds a fudgy, chocolaty icing that really takes this moist, mouthwatering cake to the next level. You'll need only a tall, ice-cold glass of milk to go with it!

CAKE

Nonstick cooking spray

2¼ cups (450g) granulated sugar

1 cup (90g) unsweetened cocoa powder, preferably Dutch process

1½ cups warm coffee or water

1 cup (220g) mayonnaise

2 teaspoons vanilla extract

1 teaspoon instant espresso powder

1 teaspoon kosher salt

2 teaspoons baking powder

1 teaspoon baking soda

2¾ cups (350g) all-purpose flour

ICING

2½ cups (300g) powdered sugar

¼ cup (23g) unsweetened cocoa powder, preferably Dutch process

½ teaspoon instant espresso powder

Pinch of kosher salt

2 tablespoons unsalted butter, cut into small pieces

3 to 4 tablespoons boiling water

> BABS SAYS
>
> Skip the icing and dust the cake with powdered sugar, a true vintage version!

1. Arrange a rack in the center of the oven and preheat the oven to 350°F. Spray a 9 × 13-inch baking pan with **cooking spray**.

2. **Make the cake:** In a large bowl, whisk together the **granulated sugar** and **cocoa powder** until smooth and no lumps remain. Add the **coffee**, **mayonnaise**, **vanilla**, **espresso powder**, and **salt** and whisk until smooth. Whisk in the **baking powder** and **baking soda**. Then whisk in the **flour** until smooth and well combined.

3. Pour the batter into the baking pan and tap the pan a few times on the counter to release any large air bubbles. Bake until the cake is puffed and fragrant and a toothpick inserted into the center comes out clean, 35 to 45 minutes. Set the pan on a rack and let the cake cool in the pan. Remove from the pan to frost.

4. **Make the icing:** In a large bowl, whisk together the **powdered sugar**, cocoa powder, espresso powder, and salt. Place the **butter** on top and pour **3 tablespoons of the boiling water** over the butter. Whisk the mixture until smooth, adding more water as needed to make a thick and fudgy frosting. Immediately pour the mixture over the cooled cake and gently spread it over the top with an offset spatula or the back of a spoon. (The cake can be stored, covered, at room temperature for up to 4 days.)

COOKIE FOR BREAKFAST
OATMEAL RAISIN BARS

Makes one
9 × 13-inch pan

PREP
15 minutes

COOK
25 minutes

This recipe smushes an oatmeal raisin cookie into a not-too-sweet bar that's perfect for an after-school snack, dessert, or even breakfast. If I'm being honest, it's a perfect way to tell your children, or yourself, that they can have a cookie for breakfast. Talking a toddler down from a "Why can't I have a cookie for breakfast?" tantrum is not something you want to do more than once, I know. These bars are sweetened with dried fruit and maple syrup and couldn't be easier to make: just a bowl, a whisk, a spatula, and a baking pan. The bars keep really well, so enjoy them all week!

Nonstick cooking spray or butter

1¼   cups pure maple syrup

1   cup melted coconut oil or neutral oil, such as avocado

2   large eggs

1   tablespoon vanilla extract

2½   teaspoons ground cinnamon

2   teaspoons kosher salt

½   teaspoon freshly grated nutmeg

½   teaspoon ground ginger

½   teaspoon baking powder

2   cups (256g) all-purpose flour

2½   cups (225g) old-fashioned rolled oats

1   cup dried fruit, such as cranberries, raisins, cherries, chopped apricots, chopped dates, or a combination

1   cup (120g) chopped toasted walnuts

1. Arrange a rack in the center of the oven and preheat the oven to 350°F. Lightly grease a 9 × 13-inch baking pan with **cooking spray or butter** and line it with a length of parchment paper that hangs over the 2 long sides of the pan.

2. In a large bowl, whisk together the **maple syrup, oil, eggs, vanilla, cinnamon, salt, nutmeg, ginger,** and **baking powder** until smooth. Fold in the **flour** until only a few streaks remain. Add the **oats, dried fruit,** and **walnuts** and fold gently until well combined.

3. Spread the dough in the pan in an even layer and bake until golden and fragrant but still soft in the center, 20 to 25 minutes.

4. Cool completely in the pan, then use the parchment pieces on the long ends to lift the cake out of the pan and place it on a cutting board and slice into bars. (The bars can be stored in an airtight container for up to 4 days at room temperature or longer in the freezer.)

BABS SAYS

To add more fiber or protein, stir in some seeds, like flax, sesame, or poppy seeds. If you want to go in the opposite direction (which I also support!), you can replace the dried fruit with chocolate chips.

CONFETTI SKILLET COOKIE

Serves 8 to 10

PREP
10 minutes

COOK
25 minutes

It's impossible to have any celebration for my grandchildren without confetti somehow being involved. It's always on the agenda. My granddaughter Finley has requested it as her birthday cake flavor every year since she could speak. And I made a cake-batter confetti dip for my grandson Scooter's third birthday. If they offered a degree in confetti, I'd have earned a PhD. So, trust me when I tell you, this confetti skillet cookie is over the top and around the block.

It has the crispy edge and chewy middle of a cookie, plus the frosting and rainbow appeal of a confetti cake. While the frosting isn't essential, it reminds me of those amazing Lofthouse cookies you find in the grocery store, with their inviting pink frosting and sprinkled tops. Now any day can be a Funfetti Day!

COOKIE

- 1½ sticks (6 ounces/170g) unsalted butter, at room temperature, plus more for the pan
- 2 ounces (55g) cream cheese, at room temperature
- ¾ cup (150g) granulated sugar
- ¼ cup (50g) packed light brown sugar
- 1 large egg
- 2 teaspoons vanilla extract
- 1 teaspoon kosher salt
- ¼ teaspoon baking soda
- 2 cups (256g) all-purpose flour
- ⅓ cup (65g) rainbow sprinkles (not the round kind)

FROSTING

- 4 tablespoons (½ stick/57g) unsalted butter, at room temperature
- 1 cup (120g) powdered sugar
- 1 to 2 tablespoons heavy cream or milk
- 1 teaspoon vanilla extract
  Pinch of kosher salt
- 1 tablespoon rainbow sprinkles, or more if you want!

1. **Make the cookie:** Arrange a rack in the center of the oven and preheat the oven to 350°F. Lightly **butter** a 9- or 10-inch ovenproof skillet.

2. In a large bowl, with an electric mixer on medium-high speed, mix the butter, **cream cheese**, **granulated sugar**, and **brown sugar** until creamy, 5 to 7 minutes. Add the **egg**, **vanilla**, and **salt** and mix until well combined. Stir in the **baking soda**, then fold in the **flour** and **sprinkles** with a flexible spatula until just combined.

3. Press the dough evenly into the baking pan. Bake, rotating the pan halfway through, until golden but still soft in the center, 22 to 25 minutes. Set the pan on a wire rack and cool the cookie completely in the pan.

4. **Make the frosting:** In a large bowl, use an electric hand mixer on medium speed to beat the butter until creamy. Add the **powdered sugar**, **1 tablespoon of the cream**, the vanilla, and salt and mix on low until the sugar is moistened. Turn the mixer up to high and mix the frosting until light and fluffy, 5 to 7 minutes. If the mixture is dry and hard to work with, add the additional tablespoon cream.

5. Spread the frosting over the cooled cookie and top with as many sprinkles as you like. (The cookie can be stored, covered, at room temperature for up to 4 days.)

BABS SAYS

If you prefer to make the cookie without the frosting, just add 1 tablespoon of sprinkles on top of the batter before baking.

SCOTCHEROOS

Makes one
9 × 13-inch pan

PREP
15 minutes

COOK
10 minutes

I'm a native of the Midwest, so my recipe box wouldn't be complete without my version of Scotcheroos. The recipe was printed on the back of Rice Krispies cereal boxes in the 1960s. They are peanut butter–coated cereal bars topped with a chocolate-butterscotch layer, and they are absolutely incredible. If you love chocolate and peanut butter, this is for you! The original recipe produced bars that were thin and hard, like a candy bar, but my rendition is thicker, like a Rice Krispie treat, and for ease, it uses a whole box of cereal. While not traditional, my recipe also adds salted roasted peanuts on top for a bit of salt and crunch.

Softened butter or nonstick cooking spray, for the pan

1   stick (4 ounces/113g) unsalted butter

2   (10-ounce) bags mini marshmallows

1   (16-ounce) jar creamy peanut butter (about 1½ cups)

1   teaspoon kosher salt, plus a pinch for the topping

2   teaspoons vanilla extract

1   (9-ounce) box Rice Krispies (9 cups)

1   (10- to 12-ounce) package bittersweet chocolate chips

1   (11-ounce) package butterscotch chips

⅓   cup (50g) salted roasted peanuts

BABS SAYS

Change the toppings, if you want. Some pretzel bits or flaky sea salt would be equally yummy!

1. **Butter** or coat a 9 × 13-inch baking pan with **cooking spray** and line with a strip of parchment paper large enough to hang over the 2 long sides.

2. In a large pot, melt the **butter** over medium-high heat. Stir frequently, until the hissing subsides and the butter smells toasted and is speckled brown, 3 to 5 minutes. (Watch closely, as the butter can burn easily.) Reduce the heat to low, add the **marshmallows**, **peanut butter**, and **salt** and stir vigorously until melted. Stir in the **vanilla**. Working quickly, add the **cereal** and stir gently until well combined. Pour the mixture into the baking pan and use a spatula to firmly press the mixture until even.

3. While the mixture cools, melt the **chocolate chips**, **butterscotch chips**, and a pinch of salt in the top of a double boiler or in a microwave-safe bowl in 30-second intervals, stirring after each interval until smooth. The chocolate chips may melt a bit before the butterscotch chips, but keep stirring and the mixture will smooth out.

4. Spread the chocolate mixture on top of the cereal, then sprinkle the **peanuts** over the top. Let the topping cool until firm, 1 to 2 hours depending on the temperature of the room. Use the parchment to lift out of the pan, and cut into squares. (Store, covered, at room temperature for up to 5 days.)

What's in Babs' Refridge & Freezer?

The refridge and freezer are my armory, my stockpile of goods for the battle of dinnertime. And lunch. And breakfast. And snacks! Everything you need for the week and then some. Trust me, it's not always this organized, but here is a peek at my refridge and freezer at their most goal-worthy.

REFRIDGE

Refridge-Friendly Sheet-Pan Farro & Kale Salad (page 75)

Aunt Mimi's Mujaddara (page 133)

Grammie's Chicken Cutlets (page 53)

Sesame Chicken Noodle Salad (page 76)

Shredded meat from one spatchcocked chicken

Fully Loaded Cheeseburger Soup (page 80)

Milk

Butter

Cheeses: Cheddar, Swiss, mozzarella, Parmesan, Pecorino Romano

Eggs

Olives

Celery

Apples

Seltzers

Dressings

FREEZER

Grammie's Chicken Cutlets (page 53)

Mom's Meatloaf (page 62)

Minnie's Meatballs (page 73)

All the soups in the book

Stout Brisket Chili (page 193)

Breakfast-for-Dinner Sandwiches (page 68)

Finally, I Nailed Falafel with Tzatziki Slaw (page 65)

Cooked rice

Frozen veggies

Sheet-Pan Dumpling Stir-Fry (page 49)

Bacon

Shrimp

Tortillas

Cookie dough

Something fun, like ice cream or frozen candy bars

Babs' Toolbox

My kitchen is packed with cooking tools of all sorts. However, I use only some of them *all of the time*. (There haven't been that many occasions to use my pineapple corer . . . just as an example.) Of course, you should have items like measuring cups, spoons, and a can opener, but here is a list of things I find essential and basic, and some you may not have thought of. These are the kinds of kitchen tools you spend a little money on and they last you a lifetime, even when you're using them again and again . . . and again!

CASSEROLE DISH: Another name for this would be a 9 × 13-inch baking dish or pan, but I like nostalgia and there is more than one comforting casserole in this book. This is the pan in which you make casseroles, lasagnas, other baked pastas of all kinds, brownies, roasted potatoes, vegetables, etc. They can be made of all different materials: aluminum, glass, stoneware. Some are simple and some are fancy. It's a hard-working dish. Kind of reminds me of a grandma!

DIGITAL SCALE: I use my digital scale almost every day. It's much more accurate for baking, for which weight is a better measure than volume. It's also a life saver when I'm portioning out ingredients like meatballs or cookie dough; it's great for making sure the balls are the same size. The scale does all the work for me. You can find scales on Amazon for as little as $10, so it's budget friendly, too!

DUTCH OVEN: These big pots are great for sitting them on the stove and simmering soups and stews for hours, or for boiling a big batch of pasta. You also can use them in the oven for anything that needs a "slow and low" cook time. I love the convenience of a "set it and forget it" slow cooker, but a Dutch oven can do the same thing, and it's a kitchen workhorse you won't regret investing in.

FISH (SLOTTED) SPATULA: This spatula can be used for more than just fish! It's a thin, flexible, and long spatula that, of course, makes it great for its original purpose, but its flexibility is literal in lots of ways. You can use it to flip anything you're making in a skillet, but because of its length, it's also wonderful for stirring anything you would with a spoon.

GLASS 4-CUP LIQUID MEASURING CUP: A liquid measuring cup is a necessity. Liquids don't measure the same as dry ingredients, and this large version can go right into your microwave for melting butter or chocolate chips. It's also big enough to mix ingredients for marinades or sauces, right inside after you've measured them into the cup (some math may be required!). It's especially handy for recipes that call for 2½ cups or 3 cups of liquid.

KITCHEN SHEARS: A sharp pair of kitchen shears can't be beat. How else would you wrestle with the spatchcocking of those chickens? These shears make it easy. They are also great for snipping herbs, cubing meats, getting through the tough parts of asparagus spears, or even cutting pizza. Kitchen shears are a multipurpose tool that are a must-have!

KNIVES: Don't spend a fortune on a whole set of knives—you know, the kind of sets that couples often put on their wedding registries because they're so expensive. You just need three knives: a good-quality chef's knife, a serrated knife for slicing bread, and a paring knife for smaller jobs. Keep them sharp, and you'll be set for life.

MEAT THERMOMETER: This is a worthwhile spend. A thermometer takes all the guesswork out of whether your chicken, pork, or beef is at the proper temperature for serving. Meat is just too expensive to mess up. This handy gadget makes sure that never happens. You can also use it for baked goods to check that your cakes aren't raw in the middle—don't ask me how I know that. I love the Thermapen® and Yummly brands.

MICROPLANE: Including this kitchen tool here was a bit of a debate, I must admit. Does it make certain tasks easier? Absolutely. Will you regret having one? You will not. Is it expensive? Not even close. And that was ultimately what put it over the line. You can get a Microplane for as little as $7, and with that small investment you will save yourself on chores like zesting citrus or grating garlic (instead of chopping or pressing). It will grate Parmesan into a fine shower of deliciousness to pile atop any pasta, or it can create the neat chocolate shavings to top desserts. See? Already it's worth it! (Just watch your fingertips!)

OVENPROOF SKILLET: A good 12-inch skillet that you can take from the stove to the oven is essential for many of the recipes in this book. It pulls double duty as a traditional skillet for things as easy as scrambled eggs and as a casserole or baking dish for a range of dishes. I love a cast-iron skillet, but carbon steel is another good option.

SHEET PAN (AKA HALF-SHEET PAN): I don't know what I'd do without my sheet pans. There's a whole chapter in this book devoted to recipes that use them for a reason! The ones we use for home cooking are actually half-sheet pans, so if you're getting yours at a restaurant supply store (where they usually come very high quality for very little money), make sure you ask for that. A sheet pan has sides (aka a rim), so make sure you are not buying a cookie sheet, which is completely flat.

Dressings for Days

I've compiled all the mouthwatering marinades and delicious dressings here in one spot for your easy reference, just in case you want to skip to the sauces and dips in the recipes!

SESAME PEANUT SAUCE (page 76): This is delightful on the Sesame Chicken Noodle Salad, but it can go on anything else. Think of this as your go-to, all-purpose sesame dressing. It can also go on green salads and it's great on coleslaw mix, or simply use it to dress some cucumbers for your rice bowls.

TERIYAKI SAUCE (page 84): This is also good for other meats, veggies, even on eggs or plain rice. You'll find this with my Skillet Orange-Sesame Beef.

RED CHIMICHURRI (page 54): This is a must for any cut of meat or even on sandwiches, so it's with the recipe for The Ultimate Red Chimichurri Sauce with Skirt Steak. But keep a batch of this on hand to liven up other grilled or roasted meats and roasted vegetables (really good on boiled potatoes, too!).

GREEN GODDESS DRESSING (page 58): This is my daughter Elizabeth's favorite recipe in the book. I don't call it Lick-Your-Plate-Clean Green Goddess Salmon for just any reason. It's super light and bright, making it great for any poached or roasted seafood or chicken, for spring vegetables like asparagus and green beans, or for light green lettuces like arugula and baby greens. You can also use it as a dip for crudités or potato chips, or as a sauce for grain bowls.

TAHINI DRESSING (page 75): My Refridge-Friendly Sheet-Pan Farro & Kale Salad shouldn't be the only salad or crudités to benefit from this dressing. My go-to tahini dressing works with all sorts of salads, whether they have hearty greens like kale, delicate greens like Little Gem, raw veggies (hello, fattoush!), grains, or roasted or fresh veggies.

PIZZA SAUCE (page 83): I'm not frowning on your favorite jarred sauce. But if you want to make a super-simple delicious homemade sauce, you can find it with my Minivan Pepperoni Pizza Chicken with Garlic Bread. You can also use it for my Grandma's Grandma Pie (page 149) or even for a humble English muffin pizza. It's definitely Nonna approved!

RUSSIAN DRESSING (page 141): You can never have too much! You'll find this with my Reuben Pastry Pockets. Also try it on burgers and fries, or slathered on deli-meat lunch sandwiches.

TARTAR SAUCE (page 169): Of course, this goes with The Best Fish & Chips, but you may have a fish stick night with the kids, and this will go perfectly.

HERBED BUTTER (page 142): I don't think I need to convince you of the versatility of butter! This is made for my Sheet-Pan Shrimp Boil, but you can use it on *anything* you would like to spread a little butter on top of: grilled pork chops, seared chicken breasts, roasted salmon, and more!

HERB RICOTTA (page 185): Can you imagine an herb ricotta toast topped with some fresh tomatoes and a little drizzle of olive oil? Now you can! Find this with the Lamb Lover's Ragu.

PESTO (page 222): I really *could* eat this by the spoonful. It's that yummy. Find it with my Pesto Rack of Lamb with Tomato-Mozzarella Salad. If you're not in the mood for lamb, just have the salad! You can also use it anywhere you use pesto, including pasta.

BUTTERMILK DRESSING (page 217): This pairs perfectly with the Lobster Roll Cobb Salad, but will work for virtually any salad or fresh vegetable that would lend itself to something creamy and delicious.

ACKNOWLEDGMENTS

Writing this book has been an absolute privilege, fun, and hard work! I couldn't possibly have asked for better partners to help me.

Of course, I must thank my husband, Bill Costello, my emotional support, my sounding board, and most important the love of my life. I can't imagine what I would do without him.

Many of the wonderful, adorable faces you see in these pages belong to my nine amazing grandchildren: Mary, Matthew, Grace, Charlotte, Finley, Charlie, Ford, Scooter, and Willa. They are my greatest blessings and make getting older a true adventure.

To my Brunch with Babs team. My daughter Elizabeth Ariola worked side by side with me to make this book come to life. The list of things she contributed to this book would honestly take up more than a few pages. So let me put it simply: you would not have this book in your hands without her!

Laura Patterson has been on my team almost from the beginning. Her creativity and positive energy in joyfully tackling anything that I needed in order to get this book accomplished, and always with a smile on her face . . . well, this journey wouldn't have been the same without her.

Stephanie Trotta brought her wonderful eye for design and served as my art director for this book. She played a key role in making sure it looks as beautiful as it does.

Virginia Leahy managed this incredible project. Her organization, attention to detail, and talent in handling all things technical were indispensable.

My amazing executive editor, Jennifer Sit, believed in this idea from the start and was there with her gentle guidance steering me in the right direction every step of the way. I was blessed to have her and the whole team at Clarkson Potter at the helm, including Elaine Henning, Abby Oladipo, and Kim Tyner, as well as Stephanie Huntwork and Mia Johnson, who helped make this book look so amazing! Publicists Kate Tyler and Jana Branson were so instrumental in making sure people knew about *Every Day*.

This book would not have come together the way that it did without the amazing support of Ali Slagle, whose expertise helped guide me through the daunting journey of narrowing down all these recipes to the very best and yummiest of the bunch.

I also wanted to make sure these recipes were tested by a "regular" mom. Someone who didn't go to culinary school but still has to cook while juggling work and family like so many of us. The kind of person who might buy this book! Sarah Arestia, my friend, neighbor, and a very busy mom of three, stepped into that role. Each one of the recipes in this book got her and her family's seal of approval.

Ashley Holt used her extensive culinary background to help me with my first book, and I'm so grateful she was there for this one, too. Her incredible talent and skill with food were so vital, and both she and her little girl were excellent recipe testers!

MacLeod Zicari made sure my kitchen was stocked with groceries so I could cook!

Having Dane Tashima behind the camera for each and every dish in the book meant having a master at the lens. He was patient, supportive, and beyond talented, and I extend my thank-yous to his wonderful team, who were a literal dream to work with. I have to give special thanks to Pam Morris, our prop stylist, and Liza Jernow, our food stylist. Liza was able to create every recipe in *Every Day* to perfection. It was very hard to keep my mouth from watering for days on end! Pam made sure every one of those dishes came alive set against her amazing collection of linens, dishware, and glassware. Thank you to Heather Taylor Home for providing some of those beautiful linens. I appreciate all of your creative souls and open minds.

Alexandra Gilleo and Desiree Leigh who helped make all of us look like the best version of ourselves. Inge Fonteyne, Yana Galbshtein, and Paul Petzy made sure I was dressed to impress with a little help from my favorite, Talbots, which I wore in some of these photos.

Index

Note: Page references in *italics* indicate photographs.

A

Apple Crisp, Caramel, *242*, 243–44
Apricot Chickpea Stew, Not-to-Be-Missed Moroccan, 174, *175*
Artichoke(s)
    Olive Bar Chicken, 34, *35*
    -Spinach Rice & Bean Bake, *106*, 107
Asparagus
    Clean-Your-Fridge Frittata, 130, *131*
    Lick-Your-Plate-Clean Green Goddess Salmon, 58, *59*
Avocados
    Lobster Roll Cobb Salad, *216*, 217
    Maple-Lime Salmon Bowls with Coconut Rice, 30, *31*
    Salsa Verde Fish Tostadas, 88, *89*
    Zesty Chili-Lime Shrimp & Corn Salad, 42, *43*

B

Bacon
    Breakfast-for-Dinner Sandwiches, 68, *69*
    Fully Loaded Cheeseburger Soup, 80, *81*
    Jalapeño Popper Taquitos, 158, *159*
    Kiss of Summer Shrimp & Grits, 224, 225
    Lobster Roll Cobb Salad, *216*, 217
    Pasta, Warm Hug, 96, *97*
Bars
    Oatmeal Raisin, Cookie for Breakfast, *250*, 251
    Scotcheroos, *254*, 255
Basil
    Green Goddess Dressing, 58, *59*
    -Lemon Chicken & Couscous, 26, *27*
    Pesto, 222
Bean(s)
    & Cheese Tacos, Put-Your-Kids-to-Work Crispy, *44*, 45
    Chipotle Chicken Nachos, 166–67, 168
    Food Truck Tamale Pie, 126, *127*
    Pasta "Fazool," 122, *123*
    Pork Tenderloin with Peach Glaze, *28*, 29

& Rice Bake, Spinach-Artichoke, *106*, 107
Slow Cooker Chicken Enchilada Casserole, 178, *179*
Stout Brisket Chili, *192*, 193
"We Have Food at Home" Giant Crunchy Taco Wrap, 154, *155*
White, & Sausage, Vincenza's "Scarole" Soup with, 70, 71
Beef
    Beth's Sloppy Joe Casserole, 114, *115*
    Chicago Dogs with Fries, *144*, 145–46
    Don't Knock It 'Till You Try It Stuffed Cabbage Soup, *98*, 99
    Family Fajita Night, *32*, 33
    French Onion Soup Pot Roast, *180*, 181
    Fully Loaded Cheeseburger Soup, 80, *81*
    Mama's Stuffed Peppers, 226, *227*
    Minnie's Meatballs, *72*, 73
    Mom's Meatloaf, 62–64, *63*
    My Super Cheesy Lasagna, *210*, 211–12
    Not a Philly Cheesesteak–Stuffed Bread, 163–64, *165*
    Orange-Sesame, Skillet, 84, *85*
    Pimento Cheese Patty Melts, 150, *151*
    Reuben Pastry Pockets, *140*, 141
    Roast, with Roasted Garlic Wine Sauce, *204*, 205–6
    Sandwiches, Mrs. Murphy's Italian Cousins Chicago, 182, *183*
    Stew, Cook's Secret Weeknight, 118, *119*
    Stout Brisket Chili, *192*, 193
    The Ultimate Red Chimichurri Sauce with Skirt Steak, 54, *55*
    "We Have Food at Home" Giant Crunchy Taco Wrap, 154, *155*
Bourbon-Glazed Pork Chops, *60*, 61
Bread
    Garlic, Minivan Pepperoni Pizza Chicken with, *82*, 83
    Not a Philly Cheesesteak–Stuffed, 163–64, *165*
Bread Bowl Broccoli-Cheddar Soup, 198, *199*

Breakfast-for-Dinner Sandwiches, 68, *69*
Broccoli
    -Cheddar Soup, Bread Bowl, 198, *199*
    Chicken & Rice Casserole for the Soul, *124*, 125
    Pasta, Kids' Favorite, *94*, 95
    Shake-It-Up Garlic Knot Drumsticks, *112*, 113
    Skillet Orange-Sesame Beef, 84, *85*
Brussels Sprouts
    Fun with Fondue Baked Potato Bar, *188–89*, 190–91
    Honey Mustard Salmon with, *102*, 103
Butter, Herbed, 142
Buttermilk Dressing, 217

C

Cabbage
    Stuffed, Soup, Don't Knock It 'Till You Try It, *98*, 99
    Tzatziki Slaw, 66, *67*
Cakes
    Chocolate Chip Loaf, 241
    Chocolate Mayonnaise Snack, 248, *249*
    Jam Swirl Loaf, 241
    Key Lime Icebox, Babs' Favorite, *236*, 237
    Lemon Loaf, 241
    Pound, The Most Delicious, 240–41, *241*
    Strawberry Shortcake Sheet, 245–47, *246*
Caramel
    Apple Crisp, *242*, 243–44
    Sauce, Homemade, 244
Carrots
    & Chickpeas, Curried Fish Bites with, 46, *47*
    Cook's Secret Weeknight Beef Stew, 118, *119*
    Easiest Chicken Pot Pie, 90, *91*
    Lemony Chicken Soup, *128*, 129
    Love by the Spoonful Chicken Noodle Soup, 194, *195*
Casserole dish, 258
Cauliflower
    Hoisin Turkey Lettuce Cups, 92, *93*
    Roasted, Samuel's Chicken Shawarma with, *36*, 37

Cheese
   Aunt Louise's Eggplant Parmesan, 230, *231*
   Baked Shrimp with Feta & Tomatoes, 38, *39*
   & Bean Tacos, Put-Your-Kids-to-Work Crispy, *44*, 45
   Beth's Sloppy Joe Casserole, 114, *115*
   Bread Bowl Broccoli-Cheddar Soup, 198, *199*
   Breakfast-for-Dinner Sandwiches, 68, *69*
   Cheater's Cheesy Pasta Bake, 104, *105*
   Chicken Cordon Bleu Pasta, *220*, 221
   Chicken & Rice Casserole for the Soul, *124*, 125
   Chipotle Chicken Nachos, *166–67*, 168
   The Classic Tuna Noodle Casserole, 134, *135*
   Clean-Your-Fridge Frittata, 130, *131*
   Egg, & Sausage Skillet, Dad's Away, 110, *111*
   Food Truck Tamale Pie, 126, *127*
   Fully Loaded Cheeseburger Soup, 80, *81*
   Fun with Fondue Baked Potato Bar, *188–89*, 190–91
   Goat, Corn & Orzo, Chicken with, *86*, 87
   Grandma's Grandma Pie, *148*, 149
   Grilled, Tomato Soup, The Ultimate, *152*, 153
   Herb Ricotta, *184*, 185
   Homemade Ricotta Gnocchi with Sage Butter and Mushrooms, 207-8, *209*
   Jalapeño Popper Taquitos, 158, *159*
   Kids' Favorite Broccoli Pasta, *94*, 95
   Kiss of Summer Shrimp & Grits, *224*, 225
   Mac &, Better Than Boxed, 116, *117*
   Minivan Pepperoni Pizza Chicken with Garlic Bread, *82*, 83
   My Super Cheesy Lasagna, *210*, 211–12
   Not a Philly Cheesesteak–Stuffed Bread, 163–64, *165*
   Pesto, 222
   Pimento, Patty Melts, 150, *151*
   Reuben Pastry Pockets, *140*, 141
   "Revenge" Big Italian Sub Salad, *156*, 157
   Slow Cooker Chicken Enchilada Casserole, 178, *179*

   Tomato-Mozzarella Salad, 222, *223*
   "We Have Food at Home" Giant Crunchy Taco Wrap, 154, *155*
Chicago Dogs with Fries, *144*, 145–46
Chicken
   Cacciatore, Cousin Jim's, 213–14, *215*
   Cordon Bleu Pasta, *220*, 221
   & Couscous, Lemon-Basil, 26, *27*
   Cutlets, Grammie's, *52*, 63
   Easy Roast, 202, *203*
   Enchilada Casserole, Slow Cooker, 178, *179*
   Nachos, Chipotle, *166–67*, 168
   Noodle Salad, Sesame, 76, 77
   Noodle Soup, Love by the Spoonful, 194, *195*
   Olive Bar, 34, *35*
   with Orzo, Corn & Goat Cheese, *86*, 87
   Oven-Fried, & Waffles, 160, 161–62
   Pepperoni Pizza, Minivan, with Garlic Bread, *82*, 83
   & Potatoes, My Grandma's Greek, 218, *219*
   Pot Pie, Easiest, *90*, 91
   & Rice Casserole for the Soul, *124*, 125
   Shake-It-Up Garlic Knot Drumsticks, *112*, 113
   Shawarma, Samuel's, with Roasted Cauliflower, *36*, 37
   Soup, Lemony, *128*, 129
   Sticky, Fried Rice, Takeout Lovers', *120*, 121
   Tikka Masala, 186, *187*
   Two Birds, One Oven, 56, *57*
Chickpea(s)
   Apricot Stew, Not-to-Be-Missed Moroccan, 174, *175*
   & Carrots, Curried Fish Bites with, 46, *47*
   Finally, I Nailed Falafel with Tzatziki Slaw, 65–67, *66*
Chiles
   Jalapeño Popper Taquitos, 158, *159*
   Slow Cooker Chicken Enchilada Casserole, 178, *179*
Chili, Stout Brisket, *192*, 193
Chimichurri, Red, 54, *55*
Chocolate
   Chip Cookies, 234–35, *235*
   Chip Loaf, 241
   Mayonnaise Snack Cake, 248, *249*
   Scotcheroos, 254, *255*
   Turtle Date Bark, 238, *239*

Coconut Rice, Maple-Lime Salmon Bowls with, 30, *31*
Cookies
   Chocolate Chip, 234–35, *235*
   Confetti Skillet, 252, *253*
Corn
   & Chili-Lime Shrimp Salad, Zesty, 42, *43*
   Kiss of Summer Shrimp & Grits, *226*, 227
   Orzo, & Goat Cheese, Chicken with, *86*, 87
   Sheet-Pan Shrimp Boil, 142, *143*
   Slow Cooker Chicken Enchilada Casserole, 178, *179*
Couscous & Lemon-Basil Chicken, 26, *27*
Cucumbers
   Maple-Lime Salmon Bowls with Coconut Rice, 30, *31*
   Tomato-Mozzarella Salad, 222, *223*
   Tzatziki Slaw, *66*, 67
Curried Fish Bites with Chickpeas & Carrots, 46, *47*

D
Date Bark, Turtle, 238, *239*
Digital scale, 260
Dill
   Green Goddess Dressing, 58, *59*
   Tzatziki Slaw, *66*, 67
Dressings
   Buttermilk, 217
   Green Goddess, 58, *59*
   Russian, *140*, 141
   Tahini, 75
   uses for, 260–61
Dr Pepper Pulled Pork, *196*, 197
Dumpling Stir-Fry, Sheet-Pan, *48*, 49
Dutch oven, 258

E
Eggplant Parmesan, Aunt Louise's, 230, *231*
Egg(s)
   Breakfast-for-Dinner Sandwiches, 68, *69*
   Clean-Your-Fridge Frittata, 130, *131*
   Lemony Chicken Soup, *128*, 129
   Lobster Roll Cobb Salad, *216*, 217
   Sausage, & Cheese Skillet, Dad's Away, 110, *111*
   Takeout Lovers' Sticky Chicken Fried Rice, *120*, 121
Escarole
   Vincenza's "Scarole" Soup with Sausage & White Beans, 70, 71

F

Fajita Night, Family, *32, 33*
Falafel, Finally I Nailed, with Tzatziki Slaw, 65–67, *66*
Family dinners, 20–21
Farro & Kale Salad, Refridge-Friendly Sheet-Pan, *74, 75*
Fish. *See also* Salmon
    Bites, Curried, with Chickpeas & Carrots, 46, *47*
    & Chips, The Best, 169–70, *171*
    The Classic Tuna Noodle Casserole, 134, *135*
    Spicy Tuna Sushi Bake, 138, *139*
    Tostadas, Salsa Verde, 88, *89*
Fish spatula, 260
Fondue, Fun with, Baked Potato Bar, *188–89,* 190–91
Fries
    The Best Fish & Chips, 169–70, *171*
    Chicago Dogs with, *144,* 145–46
Frittata, Clean-Your-Fridge, 130, *131*
Fruit. *See also specific fruits*
    Cookie for Breakfast Oatmeal Raisin Bars, *250, 251*
    Pork Tenderloin Marbella, *228, 229*
Confetti Skillet Cookie, *252, 253*

G

Garlic
    Bread, Minivan Pepperoni Pizza Chicken with, *82, 83*
    Knot Shake-It-Up Drumsticks, *112,* 113
    My Grandma's Greek Chicken & Potatoes, 218, *219*
    Roasted, Wine Sauce, Roast Beef with, *204,* 205–6
Gnocchi
    Homemade Ricotta, with Sage Butter and Mushrooms, 207–8, *209*
    Sausage, & Peppers, Roasted, *24,* 25
Grandma's Grandma Pie, *148,* 149
Green Goddess Dressing, 58, *59*
Grits & Shrimp, Kiss of Summer, *224,* 225

H

Ham
    Breakfast-for-Dinner Sandwiches, 68, *69*
    Chicken Cordon Bleu Pasta, 220, 221
    Clean-Your-Fridge Frittata, 130, *131*
Herb(s). *See also* Basil; Dill; Sage
    Green Goddess Dressing, 58, *59*
    Herbed Butter, 142
    Ricotta, *184,* 185

Hoisin Turkey Lettuce Cups, 92, *93*
Honey Mustard Salmon with Brussels Sprouts, *102, 103*
Hot dogs. *See* Chicago Dogs

J

Jalapeño Popper Taquitos, 158, *159*
Jam Swirl Loaf, 241

K

Kale & Farro Salad, Refridge-Friendly Sheet-Pan, *74, 75*
Key Lime Icebox Cake, Babs' Favorite, *236,* 237
Kitchen shears, 258
Kitchen tools, 258–59
Knives, 258

L

Lamb
    Lovers' Ragu, *184,* 185
    Pesto Rack of, with Tomato-Mozzarella Salad, 222, *223*
Lasagna, My Super Cheesy, *210,* 211–12
Lemon
    Lemony Chicken Soup, *128,* 129
    Loaf, 241
    My Grandma's Greek Chicken & Potatoes, 218, *219*
    Tahini Dressing, 75
Lentils
    Aunt Mimi's Mujaddara, *132,* 133
Lettuce
    Cups, Hoisin Turkey, 92, *93*
    Lobster Roll Cobb Salad, *216,* 217
    "Revenge" Big Italian Sub Salad, *156,* 157
    Salsa Verde Fish Tostadas, 88, *89*
    Zesty Chili-Lime Shrimp & Corn Salad, 42, *43*
Lobster Roll Cobb Salad, *216,* 217

M

Maple-Lime Salmon Bowls with Coconut Rice, 30, *31*
Marshmallows
    Scotcheroos, *254,* 255
Measuring cup, 258
Meat. *See also* Beef; Lamb; Pork
    "Revenge" Big Italian Sub Salad, *156,* 157
Meatballs, Minnie's, 72, 73
Meatloaf, Mom's, 62–64, *63*
Meat thermometer, 259
Menus, sample, 18
Microplane, 259
Mujaddara, Aunt Mimi's, *132,* 133

Mushrooms
    Cousin Jim's Chicken Cacciatore, 213–14, *215*
    Homemade Ricotta Gnocchi with Sage Butter and Mushrooms, 207–8, *209*
    Not a Philly Cheesesteak–Stuffed Bread, 163–64, *165*

N

Nachos, Chipotle Chicken, *166–67,* 168
Noodle
    Chicken Soup, Love by the Spoonful, 194, *195*
    Sesame Chicken Salad, 76, 77
    Tuna, Casserole, The Classic, 134, *135*
Nuts. *See specific nuts*

O

Oats
    Caramel Apple Crisp, *242,* 243–44
    Cookie for Breakfast Oatmeal Raisin Bars, *250, 251*
Olives
    Cousin Jim's Chicken Cacciatore, 213–14, *215*
    Olive Bar Chicken, 34, *35*
    Pork Tenderloin Marbella, *228, 229*
Onion(s)
    Aunt Mimi's Mujaddara, *132,* 133
    French, Soup Pot Roast, *180,* 181
    Pimento Cheese Patty Melts, 150, *151*
Orange
    -Sesame Beef, Skillet, 84, *85*
    Teriyaki Sauce, 84
Ovenproof skillet, 259

P

Pasta
    Bacon, Warm Hug, 96, *97*
    Bake, Cheater's Cheesy, 104, *105*
    Better Than Boxed Mac & Cheese, *116,* 117
    Broccoli, Kids' Favorite, *94,* 95
    Chicken Cordon Bleu, 220, 221
    Chicken with Orzo, Corn & Goat Cheese, *86, 87*
    "Fazool," 122, *123*
    My Super Cheesy Lasagna, *210,* 211–12
    Picky-Eater, with Sausage & Peas, 100, *101*
Pastry Pockets, Reuben, *140,* 141
Patty Melts, Pimento Cheese, 150, *151*
Peach Glaze, Pork Tenderloin with, 28, *29*

Peanut butter
  Scotcheroos, *254, 255*
  Sesame Peanut Sauce, *76*
Peas
  Chicken Cordon Bleu Pasta, *220, 221*
  The Classic Tuna Noodle Casserole, *134, 135*
  Clean-Your-Fridge Frittata, *130, 131*
  Cook's Secret Weeknight Beef Stew, *118, 119*
  Easiest Chicken Pot Pie, *90, 91*
  & Sausage, Picky-Eater Pasta with, *100, 101*
Pecans
  Caramel Apple Crisp, *242, 243–44*
  Turtle Date Bark, *238, 239*
Pepperoni Pizza Chicken, Minivan, with Garlic Bread, *82, 83*
Peppers. *See also* Chiles
  Cousin Jim's Chicken Cacciatore, *213–14, 215*
  Family Fajita Night, *32, 33*
  Mrs. Murphy's Italian Cousins Chicago Beef Sandwiches, *182, 183*
  Not a Philly Cheesesteak–Stuffed Bread, *163–64, 165*
  Olive Bar Chicken, *34, 35*
  Red Chimichurri, *54, 55*
  Sausage, & Gnocchi, Roasted, *24, 25*
  Skillet Orange-Sesame Beef, *84, 85*
  Stuffed, Mama's, *226, 227*
Pesto, *222*
Pesto Rack of Lamb with Tomato-Mozzarella Salad, *222, 223*
Pie, Food Truck Tamale, *126, 127*
Pimento Cheese Patty Melts, *150, 151*
Pizza
  Grandma's Grandma Pie, *148, 149*
  Sauce, *83*
Pork. *See also* Bacon; Ham; Sausage
  Chops, Bourbon-Glazed, *60, 61*
  Dr Pepper Pulled, *196, 197*
  Finger Lickin' Good Sweet & Sour Ribs, *176, 177*
  Minnie's Meatballs, *72, 73*
  Mom's Meatloaf, *62–64, 63*
  Tenderloin Marbella, *228, 229*
  Tenderloin with Peach Glaze, *28, 29*
Potato(es)
  Baked, Bar, Fun with Fondue, *188–89, 190–91*
  The Best Fish & Chips, *169–70, 171*
  Chicago Dogs with Fries, *144, 145–46*

& Chicken, My Grandma's Greek, *218, 219*
Cook's Secret Weeknight Beef Stew, *118, 119*
Dad's Away Sausage, Egg & Cheese Skillet, *110, 111*
Fully Loaded Cheeseburger Soup, *80, 81*
Pork Tenderloin with Peach Glaze, *28, 29*
& Sauerkraut, Snappy Kielbasa with, *40, 41*
Sheet-Pan Shrimp Boil, *142, 143*
Pot Pie, Easiest Chicken, *90, 91*

R
Ragu, Lamb Lovers', *184, 185*
Raisin Oatmeal Bars, Cookie for Breakfast, *250, 251*
Reuben Pastry Pockets, *140, 141*
Rice
  Aunt Mimi's Mujaddara, *132, 133*
  & Bean Bake, Spinach-Artichoke, *106, 107*
  & Chicken Casserole for the Soul, *124, 125*
  Coconut, Maple-Lime Salmon Bowls with, *30, 31*
  Don't Knock It 'Till You Try It Stuffed Cabbage Soup, *98, 99*
  Lemony Chicken Soup, *128, 129*
  Mama's Stuffed Peppers, *226, 227*
  Spicy Tuna Sushi Bake, *138, 139*
  Sticky Chicken Fried, Takeout Lovers', *120, 121*
Rice Krispies
  Scotcheroos, *254, 255*
Russian Dressing, *140, 141*

S
Sage Butter and Mushrooms, Homemade Ricotta Gnocchi with, *207–8, 209*
Salads
  Chili-Lime Shrimp & Corn, Zesty, *42, 43*
  Farro & Kale, Refridge-Friendly Sheet-Pan, *74, 75*
  Lobster Roll Cobb, *216, 217*
  "Revenge" Big Italian Sub, *156, 157*
  Sesame Chicken Noodle, *76, 77*
  Tomato-Mozzarella, *222, 223*
Salmon
  Green Goddess, Lick-Your-Plate-Clean, *58, 59*
  Honey Mustard, with Brussels Sprouts, *102, 103*
  Maple-Lime, Bowls with Coconut Rice, *30, 31*

Salsa Verde Fish Tostadas, *88, 89*
Sample menus, *18*
Sandwiches
  Beef, Mrs. Murphy's Italian Cousins Chicago, *182, 183*
  Breakfast-for-Dinner, *68, 69*
  Pimento Cheese Patty Melts, *150, 151*
Sauces
  Caramel, Homemade, *244*
  Pesto, *222*
  Pizza, *83*
  Red Chimichurri, *54, 55*
  Sesame Peanut, *76*
  Tartar, *169, 171*
  Teriyaki, *84*
Sauerkraut
  & Potatoes, Snappy Kielbasa with, *40, 41*
  Reuben Pastry Pockets, *140, 141*
Sausage
  Breakfast-for-Dinner Sandwiches, *68, 69*
  Egg, & Cheese Skillet, Dad's Away, *110, 111*
  Mama's Stuffed Peppers, *226, 227*
  Minivan Pepperoni Pizza Chicken with Garlic Bread, *82, 83*
  My Super Cheesy Lasagna, *210, 211–12*
  & Peas, Picky-Eater Pasta with, *100, 101*
  Peppers, & Gnocchi, Roasted, *24, 25*
  "Revenge" Big Italian Sub Salad, *156, 157*
  Sheet-Pan Shrimp Boil, *142, 143*
  Snappy Kielbasa with Sauerkraut & Potatoes, *40, 41*
  & White Beans, Vincenza's "Scarole" Soup with, *70, 71*
Scotcheroos, *254, 255*
Sesame
  Chicken Noodle Salad, *76, 77*
  -Orange Beef, Skillet, *84, 85*
  Peanut Sauce, *76*
Sheet pan, *259*
Shellfish. *See* Lobster; Shrimp
Shrimp
  Baked, with Feta & Tomatoes, *38, 39*
  Boil, Sheet-Pan, *142, 143*
  & Grits, Kiss of Summer, *224, 225*
  Zesty Chili-Lime, & Corn Salad, *42, 43*
Slaw, Tzatziki, *66, 67*
Sloppy Joe Casserole, Beth's, *114, 115*

Soups
    Bread Bowl Broccoli-Cheddar,
        198, *199*
    Cheeseburger, Fully Loaded,
        80, *81*
    Chicken Noodle, Love by the
        Spoonful, 194, *195*
    Lemony Chicken, *128*, 129
    Pasta "Fazool," 122, *123*
    "Scarole," Vincenza's, with
        Sausage & White Beans,
        70, 71
    Stuffed Cabbage, Don't Knock It
        'Till You Try It, *98*, 99
    Tomato, The Ultimate Grilled
        Cheese, *152*, 153
Spinach-Artichoke Rice & Bean
    Bake, *106*, 107
Squash
    Refridge-Friendly Sheet-Pan Farro
        & Kale Salad, *74*, 75
    Kiss of Summer Shrimp & Grits,
        224, 225
    Lemon-Basil Chicken & Couscous,
        26, *27*
    Not-to-Be-Missed Moroccan
        Chickpea Apricot Stew, 174, *175*
Stews
    Beef, Cook's Secret Weeknight,
        118, *119*
    Chickpea Apricot, Not-to-Be-
        Missed Moroccan, 174, *175*
Stout Brisket Chili, *192*, 193
Strawberry Shortcake Sheet Cake,
    245–47, *246*

T
Tacos, Put-Your-Kids-to-Work
    Crispy Bean & Cheese, 44, 45
Taco Wrap, Giant Crunchy,
    "We Have Food at Home,"
    154, *155*

Tahini Dressing, 75
Tamale Pie, Food Truck, 126, *127*
Taquitos, Jalapeño Popper, 158, *159*
Tartar Sauce, 169, *171*
Teriyaki Sauce, 84
Tikka Masala, Chicken, 186, *187*
Tomato(es)
    Aunt Louise's Eggplant Parmesan,
        230, *231*
    Don't Knock It 'Till You Try It
        Stuffed Cabbage Soup, *98*, 99
    & Feta, Baked Shrimp with,
        38, *39*
    Kiss of Summer Shrimp & Grits,
        224, 225
    Lamb Lovers' Ragu, *184*, 185
    Lemon-Basil Chicken & Couscous,
        26, 27
    Lobster Roll Cobb Salad, *216*, 217
    -Mozzarella Salad, *222*, 223
    Olive Bar Chicken, 34, *35*
    Pasta "Fazool," 122, *123*
    Pizza Sauce, 83
    "Revenge" Big Italian Sub Salad,
        156, 157
    Soup, The Ultimate Grilled Cheese,
        152, 153
    Warm Hug Bacon Pasta, 96, *97*
    "We Have Food at Home" Giant
        Crunchy Taco Wrap, 154, *155*
Tools and equipment, 258–59
Tortilla chips
    Chipotle Chicken Nachos, *166–67*,
        168
    Slow Cooker Chicken Enchilada
        Casserole, 178, *179*
Tortillas
    Family Fajita Night, *32*, 33
    Jalapeño Popper Taquitos,
        158, *159*
    Put-Your-Kids-to-Work Crispy
        Bean & Cheese Tacos, 44, 45

Salsa Verde Fish Tostadas, 88, *89*
    "We Have Food at Home" Giant
        Crunchy Taco Wrap, 154, *155*
    Zesty Chili-Lime Shrimp & Corn
        Salad, 42, *43*
Tostadas
    Salsa Verde Fish, 88, *89*
    "We Have Food at Home" Giant
        Crunchy Taco Wrap, 154, *155*
Tuna
    Noodle Casserole, The Classic,
        134, *135*
    Sushi Bake, Spicy, 138, *139*
Turkey, Hoisin, Lettuce Cups,
    92, *93*
Turtle Date Bark, 238, *239*
Tzatziki Slaw, *66*, 67

V
Vegetables. *See also specific
    vegetables*
    Sesame Chicken Noodle Salad,
        76, 77
    Sheet-Pan Dumpling Stir-Fry,
        48, 49
    Takeout Lovers' Sticky Chicken
        Fried Rice, *120*, 121

W
Waffles & Oven-Fried Chicken, *160*,
    161–62

Y
Yogurt
    Tzatziki Slaw, *66*, 67

Z
Zucchini
    Kiss of Summer Shrimp & Grits,
        224, 225
    Lemon-Basil Chicken & Couscous,
        26, *27*

Every day with Babs through the years

Published in the United States by Clarkson Potter/Publishers, an imprint of the Crown Publishing Group, a division of Penguin Random House LLC, New York. ClarksonPotter.com

CLARKSON POTTER is a trademark and POTTER with colophon is a registered trademark of Penguin Random House LLC.

Library of Congress Cataloging-in-Publication Data
Names: Costello, Barbara, author. | Tashima, Dane, photographer.
Title: Every day with Babs : 101 easy & delicious family-friendly dinners for every night of the week / Barbara "Brunch with Babs" Costello ; photographs by Dane Tashima.
Description: New York : Clarkson Potter, [2025] | Includes index.
Identifiers: LCCN 2024019727 (print) | LCCN 2024019728 (ebook) | ISBN 9780593797907 (hardcover) | ISBN 9780593797914 (ebook)
Subjects: LCSH: Cooking. | Dinners and dining. | LCGFT: Cookbooks.
Classification: LCC TX714 .C6953 2025 (print) | LCC TX714 (ebook) | DDC 641.5–dc23/eng/20240910
LC record available at https://lccn.loc.gov/2024019727
LC ebook record available at https://lccn.loc.gov/2024019728

ISBN 978-0-593-79790-7
Signed edition ISBN: 979-82-17-03410-9
Ebook ISBN 978-0-593-79791-4

Printed in China

Editor: Jennifer Sit
Editorial assistant: Elaine Hennig
Designer: Mia Johnson
Art director: Stephanie Huntwork
Production editor: Abby Oladipo
Production manager: Kim Tyner
Compositor: Merri Ann Morrell
Food stylist: Liza Jernow
Food stylist assistants: Dara Furlow and Sarah DeLange
Prop stylist: Pam Morris
Prop stylist assistants: Helen Quinn and Vicki Farrell
Digital techs: Jane Gaspar and Jack Koto
Photo assistant: Chloe Gaget
Copyeditors: Carole Berglie and Kate Slate
Proofreaders: Heather Rodino, Hope Clarke, and Penny Haynes
Indexer: Elizabeth Parson
Publicists: Kate Tyler and Jana Branson
Marketers: Stephanie Davis and Andrea Portanova

10 9 8 7 6 5 4 3 2 1

First Edition

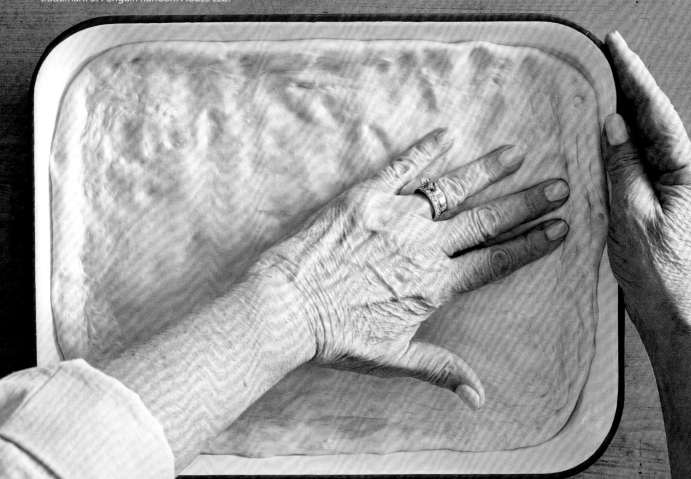